Works Righteousness

Works Righteousness

Material Practice in Ethical Theory

ANNA L. PETERSON

OXFORD

UNIVERSITY PRESS

OXFORD
UNIVERSITY PRESS

Oxford University Press is a department of the University of Oxford. It furthers
the University's objective of excellence in research, scholarship, and education
by publishing worldwide. Oxford is a registered trade mark of Oxford University
Press in the UK and certain other countries.

Published in the United States of America by Oxford University Press
198 Madison Avenue, New York, NY 10016, United States of America.

Library of Congress Cataloging-in-Publication Data
Names: Peterson, Anna L., 1963– author.
Title: Works righteousness : material practice
in ethical theory / Anna L. Peterson.
Description: New York, NY, United States of America : Oxford University
Press, 2021. | Includes bibliographical references and index.
Identifiers: LCCN 2020019149 (print) | LCCN 2020019150 (ebook) |
ISBN 9780197532232 (hb) | ISBN 9780197532256 (epub) |
ISBN 9780197532249 (updf) | ISBN 9780197532263 (online)
Subjects: LCSH: Applied ethics.
Classification: LCC BJ1589 .P445 2020 (print) |
LCC BJ1589 (ebook) | DDC 170—dc23
LC record available at https://lccn.loc.gov/2020019149
LC ebook record available at https://lccn.loc.gov/2020019150

1 3 5 7 9 8 6 4 2

Printed by Integrated Books International, United States of America

In memory of

Susan Shaffer and Zot Lynn Szurgot

We begin to think where we live.

—Raymond Williams

Contents

Acknowledgments

I am grateful to have had help from many people and institutions during the research and writing process. I was fortunate to receive a sabbatical during 2017–2018 and a Humanities Scholarship Enhancement Grant in summer 2018 from the University of Florida to work on this project. The UF Department of Religion continues to be a congenial intellectual home, and I am particularly grateful to my former and current chairs, Vasu Narayanan and Terje Østebø, for their administrative support and their friendship. I also thank my UF colleagues Jaime Ahlberg, Kim Emery, Ben Lowe, Ali Mian, and Zoharah Simmons for helping me sort through various pieces of this book. Special thanks to Ali for reading the whole book and to Jaime for countless conversations about ethics, theory, and practice. The book is far better for their insights. It is also better for the contributions of Cynthia Read and the talented, meticulous team at Oxford University Press and for the comments of three anonymous readers for the Press.

I presented an early version of chapter 8 at a July 2015 conference, organized by Donovan Schaefer, at the Ian Ramsey Center for Science and Religion at the University of Oxford. Thanks are due to Donovan and to the participants at that conference, who provided many helpful insights. I also presented a preliminary discussion of the issues discussed in chapter 6 at the University of Chicago Divinity School in 2013, where a lively audience helped me clarify my thoughts about pacifism and the relations between means and ends.

During the time I was thinking about and writing this book, I have been engaged in several other writing projects that enriched my thinking about practice and ethics in numerous ways. I am very grateful to my collaborators on those projects—Jenny Applebaum, Jaime Ahlberg, Todd LeVasseur, and Dara Wald. I must also thank the "Ethics and the Public Sphere" group at UF: Jaime Ahlberg, Elaine Giles, Rachel Grant, April Hines, Stella Kim, Chris Lomelín, Vickie Machado, and Kim Walsh-Childers. It has been a great joy to work with such a smart and talented group of people dedicated to linking research and teaching with progressive social change. It has been equally exciting to talk about many of the issues I discuss in this book with my undergraduate students, whose enthusiasm for connecting ethics and real life is a source of inspiration and hope. I also owe a great debt to my current and former graduate students—I am sure that I learn much more from them than vice versa. Very special thanks are due to Sam Snyder, with whom I have been talking about the gaps between environmental values and practices for more than fifteen years and whose insights have profoundly shaped my thinking about these issues. I am also grateful for recent opportunities to work with Todd, Chris, Ben, and Vickie and to learn about the connections between theory and practice through their work.

One of my greatest debts is to my son Gabriel Vásquez-Peterson, who read all of the manuscript, made numerous helpful suggestions, and co-wrote the sections on virtue ethics in chapter 3. I am grateful as well to my daughter Eva and my son Rafael, who bring meaning and joy into every part of my life. Thanks also to my mother Judith, my brother Brandt, and my sister Casey, who provide endless support and love. They, along with good friends, and especially Jane Fischberg, May Lehmensiek, and Carla Sabbagh, have helped me survive some difficult times in recent years.

This book is dedicated to the memory of my friends Susan Shaffer and Zot Lynn Szurgot, both of whom died suddenly during the time I was writing this book. They did not know each other, but Susan and Zot shared a contagious laugh, a talent for friendship, and a passion for making the world a better place.

1

Introduction

Ethical Theory and Practice

> Difficulties are not mastered by keeping silent about them. Practice
> demands that one step should follow another; theory has to embrace
> the entire sequence.
>
> —Bertolt Brecht[1]

Introduction

This book is framed between two conversations. The first took place more
than a decade ago, when we hosted a Thanksgiving dinner for family and
friends. It was a vegetarian feast, resplendent with Tofurky and all the
trimmings. One guest looked at the table full of food and said, "This is so
wonderful. I wish I could be a vegetarian." Our friend Zot looked her in the
eye, smiled with characteristic charm, and said, "You can."

The other conversation took place more recently, when I was beginning to
think about this book. I told my oldest son, then a college student majoring
in philosophy, about my idea for the project. He said, "Practices in ethics.
That's a great topic. Because, you know, we never think what we're doing is
wrong."

Those two conversations, with two of my favorite people, contain in em-
bryo much of what I want to explore in this book, which focuses on a decep-
tively simple question: what is the significance of what people actually do
for the ways we think about moral value? Zot's reply points to the possibility
of practicing ethics—deliberately acting on values we have carefully considered. Zot was one of those exceedingly rare human beings who strove, in
every deed and every moment, to embody deeply held moral principles. She
walked the talk more truly than anyone I have met and may be the exception
that proves the rule, revealing just how difficult and sometimes painful it is
to follow moral principles consciously and consistently. My son's comment

Works Righteousness. Anna L. Peterson, Oxford University Press (2021). © Oxford University Press.
DOI: 10.1093/oso/9780197532232.001.0001.

points to another dimension of the relationship between ethics and practices. Our actions shape what we think is good. We value not just our own deeds but also what we know (or think we know) as a result of those deeds. We talk the walk, in this sense; we develop a theory of the good from our actions.

"Walking the talk" is the main way we think about linking ethics and practices, in both scholarly literature and everyday life. In this perspective, actions are relevant to morality only as applications of intentions or mediators between intentions and consequences. People can "act on" or "apply" values, which presumably follow in a deliberate, predictable, and linear way from ideas that arise prior to and in isolation from our actions. This linear view of the relations between values and practices presumes that ideas are prior to and independent of what people do. Many influential theories share these assumptions and treat practice as inferior to and derivative of ideas and as irrelevant, or even an obstacle, to ethical thought.

This book is both a critique of these dominant idealist models and an argument in favor of putting practices at the heart of ethical theory. More precisely, I contend that what we do generates and alters values, just as often as expressed values motivate or guide the ways we act. The relationship between ideas and practices is not one of conflict, linearity, or indifference; rather, it is mutually transformative and "metamorphic," as Ali Mian writes.[2] Ethical theory's systematic lack of attention to practice is an intellectual problem because it misconstrues how people actually develop and express moral convictions. It is also a practical problem, because it harms efforts to address important moral and political issues. I aim to show that attention to practice permits more nuanced and accurate understandings both of how people think and act ethically and of the relations between their moral ideas, their actions, and the consequences of these.

This is not, or not just, an argument about particular ethical theories; I am not simply contending that Kantians or utilitarians ought to take practice more seriously (although they should). Nor do I aim to articulate a single practice-based ethic. Rather, I want to develop a kind of meta-ethic, a way of thinking broadly about the character and place of practice in ethical theory. This involves several steps: an analysis and critique of approaches that marginalize practice, an exploration of alternative theories that take practice more seriously, reflections on how practice illuminates real-life moral problems, and an initial proposal for an approach to ethical theory in which practice plays a central role.

Ethical Theory

Ethical theory is the study of what people value, the reasons they do so, and the practical and theoretical implications of their valuing. It is a way of talking about, analyzing, categorizing, and evaluating "morality," which, as Margaret Urban Walker explains, "is something that people are actually doing together in their communities, societies, and ongoing relationships. Academic philosophers don't discover it or make it up in reflection. If they discover or construct something through reflection and philosophical argument, it is a theory *about* morality."[3] Another way to put this is that if ethics or morality describes people's value systems and related practices, then ethical theory is the effort to understand them, including the way scholars talk about them. I am interested in the relationship between these two types of ethics—what people do and how to think systematically about those actions. My overall goal in this book is to put these together, by making practices central to an examination, critique, and reformulation of the ways we think about morality.

I pay special attention to several approaches that give practice a significant role in morality, including virtue, Catholic, feminist, pragmatist, Marxist, and pacifist traditions. However, I do not think that practice is or should be limited to any particular ethical theory. Practices are not something that only pragmatists or Marxists should think about but are integral to all types of morality. Thus, taking them seriously requires not just the creation of an alternative moral philosophy or theology but rather radical revisions in our overarching conceptions of ethical theory. This in some senses parallels the feminist argument that we cannot take women and gender seriously if we merely insert new themes into existing models—"add women and stir"—but leave essential structures unchanged.[4] Institutions such as the church or the state are predicated on a society in which women are unequal, sometimes invisible, figures. Integrating women into them requires significant transformations at every level. What is true of institutional change is also true of theoretical shifts. We cannot merely add women into existing theories without questioning and transforming many basic assumptions. Martha Nussbaum makes a parallel argument about disability and other novel themes for ethics, which demand "not simply a new application of the old theories, but a reshaping of theoretical structures themselves."[5]

The place of practice in ethical theory raises similar questions. Like feminists who point out that the significance of gender is not limited to the domestic sphere, I believe that practice is not only relevant when we consider specific problems. This is the assumption behind not just most specific theoretical models but also the usual division of ethical theory into three categories. The first is meta-ethics, which asks about the structure and underlying meanings of moral thinking in general. Normative ethics is more specific, addressing the content of moral claims and the justifications for those particular claims. Last, applied ethics considers the ways moral theories guide action in particular settings, usually for professionals in healthcare and bio-medical research, law, and business, although the scope of applied ethics has grown rapidly. For many thinkers, practice enters only in this last category, which is addressed after theorizing is finished and has provided conclusions that can be "applied."

Against this model of ethical theory, I argue that practice is significant in meta-ethics and normative ethics, and indeed in almost all moral reflection and judgment, not just in relation to specific real-life problems. Like race, gender, nature, and many other previously ignored aspects of our real lives, practice is woven into everything we do. It is, precisely, most of what we do, with our bodies, our time, our lives. Practice should thus be an explicit aspect of ethical thinking generally, not just a specialized compartment of it. It is applicable to every aspect of ethical thinking, which is itself a form of practical activity and one that shapes and is shaped by all our other activities. Making the role of practice explicit can help us consider what it means to think and act ethically, highlighting flaws in dominant frameworks while also revealing the strengths of other, less generally influential perspectives.

In tackling these issues, I write not as a philosopher or theologian but as a social ethicist. As a subdiscipline within religious ethics, social ethics focuses on understanding and addressing real-life problems with the help of social scientific methods and theories and attention to the social character of both human nature and moral problems. It understands moral theory as always practical, rather than purely normative, and it views people as fundamentally social animals. Thus, social ethicists draw on social sciences and policymaking to understand society, human nature, the character of ethical thinking, and the best way to address concrete problems. This stems in part from the focus on religious ethics, which are lived out or put into practice much more often than philosophical ones. At the same time, practical experiences and activities shape religious ethics more continually and powerfully than they do most secular theories. In these ways, social ethics differs from secular moral philosophy and traditional theological ethics, both of which tend to be more privatized, individualistic, and idealist. While social ethics is not identical to the practice-oriented approach I want to build, it is a uniquely valuable site for thinking about practice, because of its social, practical, and integral approach to thinking about morality and moral theory.

I was trained at one of the original homes of social ethics, the University of Chicago Divinity School, where my area of doctoral study was "ethics and society." This subfield had roots in the curriculum developed at the Divinity School by James Luther Adams, which trained students "to search for moral norms within the variegated life of society, integrating social scientific research with ethical reasoning."[6] Adams and other founders of social ethics as a field were influenced by pragmatist philosophy, which emerged during the same period of the late nineteenth and early twentieth centuries. Although I did not know much about social ethics at the time I began graduate work, I knew that "ethics and society" captured perfectly my twin interests in moral theory and religion's role in social change. That has continued to be the case, and my scholarly work over the years has included both ethnographically grounded studies of real-life communities and movements, on the one hand, and explorations of problems in ethical theory, on the other. These diverse projects all reflect my overarching desire to understand what people value, and why, and the real-life implications of that valuing. In past works, I have described this as an interest in "lived ethics," paralleling "lived religion," an approach in religious studies that examines the embodied practices of concrete religious communities.[7] This reflects a refinement of the question that first drew me to religious studies as an undergraduate: what happens to big ideas in real life? Philosophical ethics seemed, most of the time, far removed from this question, but in religious studies, I was able to learn about the ways communities interpreted, changed, and lived out their traditions' understandings of questions such as the proper purpose of community and human life and the nature of the good.

Among the most important distinguishing features of religious ethics is the fact that religious thinking, about morality and all other topics, is rooted in living communities. This makes it both social and practical, so it can never remain abstract. Religious ethics both emerge from practical experiences and are meant to be practiced. Just how they should be lived out is, of course, the subject of heated arguments within every religious community. These arguments, and religious values in general, are not exclusively the domain of an intellectual elite, as is the case for many secular philosophies. Some moral rules are the province of a small group, such as monastics or clerics, but in general, religious ethics are widely known, understood, and discussed by laypeople as well as specialists. Because religions have communal, practical, and institutional lives, they involve ordinary people who interpret the texts, commandments, rituals, and stories of their faith in diverse ways. All these features make religious ethics qualitatively different from most secular moral philosophies and especially important for a study of practice in ethics. They are important not only in themselves but also as a model for thinking about other lived ethics, such as feminism, pragmatism, and Marxism.

In this book, I undertake a comparative analysis of religious and philosophical ethics. This both highlights the intellectual traditions that have most shaped our culture's approaches to ethics and makes it possible to identify key themes, assumptions, and values across traditions. I not only understand religious ethics as rooted in particular communities and practices but also apply the same approach to secular theories. The latter are often presented as abstract, ideal, removed from material circumstances, but they are also developed by real people. Thus, religious ethics, and social ethics in particular, points us toward a model for thinking about morality as a living, collective, and active undertaking.

Defining Practices

I use the word *practice* in part to distinguish my approach from the treatment of *action* in analytic philosophy. In that model, ideas are prior to and independent of practice; the tendency to separate theory and practice is, in fact, "the key to analytical philosophy," as Alasdair MacIntyre writes.[8] In analytic philosophy, actions are of interest only when they are intentional, which assumes a particular relationship between practices and ideas. Ideas come first, and actions are the result or application of internal mental states. This model makes irrelevant the very large proportion of human activities that are not the result of explicit intentions, often with a label such as *behavior* suggesting its similarity to the presumably non-reflective, instinctive activities of nonhuman animals. Many philosophers agree, as Alfred Mele puts it, that "if there were no intentional actions, actions would be of little interest at best, and perhaps there would be no actions at all."[9] As far as actions are morally interesting, in this perspective, they consist of efforts made to implement particular intentions, understood as mental dispositions that are established in an actor's mind before she does anything. These prior intentions make an action good or bad, for ethics. My use of the term *practice* instead of *action* signals a departure from the analytic focus on intentional action and other features of philosophical action theory.

I also use the term *practice* to signal my affinity for the Marxist and pragmatist traditions. I am drawn to their expansive definitions of the practice, as in John Dewey's notion of "active operations"[10] and Karl Marx's concept of "human sensuous activity."[11] Both encompass not only deliberate actions but many other kinds of things people do, including habit and physical labor. Both pragmatism and Marxism, further, highlight the role of material conditions in the development and articulation of moral ideas. Ideas never exist in a vacuum but are always the products of real persons, influenced by their relations with other people and with the social, natural, and built environments. Furthermore, these relations always involve mutual transformation; there is no simple determinism between individuals and larger structures or between ideas and practices. These constructions of practice make pragmatist and Marxist thought especially helpful for my project here, although I also draw on a variety of other traditions of thought both to critique idealist models and to develop a practice-based approach.

The broad definitions suggested by Marx and Dewey indicate the range of activities that I want to include in my definition. Building on these approaches, it is possible to identify several important characteristics of *practice* as I use it throughout this book.

First, a practice is something that we do with and in our bodies. This includes activities we think of as mental, because the brain is part of the body, interacting with the rest of it, processing sensory experiences, expressing emotions, directing movement, and more. These sensuous activities constitute our lives and make them coherent, both personally and in collective, public ways. In and through practices, humans and other creatures use their senses to interact with, gain information about, and affect their environments and the other beings who share it. There is no disembodied mind that does our thinking and judging but only the embodied brain that is intimately connected to every other embodied part of us.[12] This means that talking is a physical activity, as are reading a book, writing an essay, playing the piano, building a house, kicking a ball, welding, walking a dog, riding a bike, chopping potatoes, washing dishes, hugging a friend, and hurting an enemy. Constructing and using ethical theories are also physical activities, because our brains are part of our bodies, and therefore all mental activity is itself physical, and also because mental activities are always connected to other bodily activities.

Second, practices are social. This is because humans are social animals, and this shapes everything we do. Practices are interactions between people, not always in the same time and place but sometimes across generations or across oceans. My apparently private practice of reading a book is an interaction with the author, with the people who suggested that I read it, with reviewers who influenced my view of it, with students and colleagues when we discuss the book, and so forth. Practices are social not only because they always involve interactions with other people but also because practices construct our relationships. We do not get to know or come to love (or hate) people in the abstract, but only in and through concrete, practical interactions.

Third, practices are always embedded in social and institutional contexts, including material structures, which are shaped and created by what people do, just as they in turn affect those doings. Economic and political conditions, which of course are the result of human practices, always shape the activities of people living within them. Practices are also ecologically embedded. We are not just social but also natural animals, dependent upon the nonhuman world and in constant, transformative interaction with it. We affect, and are affected by, natural processes and other organisms, and these practices are of great moral significance. Any ethical theory that does not take relations with nature into account in understanding human character and behavior will fall short. These relationships and contexts, further, shape not only what we are able to do and the results of our actions but also, less obviously but no less important, what we value and what we think we should do.

Fourth, practices are mediating. They are the way individuals are linked to larger structures. Practices connect us to the larger histories and institutions of which we are a part and also express and define our place in them. In other words, practices shape and are shaped by the intentions and ideas of individuals and also by the larger social forces that condition individuals' lives. The exact nature of the interactions varies widely, but they are never unidirectional. There is always a mutual influencing between the structures and practices. This mutuality does not imply equality, since power differences are almost always present, and the practices of different people or communities will also mediate in different ways. Thus, for example, the actions of Roman Catholic bishops express Church history and doctrine very differently from those of ordinary laypeople. Mediating practices can reinforce the status quo or transform it, due to a combination of factors that are internal and external, small and large, ideological and material.

Last, while practices are not always intentional, they are the ways people express their desires, values, and attitudes in everyday life. This relationship between practices and ideas, like that between practices and structures, is never linear. Sometimes practices are the ways people enact values, and other times they are the ways people construct values. We act on our ideas in multiple senses—sometimes we act *on the basis of* ideas we already have in mind before we act, but we also *act on* ideas so as to shape and change them. Our actions embody (not always consciously) particular interpretations of ideas and respond to ideas by reinforcing or challenging them. They may also generate ideas and shape our desires, attitudes, and motives, again reflecting the continuous, mutual shaping of mental states, bodily activities, and the environment in which we live.

Putting these elements together, we get a rough working definition: a practice is an activity in which humans use their bodies and senses to express themselves, relate to other people and to nonhuman nature, experience and get information about the world, and create and produce both meanings and other kinds of goods. Of course, I cannot discuss all kinds of practice, and some enter into and shape ethics more than others. I am especially interested in daily activities and habits, which are rarely discussed in ethical theory even though they constitute a large proportion of what people do. These ordinary activities often seem to involve little choice (going to work, washing dishes) while others represent decisions, often unreflective, to spend time and energy in a particular way (staying late at work rather than going home to a family dinner, for example). Many of these practices are part of long-term patterns in our lives, while others might be infrequent or temporary. Because these mundane activities define so much of our time, many of our most important moral values are embedded, created, and expressed in and through them.

I am also interested in practices that involve more reflective decisions. These include deliberate efforts to enact values, such as choosing vegetarianism or committing civil disobedience; ritual activities, such as religious services, prayer, meditation, or yoga; and group activities, including participation in organizations, sports teams, or clubs. Another important type of practice is labor, the work people do to support themselves and their families and to participate in collective projects. All of these are not just ways of expressing or enacting values but factors that shape and construct values themselves.

Organization of the Book

My argument begins with a critique of certain dominant approaches in and to ethical theory and proceeds to examine a wide array of theoretical frameworks and, in the later chapters, three quite different practical problems. In order to organize this far-ranging discussion, I keep in mind five themes that help clarify both my critique of idealist ethics and the characteristics of the practice-based approach I hope to develop:

1. The relationship between ideas and their context, including not only social structures and historical events but also personal experiences, emotions, and relationships. The idealist approaches I address in chapter 2 presume that ideas are largely independent of social context, either as the pure reason of Kant or the individual will of Augustinian Christianity. Against these approaches, I argue that ideas are never disembodied or decontextualized. This is tied to a view of knowledge as always situated. There are no absolute answers, no fixed foundations, no final solutions, and no view from nowhere. Ethics is thus partial and provisional, rather than transcendent and absolute, and it is never just about the application of neutral reason to isolated problems. Moral ideas, and ideas in general, are always shaped by and tied to practices, emotions, relationships, culture, history, and material conditions.

2. How different ethical theories relate form and content. Idealist models in ethics, including the dominant Kantian, social contract, and utilitarian models, assume that ethics is largely a matter of identifying correct procedures for decision-making. These procedures are thought to be independent from substantive norms and values. They are empty vessels or, to use Clifford Geertz's term, "thin."[13] I contend, however, that there can be no purely procedural ethic. All ways of conceiving of "ethics in general" assume and also suggest particular substantive "thick" commitments. Normative content and other details, in other words, always shape forms and procedures; the "vessel" is always altered by its content. Thus, attempts to describe ethical theory in formalist terms miss—or actively ignore—the mutual shaping of form and content and the impossibility of creating a theory that is free of values, biases, histories, interests, and other substantive details. It is best to be clear about this and analyze the origins and implications of the content rather than misdescribing theory in thin, universalist terms.

3. *How conceptions of human nature shape ethical theorizing.* Most influential philosophical ethics, and some religious ones as well, assume that moral actors are autonomous individuals who think about problems and reach decisions based only on internal reasoning or, in religious contexts, on personal faith. However, I contend that people are social animals and that ethics must also be social, in two different ways. First, we never think or act morally as isolated individuals; our ideas about value as well as our options for acting are profoundly shaped by our experiences with and relations to other people, as well as the material structures in which we are embedded. In addition, ethics itself is a social project: what we think about, when we think morally, is our relationships to others and our communities. And when we act morally, we always affect and are affected by other people, institutions, and traditions far beyond any individual actor.

4. *The relationship between ethics and other kinds of thought and action or spheres of life.* Many ways of thinking about ethics, both popular and academic, conceive of it as a peculiar aspect of human life, different and separate from other spheres of life. I believe, however, that ethical reasoning and action are linked to and similar to other kinds of thought and action. Ethics is not "modular," as Margaret Urban Walker puts it;[14] it is not a self-contained compartment off to the side of the rest of our lives but an aspect of everything we think and do.

5. *The relations between ideas, actions, and consequences.* Many philosophers and theologians assume a linear connection, such that ideas are formulated internally, conceived of as intentions which are "applied" in actions which themselves lead to predictable consequences. I show, however, that the linear model fails in several ways: it does not accurately describe the relations between moral ideas and actions, and it also fails to take into account the unpredictability of consequences. A better approach acknowledges the mutual shaping of ideas, actions, and external factors and the constantly shifting relationship between means and ends.

All five themes are relevant in each chapter, though not with the same tone or degree of significance in every case. The relations between ideas and material context, for example, is especially prominent in Marxist theory, while the tensions between thin and thick models come to the fore in debates about free speech. Further, these themes are interrelated, so it is not always possible to distinguish among them. Thus, they serve as heuristic devices rather than exhaustive analyses of the implications of practice for ethics. Nonetheless, I find these themes useful for organizing and focusing disparate arguments, clarifying comparisons across tradition and cases, and highlighting important issues that recur throughout my analyses of both different theories and different real-life problems.

* * * * *

Following this introduction, chapter 2 explores the primacy of ideas in dominant ethical theories, focusing on several influential religious and secular traditions: Lutheran Christianity, including its roots in the thought of both Paul and Augustine, and Kantian philosophy. Despite their differences, these models agree that the agent's intentions are the key to moral evaluation; what makes a decision morally good or bad is in the actor's head. Augustine and Martin Luther, following Paul, frame this in terms of faith, will, and love, while Kantians emphasize decision-making processes, which must be completed prior to any actions. Because they prioritize attitudes and intentions, these models marginalize practice. In this chapter, as throughout the book, I compare religious and secular approaches, showing how they influence each other, historically and currently, and how neither alone can fully account for either academic or popular thinking about ethics.

Chapter 3 (written with Gabriel Vásquez-Peterson) moves to models that see practice as something other than the mechanistic application of internal reasoning. The theories highlighted in this chapter—virtue ethics, feminist ethics, Roman Catholic social thought, and liberation theology—are driven by substantive, normative claims about the good and ways to achieve it. They also all share a social view of human nature and a conviction that ethics is integrated with other parts of life, not an isolated sphere of decision-making. The chapter begins with virtue ethics, including its Aristotelian roots and several contemporary interpreters. Virtue theories insist that the whole person, not just decision-making procedures, matter for ethics, and they offer substantive norms and goals to be pursued through a lifetime of good works. It then turns to feminist care ethics, which critiques the rationalism, individualism, and idealism of Enlightenment-based ethical models. Care theorists, like virtue ethicists, present a substantive vision of moral goodness in which emotions, relationships, and practices are crucial to defining the good. These themes also emerge in Catholic ethics, including liberation theology. Against Luther's reliance on faith alone, these traditions insist that in and through their practices, people may share in the divine process of creation and per-haps even help build the reign of God. All these models, in different ways, challenge the idealist, rationalist, and individualist emphases of mainstream ethics, in which the decisions of a willing actor are all that matters.

Chapter 4 looks at pragmatism, which conceives of a particular form of practice—problem-solving in concrete circumstances—as the core ethical task. Pragmatism has much to offer a practice-based ethic, beginning with its robust challenges to the static, idealist, and dualistic approach of dominant theories. I find especially helpful the pragmatist emphasis on open-ended, fallibilistic inquiry, which offers promising models for working around or through polarized ways of thinking about moral issues that can prevent ef-fective action. I also highlight William James's notion of cash value, which points to the meaning of moral ideas in real life, and Dewey's concept of ends-in-view, which challenges both linear models of action and the possi-bility of absolute, once-and-for-all goals.

Chapter 5 examines Marxist thought, which is primarily a sociological rather than an ethical framework. Even though Marx showed little interest in moral theory, both meta-ethical and normative claims run throughout his work. Later Marxist thinkers also developed theories with clear moral assumptions and goals, from their anthropology to visions of a revolution-ized society. Marxist thought makes "human sensuous activities" central to everything, and that has to include its (implicit) ethical theory. I am espe-cially interested in Marx's emphases on the role of material forces in shaping ideas and on the creative tensions between individuals and structures. To explore these issues, I engage the thought of Marx and some of his recent interpreters to understand the ways all ideas, including ideas about value, are grounded in material practices, experiences, and structures.

Chapter 6 looks at religious pacifism, mainly Christian but also Gandhian. One of my primary arguments in this chapter is that pacifism is not merely an applied ethic—a narrow approach to the particular moral problem of war—but rather a comprehensive ethical theory. The same is true, I add, of just war theory, the other main approach to the morality of war. The chapter begins with the Radical Reformation or Anabaptist stream within Christianity, which rejects consequentialist calculations of cause and effect while also insisting that practices lie at the heart of Christian morality. These themes also drive the thought of Martin Luther King Jr., who was not only an effective activist but also a sophisticated and innovative ethical theorist. King emphasizes in particular the relationship between means and ends, a theme that is important to other pacifist thinkers and to my reconceptualization of practice in ethical theory. This is also central to the thought of Mohandas K. Gandhi, a major influence on King. Gandhi insisted that practices are the only means we have for pursuing our moral ends. They are not just tools for achieving predetermined goals, however, but shape the ways we conceive of those ends and of the possibilities and obstacles we face in achieving them. This offers a radically different way of conceiving not just means and ends but ethics generally, one in which practices are central from start to finish.

Following these theoretically focused chapters, I turn to several concrete problems and explore the themes and perspectives that come to the fore when we highlight practice. Chapter 7 examines the moral problems raised by the "campus tour" of white nationalist Richard Spencer. This provides a way to reflect on some of the issues raised in and by moral dilemmas as a strategy within ethical theory, including their helpfulness for addressing real-life challenges. It also shows the power of practice to put familiar moral conflicts in a new light. In the case of Spencer, and hate speech generally, a practice-focused approach enables us to see beyond the tension between two competing values of racial equality and free speech. That dilemmatic framing leaves out the lived experiences of people who are concretely threatened by white supremacists, the actual practices of those supremacists, and the relationships and structures of the society in which both racists and their victims live.

Chapter 8 turns to one of the most important and controversial issues in medical ethics: euthanasia and physician assisted suicide (PAS). When we approach this problem through the lens of practice, we encounter the everyday actions and relationships of diverse parties as crucial influences not just on specific decisions but also on the ways the moral dilemma itself is framed. The intensely personal scale of mercy killing makes it possible to consider practice in a very concrete way, including activities that shape the situations of very ill people and their relations with a variety of other moral agents, from family members and physicians to policymakers. I explore not only human euthanasia and PAS but also killings of nonhuman animals, including both the euthanasia of beloved pets and the killing of homeless dogs and cats in shelters. This comparison highlights the difference that relationships make in ethical arguments. It also reveals how much species runs through ethical argumentation, in the form of unquestioned assumptions about what makes a life valuable.

Chapter 9 examines climate change, the most pressing environmental problem of our time. I focus on the ways practice can help us think about key issues, such as the gap between values and practices, the ways economics and technologies shape moral attitudes and actions, and the problem of moral responsibility and consequences. I also consider the question of what individuals can and should do in response to a problem that is far too big for individual actions to fix. The vastness of climate change demands that both environmental and social ethicists rethink some common assumptions and develop innovative models for understanding and mitigating humans' destructive impact on the natural world.

The conclusion, chapter 10, explores some of the features of a practice-based approach to ethical theory. I contend that rather than being isolated in one or another compartment, or ignored completely, practice should be and in fact is integral to all aspects of ethical theory. Because dominant models do not and cannot take practice seriously, we cannot foreground practice within the usual theoretical confines. To understand practice, we have to reshape ethical theory, and vice versa. We will not find real alternatives unless we put practice front and center. Beginning with practice, I contend, makes it possible to rethink our vision of ethics at the same time as it demands such a rethinking.

2

It's the Thought That Counts

The Triumph of the Will in Western Ethical Theory

> Nothing can possibly be conceived in the world, or even out of it,
> which can be called good without qualification, except a *good will*.
>
> —Immanuel Kant[1]

Introduction

In this chapter, I begin my discussion of practice in ethical theory by examining several important moral theories that largely ignore and denigrate
practice. It is impossible to explore the place of practice in ethics without understanding how some of the most influential models have ignored, dismissed,
and excluded practice. Toward that goal, this chapter analyzes the hegemony
of ideas and intentions in a broad sense. I first outline the major characteristics of the idealist model and then look at several theories that embody this
approach and have strongly influenced Western religious and philosophical
ethics generally. I start with Saint Paul, Saint Augustine, and Martin Luther,
foundational Christian theologians who prioritize faith and the "inner law"
above works. I turn next to Immanuel Kant, the thinker with the most influence on secular philosophical ethics. I then begin my comparative analysis by
highlighting some important themes that the Kantian tradition shares with
Augustinian and Lutheran Christianity.

Idealist traditions of thought have shaped a distinctive approach to moral
problems that continues to dominate many discussions in theological and
philosophical ethics today. I argue that this approach includes a polarized,
linear, and inaccurate view of moral ideas and behavior. These traits reflect
and reinforce the marginalization or exclusion of practice from Western
moral theories. It is important to show how this marginalization has developed, before turning to the possibility of a more central role for practice in
ethics.

Works Righteousness. Anna L. Peterson, Oxford University Press (2021). © Oxford University Press.
DOI: 10.1093/oso/9780197532232.001.0001.

The Hegemony of Idealism

The ethical theories with the most influence in Western religion and philosophy identify moral goodness with mental attitudes, such as intentions and
motives, which are internal to the moral actor. This idealism has roots in the
Christianity of Paul, Augustine, and Luther and is developed in the secular
philosophies of the Enlightenment, especially Kantianism. These models
differ in many important ways, but they share an assumption that it is the
thought that counts: people's mental states determine the moral quality of
their actions. This notion is certainly not unique to Christianity or the West,
but Western philosophy and Christian theology have developed particularly
influential ways of understanding the significance of intentions.

According to this approach, practice is external to morality; it enters only
after the real work of ethical discernment and decision-making has been
completed. Actions may be an application of good intentions or an instrument for achieving desired goals, but they do not enter into the creation, interpretation, or transformation of values. Instead, internal attitudes alone
decide what has value; thus, thinking and intending "constitute the essential
moral act," as Charlene Seigfried writes. The logic behind this is that while
we control our inner feelings and thoughts, "actions are accidental, not completely under our control, and morally ambiguous. Deeply embedded in this
thinking is the attractiveness of the spirituality of a hidden and inner life and
a denigration of the physicality of bodily actions."[2] The notion that willing
is the essential moral act dominates all aspects of ethical theory: normative
claims about what has value and why, applied moral judgments about particular situations, and meta-ethical reflections about the nature of ethical
theory.

The focus on ideas and intentions is part of a framework that has dominated ethical theory, particular in the English-speaking world, since the
Enlightenment. Margaret Urban Walker calls this the "theoretical-juridical
model" (TJM), which "represents morality itself as if it were, primarily or in
its most important part, a surprisingly compact kind of theory or some kind
of internal guidance system of an agent that could be modeled by that kind
of theory. It makes morality look as if it consists in, or could be represented
by, a compact cluster of beliefs."[3] The TJM is not itself a moral theory but
rather a meta-ethic, "a kind of template for organizing moral inquiry into the
pursuit of a certain kind of moral theory."[4] This parallels my interest in developing not a particular ethical theory but a more general approach to thinking

about ethics in regards to practice, one that contrasts with the TJM in crucial aspects.

Many of the traits of the TJM, as Walker describes it, entail a marginalization of practice. First, she asserts, this model is idealist, or what she calls intellectualist, "in seating morality primarily in some central, specifically moral, beliefs." Next, it is rationalist, in assuming "that the central moral beliefs are to be understood and tested primarily by reflection on concepts and logical analysis of the relations of evidential support among moral beliefs." It is individualist, in "its assumption that the central moral concepts and premises are to equip each moral agent with a guidance system he or she can use to decide upon a life or its parts." And last, it is formalistic and impersonal: "The right equipment tells one what is right to do . . . no matter who one might happen to be and what individual life one is living, no matter what form of social life one inhabits and one's station within it."[5] Substantive features of people's lives, including their histories, commitments, practices, and material circumstances, do not alter the rules or procedures by which one reflects on moral issues.

These features of the TJM overlap substantially, though not perfectly, with the idealist theories I address here. The gap stems in part from Walker's failure to address religious ethics—a shortcoming that is common to moral philosophers, who appear to find religious belief systems insignificant, uninteresting, or inadequate. In particular, religious ethics, including those I describe in this chapter and also the more practice-focused approaches I explore later in the book, do not rely on human reason as much as many dominant philosophical models. However, they often share the other features that Walker lists, including idealism or intellectualism: the notion that ethics is an exclusive quality of beliefs or other mental states. Many religious ethics, further, focus on the individual moral agent and understand goodness as a general, universal quality (often originating in the divine) that is not affected by social and personal context. These features stem from and reinforce the marginalization of practice.

The prime example of the TJM is Kantianism, which has also influenced most of the other versions of this approach, including utilitarian, social contract, and rights theories, most notably. These approaches have dominated twentieth-century Anglo-American ethics, as is evident in the ways it shapes research, teaching, publications, and scholarly discussions. An example of this dominance is the ways most philosophical discussions of moral dilemmas, hypothetical or real, are framed as choices between two types of rationalist approaches, usually Kantian and utilitarian. These are presented as the only possible ways to resolve a given conflict, and further, they appear to exhaust the ways we can and should think about moral conflicts generally. The idealist or intellectualist paradigm sets the terms of debate, the ways in which we are supposed (and allowed) to think and act morally. Thus, even alternative models frame their critiques in language set by dominant models.

This dominance is a form of hegemony, the power that enables "the cultured European classes" to make "the terms evolved by themselves accepted everywhere," as Marxist theorist Antonio Gramsci puts it.[6] To say that a culture or worldview is hegemonic is not to imply that it is the only one that exists or that it has gone unchallenged.[7] However, because this model sets the terms of debate, theories that diverge are almost inevitably framed as challenges, critiques, or alternatives to the "mainstream" model. In Walker's words, the dominance of a paradigm can be measured by "its success in making work done within its discipline but done in other ways struggle against it, thereby acknowledging and reproducing its importance."[8] This hegemonic paradigm includes several core assumptions that directly and indirectly reinforce the centrality of ideas and intentions and the marginalization of practice. These assumptions can be understood as the idealist interpretation of the themes I introduced in chapter 1: the autonomy of ideas, a division between form and content, normative and methodological individualism, the separation of ethics from other spheres of life, and a linear conception of moral action. I keep these themes in mind throughout this chapter, both to organize my analysis and critique of the moral theories discussed here and to build the foundation for a meaningful, robust comparison across traditions.

The Interiorization of Christian Ethics

Christianity began after the death of Jesus, as his disciples carved out a distinctive identity distinct from their origins as a minority movement within Judaism. During this formative period, the new religion encompassed a wide range of ideas, practices, pastoral and communal activities, and cultural identities. Early Christians argued about issues including their relation to Judaism, the nature of Jesus, salvation, the Trinity, the sacraments, and church leadership. Practice entered into many of these conflicts, though not always explicitly. One of the most important questions concerned Jesus's activities and their importance for Christian theology and ethics. During the first few centuries CE, some groups claimed that Jesus was divine and only appeared human, while others asserted that he was fully human and not really divine.

While these Christological controversies officially ended after the fifth century, their influence is still evident in varying views of Jesus among Christians today, which in turn shape ethical positions. Some groups emphasize the "historical Jesus" described in the Synoptic Gospels (Matthew, Mark, and Luke) and define Christian ethics as an effort to imitate what Jesus actually did—his practices of nonresistance, welcoming strangers and outcasts, forgiving enemies, and so forth. In contrast, others emphasize the "Christ of faith," focusing on the salvific power of Jesus's death and resurrection. Many theologians point out that the historical Jesus and the Christ of faith are not mutually exclusive and that a correct conception of Christianity will embrace both. Nonetheless, different communities prioritize one version or the other, and these choices make a difference in their ethics. Specifically, the emphasis on faith over works in some streams contributes to an interiorization of Christian ethics that still wields great influence today.

This approach can be traced to the work of the apostle Paul, a Jew who converted after Jesus's death and became Christianity's first great theologian. Paul's complex relationship to Jewish law lies at the heart of his arguments about faith and ethics. On the one hand, he insists that Jesus brought a "new law" which is written on believers' hearts and transcends the Jewish "old law." On the other hand, Paul affirms Jesus's continuity with Judaism. This approach reflects both a theological struggle and a practical tension. While not wanting to alienate the earliest (Jewish) Christians, Paul believed that it would be impossible to convert Gentiles if becoming Christian required adherence to Jewish law, including circumcision. To manage this tension, he proposed that "A person is not a Jew who is one only outwardly, nor is circumcision merely outward and physical. No, a person is a Jew who is one inwardly; and circumcision is circumcision of the heart, by the Spirit, not by the written code" (Romans 2:28–29). This dual approach to circumcision reflects Paul's broader claims about the law and works in general.

Jesus's death and resurrection offer salvation to all believers, regardless of their personal histories or practices, and render other paths to salvation unnecessary: "just as one trespass resulted in condemnation for all people, so also one righteous act resulted in justification and life for all people" (Romans 5:18). Before Christ, the Jewish law was necessary, but now salvation requires only the "inner law" of love that is written on the believer's heart. "Before the coming of this faith, we were held in custody under the law, locked up until the faith that was to come would be revealed. So the law was our guardian until Christ came that we might be justified by faith. Now that this faith has come, we are no longer under a guardian" (Galatians 3:23–25). The new law, according to Paul, is more demanding than the old one, which mandated ritual and dietary obligations but did not require the all-encompassing internal transformation of Christianity.

This internal transformation became central to later Christian thinkers, including perhaps the most important of all, Augustine of Hippo (354–430 CE). Augustine continued Paul's project of linking salvation to an internal shift, made possible by divine grace. Like Paul, Augustine emphasizes subjective inner states. As Robert Holmes puts it, "Augustine turns Christianity inward."[9] Now, Augustine declares, "not what the man does is the thing to be considered; but with what mind and will he does it."[10] In *City of God*, he argues that what a person wills or loves best determines their citizenship in the city of God or the city of man. True Christians belong to the former, because they love God above all, while the denizens of the city of man love their own interest best. It is "the character of the human will which makes the affections of the soul right or wrong," he writes. If the will is wrong, then its affections will be wrong, "but if it is right, they will be not merely blameless, but even praiseworthy. For the will is in them all; yea, none of them is anything else than will."[11]

This inward turn has sweeping practical implications, making permissible actions that were previously prohibited. Paul asserted that as long as Christians had the law "written on their hearts," they need not undergo circumcision; Augustine goes further to read much of scripture metaphorically, proclaiming "that Christ's injunctions in the Sermon on the Mount do not apply to outward action but rather to inner attitude."[12] Thus the "hard" sayings of the Gospels—Jesus' injunctions to "love your neighbors" (Matthew 5:44) or "sell your possessions and give to the poor" (Matthew 19:21) need not be read literally. Salvation is determined by believers' interior state—their will—and not their practices. Augustine thus deepened the interior shift initiated by Paul. He also added a new emphasis on the freedom of the will. Free will makes evil possible, he asserts, because it permits people to turn away from the goodness of God's creation. "The cause of evil," Augustine writes, "is the defection of the will of a being who is mutably good from the Good which is immutable."[13] Humans' ability to choose good or evil is identical with the ability to turn toward or away from God. This is determined not by physical actions but by interior motives. For Augustine, as James Pratt argues, "It is the will, and the will alone, that is essentially evil. The thing toward which the evil will turns is neither evil nor good. Nothing is evil but the evil will."[14]

Augustine's emphasis on intentions shapes his approach to concrete moral problems, including war. The physical act of killing is not the chief evil of war, he argues, because every person "will soon die anyway." Rather, he believes that "the evil to be avoided is not death, but rather an evil intention in causing death or other forms of injury in war," as James Turner Johnson writes. Just as a bad intention can render apparently good deeds worthless, according to Augustine, sometimes killing in war can be "justified because of its rightly ordered intentionality."[15] Augustine's view of war is tied to his larger theological ethic by an insistence that the agent's intention, and not the objective character of the act itself, determines its moral quality. This claim that intentions matter most in determining the morality of war remains a central theme in modern just war theory.

Martin Luther (1483–1546) is the direct heir of both Paul and Augustine, and he pushed their thought toward a more radical interiorization of Christian ethics. Before he launched the Protestant Reformation, Luther was an Augustinian monk and one of many Catholic critics of the official Church's corruption, reflected especially in the buying and selling of indulgences (exemptions from divine punishment for certain sins). Luther's attacks grew into a radical challenge not just to particular failings of the institutional church but more broadly to the theological, ecclesiological, and pastoral foundations of Catholicism. This challenge is reflected in core Lutheran concerns such as the priority of scripture, the rejection of clerical mediation, and, perhaps most of all, the elevation of individual faith as the key to salvation.

Grounding many of Luther's theological claims was an echo of Augustine's dualistic view of Christian life on earth. While Augustine posited the existence of two cities, Luther described two kingdoms, one heavenly and one earthly. In the former, humans are radically free, ruled only by Christian love—but this extends only to matters directly concerning faith and salvation. In the earthly realm, humans must be totally obedient to secular authorities and rules, even "bearing the sword" if commanded by the ruler.[16] Thus, Luther asserts, paradoxically: "A Christian is a perfectly free lord of all, subject to none. A Christian is a perfectly dutiful servant of all, subject to all."[17] This divided citizenship and dual obedience reflect what Luther calls humans' "twofold nature," one spiritual and one bodily.[18] The former is all that matters for salvation and ethics; the latter must be disciplined, so that it does not fall into sin.

Luther embraces a dualism not only between the kingdoms of heaven and earth but also within people, between the soul and the body. His dualism is more extensive than that of Augustine, who repeatedly affirmed the goodness of creation and physical embodiment, in no small part because of his conscious rejection of his Manichean roots. Luther also diverges from Augustine by dismissing the mediation of the institutional Church, including the sacraments, priests, and the pope. According to Luther, not only is individual faith all that matters, but also faith requires no institutional assistance to communicate directly with God or to discern what is right. Every Christian is a priest, needing only scripture (*sola scriptura*) as a guide to correct belief: "Not only are we the freest of kings, we are also priests forever, which is far more excellent than being kings, for as priests we are worthy to appear before God to pray for others and to teach one another divine things."[19]

These convictions are supported by Luther's insistence that faith alone (*sola fides*) contributes to salvation. More precisely, Luther claims that Christians are saved only through their faith and by God's grace, and not as a result of works. Works, for Luther, include any human activity, including acts of charity as well as more cynical or sinful behavior. This challenges the Catholic assertion that some good deeds can contribute to the fate of the doer's eternal soul. Luther's theory of salvation rests on his belief that humans are too weak and sinful to be able to save themselves, on the one hand, and his view of divine grace as all-powerful, on the other. "As the soul needs only the word of God for its life and righteousness, so it is justified by faith alone and not any works; for if it could be justified by anything else, it would not need the Word, and consequently it would not need faith."[20] Salvation is entirely a free gift of God, completely unrelated to any actions done by humans. Thus, Luther asks, "Do we work nothing for the obtaining of this righteousness?" He answers himself: "Nothing at all. For the nature of this righteousness is to do nothing, to hear nothing, to know nothing whatsoever of the law or of works, but to know and to believe this only, that Christ is gone to the Father and is not now seen."[21] Only what is in a person's heart matters, and this inner conviction or faith has no functional relationship to the believer's deeds.

Works, for Luther, are associated with "the law," meaning in particular Jewish law but more broadly any set of rules that links justification to certain actions and rituals. For Luther, those who embrace true faith not only do not need the law, but in fact they must abandon the law: "To live unto the law is to die unto God; and contrariwise, to die to the law is to live unto God."[22] This echoes Paul's assertion that "a person is not justified by the works of the law, but by faith in Jesus Christ" (Galatians 2:16). However, Luther, like Paul, recognizes the risks of complete freedom from rules and seeks to balance freedom from the law with the demands of proper Christian behavior. While practical activities cannot affect the status of the soul, he contends, freedom from the law does not liberate Christians from all moral rules. This creates ambivalence regarding ethical action, reflected in Luther's own writings. Most notably, he rejects the claim of the Book of James that "faith without works is dead," as the common shorthand version asserts. When Luther translated the Christian scriptures (New Testament) into German, he omitted James, which he called "an epistle of straw." In his view, James places too much emphasis on the law, which for Luther is inextricably tied to works and to the false (in his view) conviction that human actions could affect God's decisions about salvation. Faith in Christ, for Luther, frees Christians "from the foolish presumption that justification is acquired by works."[23]

Luther's stance on works creates a conflict, which he acknowledges. He does not want Christians to believe that they may sin freely just because works are ineffective for salvation. However, it is not clear why Christians should do good deeds, if all that matters ultimately is what is in the believer's heart. Luther makes explicit the moral challenge implied by his theology: "If faith does all things, why are good works commanded? Why not just take our ease and do no works and be content with faith?"[24] He offers various replies to this question. Perhaps most important, the law serves "to bridle the wicked."[25] While Christians will refrain from sinning because they are ruled by love, others require the force of law and the threat of violence to refrain from wrongdoing. This use of the sword, however, does not make men righteous, according to Luther, but rather underlines their sinfulness, by revealing that only force keeps them from evil: "For in that I do not kill, I do not commit adultery, I do not steal, or in that I abstain from other sins, I do it not willingly or for the love of virtue, but I fear the prison, the sword, and the hangman. These do bridle and restrain me that I sin not, as bonds and chains do restrain a lion or a bear, that he tear and devour not everything that he meeteth; therefore the restraining from sin is not righteousness, but rather signification of unrighteousness."[26] Christians do not need the rules that keep society safe from the wicked, but they must follow them nonetheless.

They do so, Luther explains, because just as a good tree bears good fruit, so good Christians will naturally do good deeds, even though they gain nothing by their actions. As he writes, "Good works do not make a good man, but a good man does good works; evil works do not make a wicked man, but a wicked man does evil works."[27] In other words, inner good or sinfulness is prior, both chronologically and ontologically, to action. Thus, for Luther, "a man must first be good or wicked before he does a good or wicked work, and his works do not make him good or wicked, but he himself makes his works either good or wicked."[28] More directly, true Christians will do good deeds not because they find the deeds good by some independent measure but because the actions of a true Christian are, by definition, good. Actions are not just external to the person but empty of moral content other than as an expression of the actor's previously established qualities. Deeds are good only if, and because, they are the actions of a good person.

This view of the relationship between interior attitudes and actions leads to a linear conception of moral action: good or bad intentions will make deeds good or bad. Many secular philosophical ethicists share this belief in a simple, straightforward cause-and-effect relationship between ideas and actions. Mental states such as intentions or faith come first, independent of actions, and can give actions a corresponding moral quality. If this linear model truly describes the relationship between ideas and actions, then it makes sense for ethicists to focus on internal attitudes. The problem, as both history and empirical studies show, is that the relationship between intentions and actions is far from straightforward. On the individual level, it is often hard to act on good intentions, as Paul himself acknowledges: "For I do not do the good I want to do, but the evil I do not want to do—this I keep doing" (Romans 7:19). Knowing the good and wanting to do it, in other words, does not always lead to good deeds. This is the problem of akrasia, which I discuss in more detail in chapter 9. Sometimes, further, the relationship between knowing and doing is more complicated: we cannot even know the good before we act. In the doing, we come to see and understand the values.

The notion that the proper will or intention must be in place before, and as a condition of, moral action became central as Christian ethics developed from Paul through Augustine and Luther. This aspect of Christianity, in particular, was crucial for the emergence of modern philosophical ethics, which emphasizes will or intentions and a linear relationship between ideas, actions, and consequences. Thus, even though the philosophical Enlightenment and in particular its most famous thinker, Kant, are widely seen as rejections of religion, in fact they follow directly from a particular stream of Christian moral thinking.

Kantian Ethics

The influence of Immanuel Kant (1724–1804) on Western ethics and philosophy in general cannot be overstated. His ideas have played a central role in philosophical thinking since the Enlightenment and still loom large in scholarly discussions today. The foundation for Kant's ethics is his belief that moral decisions must be based on "non-factual, a priori criteria by which maxims of conduct can be assessed as to their ethical standing."[29] This leaves no room for consequences, feelings, or other empirical considerations, including psychological, historical, or anthropological factors. Those are all external to the will, according to Kant, which is the only thing that can be inherently good in itself. The echo of Augustine is unmistakable here:

> A will is not good because of what it effects or accomplishes—because of its fitness for attaining some proposed end: it is good through its willing alone—that is, good in itself. Considered in itself it is to be esteemed beyond comparison as far higher than anything it could ever bring about merely in order to favour some inclination or, if you like, the sum total of inclinations. Even if. . . this will is entirely lacking in power to carry out its intentions; if by its utmost effort it still accomplishes nothing, and only good will is left (not, admittedly, as a mere wish, but as the straining of every means so far as they are in our control); even then it would still shine like a jewel for its own sake as something which has full value in itself.[30]

In addition to his emphasis on the will, Kant insists that morality must rest on rational, universal principles. Embodied experience, including information gained through our senses as well as practical activities, cannot provide the kind of universally true knowledge that must ground morality. The only activity that matters for ethics, or for philosophy generally, is mental activity that is deliberately separated from bodily actions. Thus, he writes, "Not only are moral laws with their principles essentially distinguished from every other kind of practical knowledge in which there is anything empirical, but all moral philosophy rests wholly on its pure part. When applied to man, it does not borrow the least thing from the knowledge of man himself (anthropology), but gives laws a priori to him as a rational being."[31]

The sole role for experience in Kant's moral theory lies in its capacity to sharpen the judgment used to evaluate situations and discipline agents to act on the correct laws. In this sense, experiences can help people tame the many "inclinations" that challenge reason, so they are better able to make "practical pure reason . . . effective *in concreto*" in their lives.[32] This experience appears to be primarily intellectual, however—a honing of mental capacities of discernment and judgment. Material practices, including daily activities, physical labor, or social interactions, are not just irrelevant but actively detrimental to correct moral reasoning. They are part of "anthropology," according to Kant, with no place in ethics.

Because he finds moral value only in ideas that are rational, abstract, and decontextualized, Kant concludes that even apparently charitable acts are not truly good unless they are motivated by the proper intentions. This is crucial to his ethical theory: "In order that an action should be morally good, it is not enough that it *conform* to the moral law, but it must also be done *for the sake of the law*, otherwise that conformity is only very contingent and uncertain; since a principle which is not moral, although it may now and then produce actions conformable to the law, will also often produce actions which contradict it."[33] This echoes Luther's insistence that the problem with works is false ideas about them. Works can be valuable only if they stem from right ideas and proper faith.

Since circumstances cannot enter into moral reflection, we must not consider the potential consequences of our actions. Kant's disregard for consequences is most famously crystallized in his response to the "murderer at the door," where he insists that it is never morally acceptable to tell a lie, even with the goal of saving an innocent life.[34] The imperative to tell the truth yields no exceptions, and "benevolent purposes" cannot justify wrongdoing. Kant called the Latin phrase *Fiat justitia, pereat mundus* ("Let justice reign even if the world should perish from it") a "stout principle of right."[35] This exemplifies Kant's rejection of empirical considerations. Even in the direst situations, moral agents must follow the law without concern for what happens after they act. And if they do, as Christine Korsgaard writes, "bad outcomes are not [their] responsibility."[36]

People can only follow rules in this blinkered way if they are unaffected by emotions, past experiences, relationships, or social context. The self-contained character of the moral actor is essential to Kant's categorical imperative: "Inexperienced in the course of the world, incapable of being prepared for all its contingencies, I only ask myself: Canst thou also will that thy maxim should be a universal law?"[37] Social experiences and relationships are all considered external to the self which is defined by and presumed to be in control of internal mental states. An individual may choose to enter into relationships, out of duty or self-interest, but these relationships do not constitute or alter the essential self. That self is affected, and even constituted, by "inner" factors such as the soul, reason, or the will.

The Kantian model of ethics as rational, intentional, individualistic, and separate from the partiality of ordinary life makes material practice irrelevant in several ways. Most obviously, it confines ethics to the interior life of each moral agent, separate from the rest of life. Material practices, like other aspects of bodily existence, cannot enter into and must in fact be carefully separated from both the articulation of the moral law and the mental attitudes that make its fulfillment possible. There can be rules about the body, but the body and its practices have no part in generating the rules. Actions themselves have no value apart from the intentions that inspired them. In addition, Kant separates means and ends, as expressed in his "practical imperative" (often called the second formulation of the categorical imperative): "Act in such a way that you always treat humanity, whether in your own persons or in the person of any other, never simply as a means, but always at the same time as an end."[38] Being an end is not a result of other people's actions or ideas but an essential quality of persons, just as being a means is an essential characteristic of nonpersons, such as inanimate objects or natural entities. Thus, treating a person only as a means is a category mistake, a failure to recognize intrinsic value.[39] This presumption that we can clearly distinguish between means and ends is an important part of idealist models, particularly in relation to the presumed autonomy of ideas and the linear model of behavior. This is challenged by practice-oriented theories, especially pragmatism and religious pacifism, which see ends and means as intimately related and often indistinguishable.

Moral Dilemmas and Dilemmatic Thinking

Idealist ethical theories do not incorporate practice into normative definitions of goodness or meta-ethical questions about what constitutes moral thinking. They address practice, or practical implications, in two primary ways. The first is applied ethics, which considers the ways moral theories guide action in particular settings, especially for professionals in healthcare and biomedical research, law, and business. I discuss applied issues in legal, medical, and environmental ethics in chapters 7, 8, and 9.

The other main way practice is addressed, particularly in mainstream philosophical approaches, is in relation to moral dilemmas. Dilemmas describe situations in which mutually exclusive values, duties, or goods are at stake but the moral actor can choose only one. Often, they are framed as conflicts between values that take priority in different ethical theories, for example, between individual liberty and social utility, or between rule following and cost-benefit analysis. Many philosophers find dilemmas useful to focus attention on issues about the character and also the practical implications of different theories, rules, and principles, such as how we can choose between two similarly bad consequences or when it is acceptable to break a moral rule. They also make it possible to isolate concepts and arguments.

In relation to practice, dilemmas are helpful because they ask how ethics guides reflections about what to do—what practices should follow from different theories and what happens when we put those theories into practice. As Judith Jarvis Thomson puts it, dilemmas help us grapple with what William James might call the "cash value" of important yet problematic moral concepts.[40] This cash value hinges on what the concept means in practice: what might be the real-life implications, including harms and benefits to different parties, of acting in accordance with particular moral guidelines. In asking about these practical dimensions, dilemmas highlight the relations between intentions, actions, and consequences in different theoretical models.

To explore these issues further, it is helpful to consider a few well-known hypothetical dilemmas. One of the most famous is Philippa Foot's famous trolley problem, presented in an article about the morality of abortion.[41] In the original and simplest version, the driver of a runaway trolley "can only steer from one narrow track on to another; five men are working on one track and one man on the other; anyone on the track he enters is bound to be killed." Foot is interested in "why we should say, without hesitation, that the driver should steer for the less occupied track," when most people would be appalled at the idea of directly killing an innocent person in order to save five others.[42] In other words, she begins by assuming a common response and searches for its underlying logic. The logic, Foot believes, hinges on "the distinction between avoiding injury and bringing aid."[43] For Foot, the negative duty to avoid causing injury is more pressing than the positive duty to provide aid. Other philosophers interpret the moral choice in different ways. Thomson, for example, appeals to rights theory and the Kantian principle that we may not treat people only as means to our ends.[44] The crucial feature of morality, in this view, is the agent's intentions, reflected in her view of others.

Thomson invented another famous dilemma, which was first introduced, like Foot's trolley story, in an article about abortion. It is interesting and revealing that they address this difficult real-life problem by recourse to highly unreal hypothetical dilemmas, in efforts to find underlying principles that would justify their moral claims, instead of seeking the principles in the course of thinking about the actual problem at hand. Thomson gets at the issue in a roundabout way, imagining a famous violinist, unconscious and seriously ill with a fatal kidney ailment, who can be saved only if he is hooked up to a specific person's kidneys. In order to save the violinist, the music lovers' society has strapped the violinist to the unsuspecting person's back during the night, without her knowledge or permission. If the violinist is unhooked, he will die. Thomson asks whether the savior is morally obligated to live out her days strapped to the violinist, in order to respect the violinist's right to life. Her answer is no, because "having a right to life does not guarantee having either a right to be given the use of or a right to be allowed continued use of another person's body—even if one needs it for life itself."[45]

An almost equally far-fetched dilemma features in Bernard Williams's argument against utilitarianism. Williams describes the plight of Jim, a botanist conducting research in a tropical country who wanders onto a shocking scene: a cruel army officer has gathered a number of innocent villagers and is planning to kill them all. When Jim appears, the officer makes him an offer: if Jim kills one of the innocent men, the rest will be able to go free. If Jim refuses, the officer will continue with his plan, and all the men will die. (We are supposed to believe that the officer will keep his word.) A utilitarian, Williams asserts, would say that Jim should agree to the offer, horrible as it is, in order to save most of the men. Williams, however, rejects this solution, because it does not take into account "the idea, as we might first and very simply put it, that each of us is specially responsible for what *he* does, rather than for what other people do."[46] In her article on abortion, Foot makes a similar point, reflecting on yet another imaginary situation, in which a mob threatens to kill many people if a judge does not frame and execute one innocent person. Her analysis relies on the duty not to inflict harm, which permits us to "refuse to be forced into acting by the threats of bad men. To refrain from inflicting injury ourselves is a stricter duty than to prevent other people from inflicting injury, which is not to say that the other is not a very strict duty indeed."[47] The hierarchy of values makes the dilemma not really a dilemma—the answer is clear, at least to the writer, and the task at hand is to identify the reasons that it is correct.

Perhaps the most famous of all is Lawrence Kohlberg's "Heinz dilemma." This case involves a (nameless) woman who is dying from a rare disease. The only medicine that can save her life has been discovered by a pharmacist who happens to live in the same town as the sick woman and her husband, Heinz. The inventor charges ten times the (already high) cost of production for the drug. Heinz tries to borrow the money but can raise only half the cost. He asks the pharmacist to sell him the drug for a lower cost or let him pay later in order to save his wife's life, but the druggist refuses. Desperate, Heinz breaks into the man's laboratory to steal the drug for his wife. The moral question is whether Heinz was justified in stealing the drug to save his wife's life.[48] Kohlberg suggests that the highest morality is a Kantian adherence to abstract rules, so that it is best to forbear stealing. Analyzing responses to this dilemma among adolescent and young adults, Kohlberg found that male respondents more often gave the "correct" answer rejecting theft, while women frequently looked for alternative solutions that might save the wife's life. This prompted an influential critique by Carol Gilligan regarding different modes of moral thinking, which provided important seeds for feminist care ethics.[49]

All these dilemmas are supposed to offer guidance about action, helping us see the implications of different theories in a concrete situation. As Thomson points out, moral theory requires stories about real people in real situations (actual or invented), because "we do not even know what accepting this or that candidate moral principle would commit us to until we see what it tells us about what people ought or ought not do in this or that (so far as possible) concretely described set of circumstances."[50] Here Thomson diverges, to some extent, from most philosophers in acknowledging that we do not always come to concrete situations with a fully articulated plan for moral action. She does not pursue this insight, unfortunately, but declares that moral theory must explain "what makes those acts right which are right, and what makes those acts wrong which are wrong." This begins in the middle of the story, before we have asked, let alone answered, the crucial questions about which acts are right or wrong. Thomson takes these as rhetorical questions: "among the right ones are the ones which strike us as clearly, plainly, on any plausible moral view, right; and so also for the wrong ones."[51] In other words, we already know what is right or wrong; the task of ethical theory is to find support for these intuitions. As Kwame Anthony Appiah writes, philosophers use dilemmas not to examine equally plausible options but rather "to discover principles that will explain why [theirs is] the right answer."[52]

This approach to dilemmas reflects a larger pattern in the way many philosophers approach the relationship between ideas and practices. They separate the two and build their ethical theories in the abstract, without any interest in what Kant called empirical matters. These theories are then applied to specific problems by being dropped upon the actors from on high as preformed guides to moral behavior. In moral dilemmas, we see the complementary inverse of this pattern, where ethical theory comes in after the fact. Confronted with a hard moral problem, people follow their hunches about the right thing to do and invoke theory after the fact to support their intuitions. Practice and theory do not interact directly: theory instructs beforehand or justifies afterward, but it is absent in practice itself. We do not learn from what we do or improvise, test, discover, or change our values as we act.

Even Thomson, who touches on the possibility of a more complex, mutualistic relationship between ideas and actions, shies away. In the end, she settles for the nearly universal approach: "It is precisely our moral views about examples, stories, and cases which constitute the data for moral theorizing."[53] Not actions but rather ideas are the data for theorizing. Thus, even though dilemmas bring ethics to bear on practical issues, they ultimately reinforce the separation between ideas and practices and the subordination of the latter which dominate ethical theory generally. Too often, philosophers suggest that dilemmas involve disagreement or uncertainty only about the reasons underlying the right decision, not about what that decision is. Most seem incapable of conceiving of a truly open-ended dilemma, one in which we work out the right thing to do in the course of action, rather than via pre-established principles that we can apply in every real-life case.

A good example is a case presented by Tom Regan, a philosopher of animal rights, who describes a lifeboat that contains several humans and one dog, all of approximately the same weight. The lifeboat will sink if the group does not cast one of the occupants overboard. Regan poses what at first seem to be serious questions about the implications of his arguments for animal rights: "If each [humans and dog] have an equal right to be treated respectfully, must we draw straws? Would it not be unjust, given the rights view, to choose to sacrifice the dog in preference to one of the humans?" That does appear to be a reasonable question, after nearly three hundred pages of detailed arguments that nonhuman animals "are never to be treated as if they exist as a resource for others; in particular, harms intentionally done to any one subject cannot be justified by aggregating benefits derived by others."[54]

The reader might think this argument would lead Regan to consider, at least for a moment, the possibility of giving the dog a shot at survival. However, Regan does not hesitate to throw the dog metaphorically under the bus and literally out of the boat. He does so, he explains, because to do otherwise would doom his argument in favor of animal rights by associating it with an unpalatable conclusion. "No reasonable person would suppose that the dog has a 'right to life' that is equal to the humans' or that the animal should be given an equal chance in the lottery for survival."[55] Like Foot and Thomson, Regan starts with a conclusion—obviously, the dog should go overboard—and then constructs an argument to support it. This argument rests on the assumption that death is a greater loss for humans than for dogs. Once again, the "reasonable person" cannot deny that "the death of any of the four humans would be a greater prima facie loss, and thus a greater prima facie harm, than would be true in the case of the dog. Death for the dog, in short, though a harm, is not comparable to the harm that death would be for any of the humans."[56] This is assumed, not supported. Regan does not offer any reasons for this claim about the harm of death, even though it plays a central role in his argument.

This example is especially revealing because, despite the potentially radical nature of animal rights in general and Regan's arguments in particular, he does not escape the binding structures imposed by Kantian theory. Morally correct answers must be devised in abstract mental processes, with nothing left to be worked out in and through practice. Regan's dilemma also reveals the power of assumptions about reasonableness to shut down even serious philosophers. The hegemonic way of framing and deciding moral problems, in other words, constrains what appears, at first, to be a radical challenge. The assumption that humans must always come first, which Regan attacks throughout his book, ultimately sabotages his argument. The abstract ideas that he supports—the equal moral rights of nonhuman animals—are rejected and dismissed because of the action to which they might lead. Thus, despite Regan's efforts to remain abstract, practice creeps in and profoundly shapes his ethical analysis.

The Problems with Dilemmas

While dilemmas are beloved by many philosophers, they can be unhelpful and even harmful in the way they teach us to think about moral decision-making and action. There are two clusters of problems: one concerns the philosophical weaknesses of dilemmas, and the other concerns their inaccurate depiction of moral reasoning. The philosophical defects begin with the fact that dilemmas, as Anthony Weston writes, "pose narrow and limited questions that leave us, not surprisingly, with narrow and limited answers."[57] For advocates of dilemmas, this is part of their appeal. The point of dilemmas is to "arbitrarily cut off and restrict the range of alternative courses of action," as Williams explains.[58] This is supposed to sharpen our moral reasoning, so that we focus on the most relevant factors. However, the problem is that the one who poses the dilemma has already decided what is relevant and what is not. This precludes consideration of factors, including empirical data, historical context, emotions, or personal relationships, that usually enter into real-life moral reflection and decision making.

The initial step of framing a problem as a dilemma leads people to view it as a clash of mutually exclusive options. There is no middle ground, chance of compromise, or unexplored possibilities, and moral actors are not supposed to be ambivalent or uncertain. This polarized framing leads us to imagine that there are only two possibilities, which are fairly extreme and unamenable to compromise. Usually, the options are Kantianism and utilitarianism: either we obey a universal moral law that requires individuals to keep their hands clean, or we calculate costs and benefits in order to find the least bad option. Because the options are presented as mutually exclusive, we must treat one as completely wrong and the other as completely right.[59] This discourages us from finding common ground with people who have other opinions, integrating different values, or acknowledging that another position may have valid points.

The usual framing of dilemmas also discourages us from considering the complex collective and structural contexts that shape not just the immediate situation but also moral thinking and action more generally.[60] Some philosophers hint at them, as when Thomson points out that it may be relevant to learn why and how the potential victims ended up on the trolley track.[61] Are they well-paid, highly trained workers who knew the risks they took? Innocent children who were lured to the tracks by a villainous liar? Those histories often matter not only for moral judgment but also for the feasibility of different solutions.[62] More profoundly, we have to consider structural conditions if moral challenges are to inspire action with the goal, as Ruth Marcus writes, of learning how "to arrange our lives and institutions with a view to avoiding such conflicts."[63] The abstraction and thinness of mainstream ethical theories, however, limit the possibility of asking such questions, much less of permitting the answers to shape moral decisions.

The polarization, oversimplification, and narrowness of dilemmatic thinking are evident in many famous dilemmas. A good example is Kohlberg's Heinz dilemma. Heinz faces a terrible situation—his wife is dying—and is permitted only two options, both bad: steal a drug, or watch his wife die. Weston points out that the description of the problem precludes any structural solutions that might have prevented the problem, noting that if Heinz and his wife had health insurance, he would not be tempted to steal to save her life.[64] Even once we are in the midst of the problem, creative thinking can identify other possible solutions. Some of Kohlberg's subjects suggested this, looking for ways to get the medicine besides stealing it. Sara Ruddick describes one participant in Kohlberg's research, an eleven-year-old named Amy, who looked carefully and concretely at the details of the situation to try to find a way out. However, this is not how the dilemma is supposed to work. "Amy doesn't get it," Ruddick comments. "She doesn't realize that the dilemma is meant to foreclose options."[65] By attending to the details of the problem and resisting abstractions, Amy failed to think morally, in Kohlberg's terms. For Kohlberg and many philosophers, moral reasoning must follow universal and rationalist models. "To think concretely," as Ruddick explains, "is to refuse to 'get it,' to accept abstraction's terms," and to insist on "looking, talking, and asking troublesome questions" rather than accepting the narrow, polarized, and formalistic approach enshrined in dilemmas.[66] To think in this way, in sum, is to challenge the hegemony of the intentionalist, idealist model which excludes practice, commitments, histories, and other "empirical" matters from the process of ethical decision-making.

These weaknesses of dilemmas are related to a second problem, the accuracy with which they describe reality. Dilemmas generally misunderstand how people actually make decisions. Recent research in cognitive science and behavior portray moral reasoning and action in very different terms from the abstract, rational, dualistic model implicit in dilemmas. In particular, the research shows that the brain and the rest of the body are a single organism; there can be no dualism, because the mind is part of the body. What we think of as mind, further, is not the brain alone but the brain interacting with the rest of the body and the body's environment.[67] This undermines standard philosophical conceptions of interior dispositions such as intentions or faith as independent of bodily actions and social and natural contexts. It also challenges the assumption that these mental attitudes are related in linear, predictable ways to human actions. Instead, mental attitudes are products of and also participants in the ongoing interactions between people and their environment, other people, other creatures, and social institutions.

This means that people think about ethical issues in embodied, emotional, and imaginative ways. The most basic claim of neuroscience is that the mind and cognitive processes are embodied, and the common philosophical idea of a disembodied mind (spirit, soul, reason, *Geist*) is simply wrong.[68] Mental processes such as "the capacity to conceptualize, to understand, to reason, to know, and to will" are all bodily processes.[69] This throws into question the supposed "transcendence of mind over body," as Mark Johnson writes,[70] which presumes that people have mental faculties that make decisions and then tell the body what to do.

Contemporary research, in sum, demands that we recognize what John Dewey called "the *essential unity of the self and its acts*."[71] Moral actors are unified persons, in which mind and body, reason and emotion, are integrated rather than mutually exclusive opposites. In other words, we must reject the dualism that is intrinsic not only to the dilemma model but also to many Western philosophical traditions, particularly those rooted in the philosophical Enlightenment. The notion that mind and body or reason and emotion are opposed and mutually exclusive simply has no empirical basis. This echoes the pragmatist argument that, as James put it, we do not have two substances, mind and body; instead, mind is "an emergent process, never separate from body."[72] Similarly, feminists have long argued against mind-body dualism, partly because it is associated with a polarized and essentialized understanding of men and women, culture and nature, reason and emotion.

In addition to misdescribing human behavior, dilemmatic thinking is wrong about the actual situations in which people face moral challenges. It assumes that real-life moral decisions are made in the kind of dramatic, thinly described situations that characterize hypothetical dilemmas. It takes only a moment's reflection to conclude that ordinary people rarely face runaway trolleys, murderers at the door, or comatose violinists. Because these hypothetical scenarios do not seem relevant to most people's real-life circumstances, they appear more as fairy tales or games than as cause for serious reflection. Perhaps more important, repetition of fantastical dilemmas makes moral decisions in general seem both overly simple and removed from our real lives. Thus, philosophical discussions of trolleys do little to prepare people to make thoughtful, well-grounded, and constructive decisions about the actual moral conflicts we face.

Dilemmas focus on the person confronted with the difficult choice between conflicting duties. The others involved are either villains (the murderer, the rogue army officer) or anonymous, passive objects of moral concern (Heinz's wife, the murderer's would-be victim, the hapless people on the trolley track). There is never any meaningful interaction between the main character and the rest of the players. The focus is on how this individual moral actor will answer certain abstract questions: Do I follow rules? Or should I maximize good consequences? In facing these questions, the actor stands alone, without advice, support, critique, or hindrance from others. Whatever decision the actor makes will be decisive—his yea or nay alone will determine what happens. This presumption of an isolated, all-powerful moral actor is even more fantastical than runaway trolleys and wandering botanists.

Building a Practice-Based Ethical Theory

Moral dilemmas do not really prepare us to make good decisions and act morally in our everyday lives. The problem is not so much the dilemmas themselves but the approach they embody. They both arise from and reinforce a misconception of ethics as composed mainly of abstractions and stark polarities, rather than the ambiguous, content-filled realities we usually face.[73] They also present a false view of the relations between intentions or ideas, actions, and consequences in real life. These misconceptions are rooted in idealist ways of thinking about morality.

1. Most important is that idealist or intellectualist theories assume that ideas, including mental states such as attitudes, intentions, or the will, are separate from material practices and other embodied experiences. Ideas are prior to and independent of material experiences, social context, and embodied actions. Ethics is a matter of ideas and internal states. This is made clear in

Augustine's and Kant's insistence that the only thing that can be good in itself is the will. In all these models, rightness depends on the actor's prior decision to put faith in God. We know something is good, as Luther might argue, because we know it came from an attitude of correct faith. These disembodied ideas, and especially intentions, determine the moral quality of persons, decisions, and actions. This means that moral principles cannot and should not be understood in social and historical context; they are neutral, transcendent, and universal. This rejection of what Kant calls "empirical" matters also requires the dismissal of physical bodies, emotions, and personal relationships as irrelevant and even a hindrance to proper ethical reflection.

2. The autonomy and priority of ideas undergird a formalist approach, in which moral quality is determined not by substantive content but rather by correct procedures. This is most obviously true for Kant, for whom moral reflection seems exhausted by the search for and adoption of the proper rules. We might say that for Kant, decision-making has a normative value in itself, because moral goodness or badness lies in the mode of decision-making. This sort of ethical theory resembles what anthropologist Clifford Geertz calls "thin description." Thin descriptions attempt to explain data in highly abstract, decontextualized ways; as Geertz puts it, they separate interpretations of what happens from what happens and codify abstract regularities.[74] Kantian ethics, perhaps the thinnest of all, does not need and in fact cannot admit of content-full descriptions. This minimalist type of moral theory aims for universal appeal and relevance and fears that the details and substance of "thick" ethical systems make them only narrowly relevant.[75] It is important to note that religious ethics are rarely purely formalistic, because they rest on content-filled claims about God, human nature, sin, grace, and more. Thus, even though Augustine and Luther share many features of liberal philosophical idealism, they cannot be as formalist in their approach to decision-making or to the ultimate foundation for moral knowledge.

3. Idealist models share a methodological and normative individualism, according to which the moral agents act as individuals, making decisions for and by themselves. Tied to this is an assumption that ethics is about the individual's effort to answer questions such as "How should I live?" Like all moral philosophies, idealism presupposes particular kinds of answers to this question, which are grounded in and continually refer back to the individual's quest for moral improvement and even purity. These idealist or intellectualist models understand ethics as the project of individuals, who think and act

autonomously. This is especially obvious in hypothetical dilemmas, which present us with a single moral actor who must make a momentous decision alone. Emotions, relationships, and community life do not affect what is morally right. The moral agent of liberal philosophy is an "unencumbered" self, in the phrase of Robert Bellah and his colleagues, who moves through life with absolute freedom and open-ended potential.[76] The self-precedes social relationships and is not fundamentally constituted or altered by those relationships, by interactions with other people or institutions, or by material practices.

4. Idealist models generally characterize ethics as qualitatively different from other kinds of thinking and acting. Morality appears as a separate, compartmentalized sphere of human activity. Thus, ethics appears to have little to do with the practices that make up everyday life. Again, this is most obviously true for Kant, whose insistence on extreme abstraction, universality, and impartiality divides moral decisions from the partial, concrete messiness of everyday life. Luther and Augustine effect this division with their split between the two kingdoms or cities, which are directed by very different rules and values. People have a foot in both realms, but true morality exists only in the city or kingdom of God, where ordinary concerns and experiences do not enter.

5. All these assumptions about ethics contribute, in idealist models, to a linear model of action, according to which mental attitudes lead directly to actions which in turn lead directly to predictable consequences. Because people are always surrounded by other actors and embedded in larger contexts, they do not control the results of their own actions or what others do. Very often our plans go awry; we act with the intention of causing one effect, but something else happens, in addition to or instead of what we intended. The closest mainstream ethics comes to acknowledging the messiness of real life is in relation to unintended consequences. Here the discussion focuses on the expected but undesired results of actions, often called double effect. The doctrine of double effect asserts that it is sometimes acceptable to act in a way that leads to harmful consequences if the actor's direct or primary intention is to produce desirable or beneficial consequences. These arguments still assume that we can accurately predict the results of actions, however, which is rarely the case in real life.

For this linear understanding of moral action, the moral agent creates mental constructs—intentions, attitudes, or the will—which are fully formed prior to any action. The agent then "enacts" or "applies" these in consistent, controlled ways, and then desired consequences predictably follow. This linear framework requires the separation of means and ends, as exemplified in Kant's second categorical imperative. When means and ends are independent of each other, practices are merely instruments for achieving intrinsically desired goods. This separation makes it possible to assert that good results can justify the use of harmful means, the foundational claim of just war theory, as I discuss in chapter 6. Less obviously, but perhaps more insidiously, this separation makes it possible to assert that good intentions justify damaging actions or results, as Kant himself claims.

The religious ethics that I have discussed echo this linear view of the relationship between ideas and actions. In particular, Luther's insistence that works are irrelevant and faith alone is spiritually and morally efficacious reflects a division of means and ends that pervades mainstream Christian thought more generally. According to this view, attitudes lead in a direct way to actions: if a believer adopts a truly faithful attitude, good deeds will follow. The assumption, again, is that the hard work is done by the moral actor who has to decide which theory to follow. Once that decision-making process is done, it is a simple matter to apply the theory to the problem at hand and act in accord with it, even though sometimes, as Paul confesses, believers fail to do the good they desire. These notions permeate philosophical discussions of moral conflict, where we see the practical implications of both the emphasis on intentions and the linear model of moral action.

Conclusions

The traditions of ethical thought analyzed in this chapter vary greatly, and I do not want to suggest that they are identical in their approach to practice or any other particular. Still, considering them together offers important insights into the place of practice in ethical theory, particularly because these religious and philosophical models have played an outsized role in both academic and "lay" ways of thinking about morality in the West. We cannot understand how particular approaches to ethical theory or to morality in everyday life have developed historically without attending to these traditions. In addition, Augustinian, Lutheran, and Kantian ideas have marginalized practice in distinctive ways, centered on the notion that moral quality depends, above all, on the will, understood as the actor's intentions or motivations. Internal states, seen as independent of bodily and empirical factors, are what make a person, a decision, or an action good or bad. This is true both for the faith-based theological ethics of Augustine and Luther and for Kant's rational rule-based model.

There are many critiques of and alternatives to both these models. I will be discussing a number of these in the next several chapters, but there is one that I do not examine: utilitarianism, which is usually presented as the major alternative to Kant. This is a significant omission, and I want to explain, briefly, my reasons for leaving it out. Like all consequentialist ethics, utilitarianism locates moral goodness or badness in the results of actions. Philosophers see this as sharply contrasting with deontological models, such as Kantianism, which emphasize following rules without regard for the outcome. This is why utilitarianism and Kantianism are often presented as mutually exclusive options, for example, in many moral dilemmas.

Despite these real and significant differences, the two theories share important commonalities as well, which are relevant both to their treatment of practice and to my decision not to discuss utilitarianism here. Both models are rationalist and focus on decision-making procedures—following rules or weighing consequences—as the core of ethical thinking. Both, further, marginalize practice by failing to acknowledge that what we do shapes what we intend as well as the results of moral action. This is obvious for Kant but perhaps not so much for utilitarianism, which seems more "practical" with its attention to outcomes and concern for social reform. The outcomes that matter to utilitarians, however, are intended ones; it is still the thought that counts, but the thinking that matters involves expected or hoped-for results rather than rules to be followed. Without denying the significance of this distinction in many settings, it is not momentous for their treatment of practice. Utilitarians, then, do not offer a critique of the Kantian approach to practice that I have outlined here but instead replicate its primary weaknesses, most notably their linear view of moral behavior. The same is largely true of other Enlightenment models, including social contract theory. Without dismissing the real differences among these ethical theories, my main critiques of their treatment of practice are captured in my discussion of Kant.

Although utilitarianism is not a real alternative to Kantianism in regard to practice, there are a number of other moral philosophies and theologies that do offer very different views of practice and the related issues identified in my five themes. Perhaps the most influential of these, at least among philosophers, is virtue ethics, often identified as the third major ethical theory after Kantianism and utilitarianism. Virtue has many historical and conceptual links to Catholic moral theology, including some incorporation of practice into ethical theorizing. These two traditions, probably the most influential alternatives to Enlightenment and Lutheran models, are my main focus in chapter 3. I also discuss feminist ethics, which includes important criticisms of the hyper-rationalism and individualism of Enlightenment models as well as other themes that are relevant to practice.

3

Virtue, Catholic, and Feminist Ethics

Character, Community, and Care

With Gabriel A. Vásquez-Peterson

> Far from thinking that works produced by man's own talent and en-
> ergy are in opposition to God's power, and that the rational creature
> exists as a kind of rival to the Creator, Christians are convinced that
> the triumphs of the human race are a sign of God's grace and the
> flowering of His own mysterious design. For the greater man's power
> becomes, the farther his individual and community responsibility
> extends. Hence it is clear that men are not deterred by the Christian
> message from building up the world, or impelled to neglect the wel-
> fare of their fellows, but that they are rather more stringently bound
> to do these very things.
>
> —Second Vatican Council, *Gaudium et spes*[1]

Introduction

Chapter 2 documented the marginalization of practice in some of the most influential Western ethical theories, both religious and secular. In these models, morality is determined by intentions, from which practices are to follow in a derivative, often mechanistic fashion. In this chapter, I begin to explore alternatives that give practice a more significant and complex place in ethical thinking. While these models differ in important ways, they share several key traits that are particularly relevant to practice and thus help us move from "it's the thought that counts" to the more practice-focused models that I examine in the following chapters. In particular, virtue, Catholic, and feminist thinkers challenge the Kantian and Augustinian-Lutheran em-phasis on the priority of the will, the autonomy of individual moral actors,

Works Righteousness. Anna L. Peterson, Oxford University Press (2021). © Oxford University Press.
DOI: 10.1093/oso/9780197532232.001.0001.

the separation between ideas and practices, and the compartmentalization of morality from other spheres of life. They insist, instead, that ethics must take into account emotions, social relationships, and historical context. In their approaches to these and other issues, virtue, Catholic, and feminist ethical theories help lay the foundation for understanding moral goodness as a quality of relationships, persons, and communities that is shaped by practice well as ideas.

This account starts with Aristotelian virtue ethics, the most prominent philosophical alternative to rationalist models, often the third wheel discussed after Kantianism and utilitarianism. Virtue ethics emphasizes the social character of human life, the importance of habit or habituation, and the identification of morality with entire lives rather than just decision-making procedures. I then explore modern Catholic social thought, which shares a social definition of human nature and adds, further, a view of works as valuable for people and God and society. As an aspect of Catholic thought, I also discuss liberationist theologies, which highlight the influence of structures in shaping morality. Finally, I look at feminist approaches that draw attention to emotions, bodies, and intimate relationships, as well as to political critiques of unjust structures. The chapter concludes with a discussion of the new perspectives that these models offer on central questions about the autonomy of ideas, the social nature of ethics, the links between form and content, the relations between ethics and other spheres of life, and the connections between ideas, actions, and consequences.

Aristotelian Virtue Ethics

Aristotle (384–322 BCE) was not the only or even the first philosopher to develop a virtue ethic, but he is certainly the most influential. Aristotelian virtue ethics is distinct from the dominant Kantian and utilitarian traditions of moral philosophy, because it is concerned not just with the process of ethical decision-making but also with the character of the agents making these decisions and the links between actions and character. Central to this account of the way we are and the things we do are the virtues, which are dispositions toward a certain way of being and acting. For Aristotle, an action is right if it is done as a virtuous person would do it, just as for Kant, an action is right if it is the result of a good will. There is a similarity here in the appeal to an internal feature of an agent as the right-making feature of action. Yet this similarity belies a significant difference: the virtues, as ethical concepts, have a much richer connection to practice and to human activity. Thus, virtue ethics helps us begin fleshing out a different view of practice's role in ethical theory.

Several features of Aristotle's ethics are particularly relevant to the place of practice in ethics. First, Aristotle does not conceive of ethics as separate from everyday life, something we engage with only when there is a moral decision to be made. Rather, for him, ethics is about making good the activities that constitutes a human life in its entirety. The virtues do not turn off and on but are always present, in our actions, our habits, and our inner life, and the same is true of their opposite numbers, the vices. Aristotle's ethical thought is broadly concerned with the ultimate good for human beings, which he identifies as happiness or "living well." Importantly, Aristotle understands happiness not as an emotional state but as a kind of activity. Human life, in general, is distinguished from other forms of life by the distinctly rational kind of activity that is characteristic of it. For Aristotle, the human good is to be found in the excellent performance of this kind of activity. To understand what this type of action looks like, Aristotle turns to the virtues. The virtues are excellences of character, which perfect different areas of human activity. Bravery, for example, is concerned with fear, danger, and risk and the ways in which we respond to them. The brave person acts rightly in regard to these things, and so on for the other virtues. Thus, Aristotle asserts that happiness, the human good, is rational activity in accordance with virtue.

Second, the virtues arise through habituation, a kind of directed practice. Our practices and activity in the world structure and shape our internal character. We are what we do, just as much as we do what we are. We must act in the right ways to become good, just as much as we must become good people in order to do good. Aristotle begins book II of the *Nichomachean Ethics* by pointing out an etymological tie between the Greek term for habit, *ethos*, and the word for ethical virtue, *ethike*—the latter is derived from the former.[2] This connection, he maintains, is mirrored by a similar link between the two in the real world. Moral virtue and states of character in general arise from the kind of activities they themselves are associated with and in some sense produce. As Aristotle puts it, "this is why the activities we exhibit must be of a certain kind; it is because the states of character correspond to the differences between these."[3] Our habits, or the patterns that structure and define our activities, are therefore of central importance to who we are, and because of this, we must form and practice the right habits from childhood. Aristotle makes an analogy here to craft: to become a lyre player or a builder, good or bad, one must play the lyre or build. In the same way, "by doing the acts that we do in the presence of danger and being habituated to feel fear or confidence, we become brave or cowardly."[4]

A distinctive feature of ethical habituation is that it involves shaping and educating desire and emotion. For Aristotle, virtue is not just a kind of expertise or a rote habit. Rather, it is crucially concerned with the internal condition of an agent. A virtue is disanalogous to craft in this, for its activity requires more than the mere technical skill required by craft. A virtuous person's internal life must be in order: the person must take pleasure and pain in the right things and feel and desire in the right ways. A person whose internal life is disordered, Aristotle thinks, will be at risk of incontinence. Such a person may recognize the right thing to do but be unable to do it because of opposing desires or drives. Furthermore, Aristotle thinks it is impossible to be fully practically rational or wise without proper habituation, for internal disharmony perverts one's moral perception and leads people to reason from the wrong starting points. Thus, although Aristotle does believe that reason is ultimately what should direct activity and is deeply concerned with how we are internally, he does not marginalize practice or take activity in the world to be merely secondary. Rather, he sees the external and internal as mutually reinforcing, where who we are shapes what we do, and what we do shapes who we are.

Third, Aristotle's ethics does not offer a clear decision-making procedure or any absolute action-guiding principles. He does not think such a thing is possible or desirable. Aristotle tells us that virtue, as a disposition, is characteristically concerned with an intermediate or mean between too much and too little. Faced with a choice, the virtuous person finds "that which is intermediate" and chooses it.[5] For example, the courageous person acts in a way that is neither cowardly nor foolhardy but appropriate to the situation. Though the numerical language of excess, defect, and intermediate suggests a kind of calculation, Aristotle's mean should not be read as a decision procedure. Indeed, he thinks it is impossible to set clear guidelines for what one should do, as there "is no fixity" about what is good for us.[6] The idea of finding the intermediate is most usefully read as saying that the virtuous person finds what is appropriate given the situation, which often presents itself as a matter of avoiding extremes.

The idea that the virtuous person just gets it right is often seen as intolerably vague. We expect a system of ethics to be there in the moment, telling us how to act. However, Aristotle's ethics is not about telling us what the right thing to do is but rather about understanding how virtuous people are able to find and interpret the right thing to do. The key point for virtue is not the moment of decision but the whole life of the agent, in which she has been shaped internally by habituation and practice. The idea of the mean captures a kind of "knowing in the doing." For both a master craftsman and a virtuous person, knowledge cannot be codified. It can only be expressed in activity. A master mason cannot enumerate rules for others to follow and become experts, yet in every situation, he knows what is right. It is just the same for the courageous person, and in both cases, what is just right often lies between too much and too little. They know this not because they have internalized certain principles but because of the knowledge and internal harmony gained through practice.

Aristotle's idea of human activity as the location of the good makes practice an unalienable component of goodness. Even though virtue, an internal state, ultimately makes activity good, there is a necessary connection between the internal and the external. The most salient feature of this connection is the idea of habituation, wherein it is what we do that shapes who we are and how we think, rather than the other way around. Even more important is the idea underlying habituation: that the morally relevant internal states are by their nature linked to practices, actions, and activity. This is because virtues are active dispositions to do something and because they are inculcated by the same kind of practices in which they manifest. These practices structure the active lives of the virtuous and the not so virtuous, just as the virtues and vices structure internal life.

Aristotelian virtue ethics thus challenges moral theories that focus on instances in which a decision must be made and considers intentional actions the proper subject of ethics. Aristotle's ethics is expansive. It does not begin and end with decisions and actions, despite their obvious importance. Rather, for Aristotle, the good is contained in all the activity that constitutes human life—internal and external. This activity must be developed and structured properly, and this cannot be done just by internalizing a theory of right action. Aristotle tells us that people cannot become good by "taking refuge in theory" while ignoring practice. The sick are not made well again by merely listening attentively to their doctor. To be "made well in soul," we must act, and act well.[7]

Contemporary Virtue Ethics

In contemporary philosophical discussions, virtue ethics is often described as an alternative that contrasts in important ways with Kantian and utilitarian models. These dominant approaches view ethics as primarily a mode of decision-making, or what Julia Annas calls "the technical manual model," which aims to provide a "systematic and theorizable way of telling us what to do."[8] Virtue ethics, according to Annas, "regards it as misguided to try to produce a theory-based decision procedure for anyone at any stage to use." A one-size-fits-all model of ethics, she argues, "would be like trying to improve building by insisting that all builders learn from the same books. These might be helpful, but they don't produce expert builders; it is people who have to make themselves into expert builders. Similarly, each of us has to do the work in our own case, aiming to become a virtuous person with understanding and not just derivative copying of others. No manual will do it for us."[9]

The lack of a manual is an advantage for virtue thinkers, but others find the "technical manual" model not only more familiar but preferable. The problem with virtue ethics, in this view, is that it is inaccessible and imprecise, in that it cannot tell non-virtuous people what to do. In virtue ethics, the right action is what the virtuous person does, as a virtuous person. Non-virtuous people, then, seem to lack guidance. Insofar as people take this as a problem, it demonstrates a certain assumption about what ethics should do: tell people how to make decisions.

In contrast to the decision-making model, virtue ethicists insist that the purpose of moral theory is not to provide rules for isolated incidents but to nurture the development of persons who have the disposition and skill to make good decisions in all kinds of circumstances. One example is Annas's developmental account of virtue, which has three parts: "the virtuous person, right action, and the relevant developmental process."[10] Just as we understand skill as the result of a continual process of development through both practice and intellectual examination, we should understand virtue as such. Here we have a way of understanding and examining the moral significance of what we do and who we are together and putting actions in that context. Good character is seen in the context of the practice and development that goes into it, just as skill is. We can then see better why what a virtuous person does is right. Furthermore, by understanding virtue in terms of development, we get a picture of what people at different stages in moral development should be doing. In other words, by incorporating both moral character and the practices that go along with it, virtue ethics gives us resources to explore minimized elements of moral life and also to re-examine features such as right action from a new angle. These features define virtue ethics as a coherent alternative to rationalist models, despite the many significant differences among contemporary virtue thinkers.

The importance of practice for virtue ethics comes to the fore in the work of one of the most prominent contemporary virtue thinkers, Alasdair MacIntyre. MacIntyre's 1981 book, *After Virtue: A Study in Moral Theory*, is one of the most influential works in twentieth-century ethics. The book is a critique of modern individualism, an argument for a particular way of doing philosophy and ethics, a rethinking of Aristotle, and more. It is helpful for my project here because MacIntyre makes practice an important part of all these issues.

Central to MacIntyre's ethics is a conception of human nature and behavior as highly social, in contrast to the hyper-individualism of liberal models. He understands human character as formed within a historical, social, and narrative context. "The story of my life," he writes, "is always embedded in the story of those communities from which I derive my identity. I am born with a past; and to try to cut myself off from that past, in the individualist mode, is to deform my present relationships."[11] We do not merely choose how to act and what to do; we inherit much of our identity and our fate. This means, as MacIntyre proclaims, that "I can only answer the question 'What am I to do?' if I can answer the prior question 'Of what story or stories do I find myself a part?'" This provides a context for understanding the place of practice in ethics. MacIntyre defines practice as

> any coherent and complex form of socially established cooperative human activity through which goods internal to that form of activity are realised in the course of trying to achieve those standards of excellence which are appropriate to, and partially definitive of, that form of activity, with the result that human powers to achieve excellence, and human conceptions of the ends and goods involved, are systematically extended. Tic-tac-toe is not an example of a practice in this sense, nor is throwing a football with skill; but the game of football is, and so is chess. Bricklaying is not a practice; architecture is. Planting turnips is not a practice; farming is. So are the enquiries of physics, chemistry and biology, and so is the work of the historian, and so are painting and music.[12]

MacIntyre's definition is narrower than my understanding in this book, which considers the role of diverse practices in ethical theory more broadly. One difference is that his definition is biased toward intellectual labor. Most of his practices require specialized knowledge—chess, painting, biology, and so forth. He includes physical pursuits such as football and farming, but only because these require knowledge of rules, schedules, and so forth. I would define practice to include at least some activities that do not require explicit prior knowledge or intentionality. In addition, and related to this, MacIntyre does not consider small-scale actions—planting turnips or bricklaying—as practices. He defines as practices only the larger context that gives meaning to individual activities. Thus, kicking a ball is not a practice for him, though the game of soccer is.

In contrast, I contend that throwing, planting, and laying bricks are in fact practices, and I would use the term *disciplines* to describe the larger constructs or institutions that hold diverse practices together and give them meaning. Mental as well as physical activities can be included here. Thus, solving a math problem is a practice, which has meaning within a discipline such as accounting, theoretical physics, or household budgeting. Similarly, kicking a ball is a practice which may occur in the larger context of a professional soccer match, a playground kickball game, or an individual's efforts to improve dribbling skills. Solving a math problem or kicking a ball is a practice in any event, and it is also a practice if it is done absentmindedly, as a way to pass the time without any larger purpose or design. This is important because all our practices, regardless of whether or not they are formally organized or deliberately planned, help shape how and what we value.

Despite the limits of MacIntyre's definition of practice, his work is crucial for the construction of a practice-centered approach to ethical theory. He insists that ideas and actions cannot be separated, historically or in theory: "Every action is the bearer and expression of more or less theory-laden beliefs and concepts; every piece of theorizing and every expression of belief is a political and moral action."[13] Thought, including ethical reflection, is shaped by action, and it is itself an action. Not only beliefs but also practices have their own histories and social contexts. By emphasizing humans' social nature, the historical and narrative context of moral identity, and the connections between ideas and actions, MacIntyre's reworking of virtue contributes to a clearer understanding of the place of practice in ethical theory, particularly but not only virtue ethics. Some parallels to his model, as well as developments in other directions, are found in Catholic social thought.

Catholic Social Thought

It does not involve a great leap to go from virtue ethics to Catholic moral theology. Aristotle was a major influence on the Church's official theologian, Thomas Aquinas (1225–1274), whose thought still shapes Catholic theology and ethics. Thomas had access to new Latin translations of the work of Aristotle, whom he called "the Philosopher." Aristotle provided Thomas with both affirmation for some of his core convictions and inspiration to extend his thought. In particular, Thomas found echoes of important Christian themes in Aristotle's view of humans as social and political animals and his conviction that human flourishing requires a life of virtue in pursuit of an ultimate *telos*. Aristotle's naturalism and his intellectual breadth helped Thomas develop an overarching system, natural law, that finds logic and meaning in the created world and human life.

These ideas enter modern Catholic social thought in the insistence that humans are created in the image of God, which gives them particular traits— sociability and an orientation toward the good—as well as an inviolable dignity. Concrete actions are necessary to live a fully Christian life, to develop the appropriate personal virtues, and to build a society that is in keeping with God's vision for human life. Active participation in "the cultural, economic, political and social life of the civil community" is thus not only a right but "a duty to be fulfilled consciously by all, with responsibility and with a view to the common good."[14] Practices are good in multiple ways: they contribute to the common good, to a happy, fulfilled life, to personal virtue, and to individual spiritual development. This contrasts starkly with Luther's conviction that human works cannot contribute toward personal salvation and that efforts to build a Christian society are inevitably doomed to failure.

We can understand the Catholic conception of practice better by looking at a particular kind of activity: labor. In the Catholic view, work is not a punishment for sin, as some Christian approaches suggest, but rather a natural, necessary, and positive expression of human nature. It is both a subjective expression of personal dignity and creativity and an objective fact of social life. Modern Catholic approaches to labor go back to Pope Leo XIII's encyclical *Rerum novarum*, written in 1891 and affirmed in more recent Catholic social thought. *Gaudium et spes* (1965) asserts that labor is superior to other elements of economic life, since the latter are only tools; labor is the way people stamp the things of nature with their seal; also by offering his labor to God, "a man becomes associated with the redemptive work of Jesus Christ," who was a carpenter.[15] By their nature and according to God's plan, all people have the right and the duty to work. Their labor is important for personal dignity as well as sustenance. It is, further, not just of personal importance but also a vital part of the common good. As *Gaudium et spes* puts it, people "can justly consider that by their labor they are unfolding the Creator's work . . . and contributing by their personal industry to the realization in history of the divine plan."[16]

The importance of labor is reflected in Pope John Paul II's decision to devote an entire encyclical to the topic: *Laborem exercens*, published in 1981. In it, he reiterated long-standing Catholic themes, summarizing the Church's view that "Work is a good thing for man—a good thing for his humanity—because through work man not only transforms nature, adapting it to his own needs, but he also achieves fulfilment as a human being and indeed, in a sense, becomes 'more a human being.'"[17] Practices, including labor, are how people express their dignity, their connections to others, and their relationship to God. By their work, people share "in the activity of the Creator" and continue to develop and perfect it.[18] Labor is thus central to both personal and social ethics in the Catholic tradition.

Catholic conceptions of labor illuminate the tradition's conception of works more generally. Material practices are part of what makes human life morally good and personally satisfying. "Human work has an ethical value of its own," as John Paul II wrote, and this value is directly connected to the meaning of human life and subjectivity.[19] Practices reflect human identity and help create it; they express spiritual and moral virtue and increase it; they are made possible by community, and they strengthen good communities; and not least, practices bring people closer to God in the course of "imitating" divine activity. Practices echo God's interventions in human history to bring about the fulfillment of the reign of justice and peace. As a recent Vatican statement on social doctrine asserts, "Human activity in history is of itself significant and effective for the definitive establishment of the Kingdom, although this remains a free gift of God, completely transcendent. Such activity, when it respects the objective order of temporal reality and is enlightened by truth and love, becomes an instrument for making justice and peace ever more fully and integrally present, and anticipates in our own day the promised Kingdom."[20]

The notion that human activity helps establish the reign of God on earth is absolutely foreign to Lutheran theology and reflects the great divide between the two traditions in regard to practice. Luther's rejection of works and his insistence on *sola fides* radicalized the inward focus of Pauline and Augustinian thought, which makes practices external to both ultimate salvation and moral character. The "inner man," according to Luther, "cannot be justified, freed, or saved by any outer work or action at all." Because they are external to the true self, works, "whatever their character, have nothing to do with this inner man. On the other hand, only ungodliness and unbelief of heart, and no outer work, make him guilty and a damnable servant of sin."[21] Catholicism rejects this division between the inner and outer person, insisting that the person is a unity and that bodily existence and practices are a meaningful part of life, not just for worldly matters but for spiritual and moral development as well.

Like virtue ethicists, Catholic theologians see practices as necessary aspects of both moral life and ethical theory, in contrast to its absence from Kantian and Lutheran ethics. While human activities are secondary and sometimes distracting aspects of morality in those traditions, virtue and Catholic ethics see practices as integral aspects of human personal and social life which contribute to individual moral capacity and to the common good. These themes are heightened in a contemporary Catholic approach, liberation theology, which makes practice central to its theological method, conception of God, and moral theory.

Liberation Theology

Liberation theology is both a broad term referring to diverse progressive Catholic and Protestant movements in different parts of the world and also a specific theoretical model that emerged in Latin American Catholicism beginning in the late 1960s.[22] I focus here on the latter, which is rooted in Catholic moral theology, including normative claims about the value of community, the social nature of human beings, and the common destination of created goods. However, liberation theologians diverge in important ways from traditional Catholic social thought. In particular, they overturn the hierarchical and deductive approach, inherited from Thomas Aquinas, in which theology begins with doctrine and moves to application. Liberation theologians, in contrast, believe that theology is a "second step," a reflection that follows political and social practices.[23] This method is rooted in the work of Cardinal Joseph Cardijn, a Belgian priest who founded Young Catholic Workers in the 1920s. Cardijn developed not only a novel method for theology but also a new theological subject, as he insisted that ordinary Catholics, such as working-class youth, should engage in moral and theological reflection in conjunction with their action in the world.

Cardijn called his method see-judge-act. Seeing entails engagement, even immersion, in the social situation at hand, and particularly the lives and conditions of the poor. Judging involves theological and moral reflection in the light of Christian scripture and tradition, as a basis for evaluating the moral quality of institutions, actions, and experiences involved in the "reality" being seen. For Cardijn, judging should be "done in solidarity with those one seeks to help; it is therefore a community that works together toward this goal, rather than a particular person or group working on behalf of others," as Justin Sands explains. This approach to moral discernment and action thus rejects the methodological individualism of many dominant models. "Once the proper judgments and/or discernments have been made, then and only then can one 'act' in solidarity with the community toward alleviating suffering—or, better still, act toward empowering those who suffer to alleviate their own suffering."[24] This action then becomes itself part of the social reality in which theological reflection takes place and which it must judge.

Cardijn's method helped structure the conclusions of the influential 1968 Latin American bishops' conference in Medellín, Colombia. The bishops adapted Cardijn's approach to address reality, reflection, and pastoral consequences. Following the see-judge-act model, they began with concrete experiences and not abstract concepts or absolute values. Their "seeing" involved detailed analyses of the contemporary political and social crises in Latin America, upon which they then reflected "in the light of the Gospel" and of Church tradition.[25] Their judgments led to conclusions that condemned institutionalized violence and human rights abuses and encouraged progressive pastoral innovations and collective action.

Latin American theologians found in Cardijn's see-judge-act model a new way to think about the relationship between theological reflection, social injustice, and Christian action in the world. Gustavo Gutiérrez, a Peruvian theologian widely seen as the "father" of Latin American liberation theology, highlighted this relationship in his assertion that liberation theology is not a new topic for theology but rather a new method of doing theology.[26] Uruguayan theologian Juan Luis Segundo elaborates on the centrality of method, asserting that liberation theology "is more interested in *being liberative* than in talking about liberation. In other words, liberation deals not so much with content as with the method used to theologize in face of our real-life situation."[27] This method understands theology not as discernment of eternal truths but as critical reflection on Christian praxis in the light of the word.[28] According to this model, practice takes priority, chronologically as well as normatively. "First comes the commitment to charity, to service," as Gutiérrez writes. "Theology comes 'later.'"[29] This resembles the model of *imitatio Christi*, which is central to many Christian pacifist traditions, with its emphasis on following, rather than "thinking about," the path of Jesus.[30] It also challenges the linear model of idealism, according to which ideas produce (or are applied in) action.

Segundo deepens this challenge by developing an explicitly practice-based method which he called the "hermeneutic circle."[31] As he explains, the hermeneutic circle is "the continuing change in our interpretation of the Bible, which is dictated by continuing changes in our present-day reality, both individual and societal."[32] The Bible is reinterpreted by new reality, and the new reality is changed by the Bible—or, rather, human practices of reading and discernment reinterpret the Bible in light of the concrete situation, and in turn this situation is changed by human practices that are shaped by biblical reflection. Practice is primary, in theory as in real life. This perspective also undergirds Gutiérrez's definition of theology as a second step.

The emphasis on practice places theology firmly "in the world," in contrast to Augustinian and Lutheran conceptions of two cities or kingdoms, which see the world and church as separate spheres. While Catholic social thought challenges Luther's devaluation of the "earthly kingdom," it limits the function of the Church in the world to evangelization and inspiration. Liberation theologians such as Gutiérrez, in contrast, insist that the Church must be fully immersed in all aspects of human life: "There are not, then, two histories, one profane and one sacred, juxtaposed or interrelated, but a single human progress, irreversibly exalted by Christ, the Lord of history."[33] Thus, it is incorrect to separate theology and other systems of thought from concrete practices. Theology must find and interpret God's word in everyday life, as Mexican theologian Enrique Dussel insists.[34] This suggests that ethical theory, similarly, must find and interpret the good in everyday life and, particularly, in concrete practices.

While liberation theologians are not, for the most part, explicitly building ethical theory, many of their core ideas, especially in regard to theological method and the place of human action in history, are directly relevant to ethics. In particular, the rejection of the "two planes" model makes morality inseparable from other spheres of life. This is supported also by the liberationist claim that salvation is not a purely individualistic and otherworldly goal, but rather it is linked to all aspects of human life, and particularly to the "communion" among people, as well as that between people and the divine.[35]

If sacred and secular history are intertwined, and if people's work in the world is linked to their ultimate salvation, then practice must play a central role in ethics. Liberation theologians often support the elevation of practice with reference to the Hebrew prophets, such as Jeremiah 22:15–16, in which God asks: "Does it make you a king to have more and more cedar? Did not your father have food and drink? He did what was right and just, so all went well with him. He defended the cause of the poor and needy, and so all went well. Is that not what it means to know me?" The liberationist interpretation of this passage is that, as Gutiérrez writes, "To love Yahweh is to do justice to the poor and oppressed."[36] In this perspective, concrete practices, and particularly work on behalf of the "least well off," are necessary not just as "works of mercy" or expressions of self-discipline but as ways to gain knowledge of and closeness to God. True faith and love of God cannot be reduced to internal mental states, Gutiérrez explains: "Charity cannot exist in the abstract, outside our human scope for loving. Charity exists only incarnated in human love, raising it to its fulfillment. Loving the neighbor is a necessary application of loving God; in fact, it is loving God."[37]

Liberation theology makes important contributions to thinking about practice in ethics. Most obviously, many liberation theologians are deeply concerned with the practical and political implications of ideas about God, Jesus, and the Church, and they often relate them to moral issues such as human rights, violence, economic justice, and democratization. In addition, liberation theology offers a model for relating ideas and actions. It gives practice a central role in both theology (knowledge of God) and ethics (efforts to know and do the good). In this perspective, "Theology is an utterance that seeks to be coherent with practice," as Gutiérrez writes.[38] This reverses the relationship between these terms in idealist models, according to which practice "enacts" previously articulated moral ideas. Liberationist concepts such as the hermeneutic circle provide models for thinking about how to relate ideas and practices in ethics more generally. Additional resources for reflecting on this issue come from the next type of moral theory I consider here: feminist ethics.

Feminist Care Ethics

Like liberation theology, feminist ethics begins with an explicit commitment to the liberation of subjugated groups and critique of dominant theoretical and social systems. Whereas liberation theology directs its critique primarily to oppressive class and colonial relations, feminist thought focuses on the experiences of women and the power structures that limit their opportunities. For many feminists, the hyper-rationalism of dominant philosophical models is part of the problem, because it excludes bodily experiences, emotion, and personal relationships. The best-known feminist moral theory, care ethics, emerged in the 1980s in a challenge to what Marilyn Friedman calls "the lopsided obsession of contemporary theories of morality . . . with universal and impartial conceptions of justice and rights and the relative disregard of *particular*, interpersonal relationships based on partiality and affective ties."[39] This lopsidedness characterizes idealist and rationalist ethical theories that define the good in relation to abstract norms and deliberately exclude personal relationships, preferences, and experiences. While care is not the only feminist approach to ethical theory, it is an important one and especially relevant for thinking about practice.

The roots of care ethics are often traced to the work of moral psychologist Carol Gilligan. In her research on women's and men's, and girls' and boys', modes of moral decision-making, Gilligan found important differences between the styles of decision-making and the conclusions drawn by male and female participants. In particular, men tended to conceive of moral problems as conflicts between different rights or other absolute rules, which were often mutually exclusive. Thus, they saw ethical decisions as choices between two opposed options. Women, in contrast, were more likely to understand moral problems as conflicts among various responsibilities, which means that the resolution requires not an either-or choice but rather a contextual, narrative, and nuanced form of moral reflection.[40] While women often see moral choices in the context of a "narrative of relationships that extends over time,"[41] men tend to view moral problems more abstractly, in terms of rules and principles.

Gilligan calls impartial, rationalistic, rule-based ethics the "justice model," which is exemplified in Kantian and social contract theories. Care ethics, in contrast, finds moral value in responsiveness to particular persons and a commitment to them as such.[42] Many feminist thinkers, including Gilligan, find the two perspectives complementary. Often their goal is not to replace rationalist models entirely but rather to open a space for emotions and relationships as legitimate sources of moral guidance. Some care theorists, however, reject justice approaches as inadequate in any context. Nel Noddings, for example, believes that care ethics should largely replace rationalist accounts, because "the very wellspring of ethical behavior lies in human affective response."[43] She finds the impartiality sought by Kant and other rationalist models inadequate, because they dismiss the moral significance of emotions and intimate relationships.

For care ethicists, intimate relationships, especially in the family, provide models for moral theory and action more broadly. They share with virtue and Catholic thinkers a conviction that humans are social animals who can find happiness and develop morally only in relationship with others. This leads to a further common theme among the three models: that there is no hard division between private and public lives and that personal experiences are connected to larger realms. Like a number of Catholic and virtue theorists, further, many feminists link the morality of individuals and their ability to lead fulfilling lives with their social relationships and participation in larger communities. For some feminist thinkers, as for liberation theologians, this connection takes an explicitly political character. This is true of the maternal ethic developed by Sara Ruddick, which brings together practices of activism, caring for children, and creating supportive communities. She describes this ethic as a discipline rather than an attitude, and one that is applicable to all aspects of life, including the public sphere. "Out of maternal practices, distinctive ways of conceptualizing, ordering, and valuing arise. We *think* differently about what it *means* and what it takes to be . . . a person, to be real."[44] Particular practices, in other words, give rise to distinctive ways of understanding goodness in the public sphere as well as in the home.

The integration of personal and public, along with other features of feminist care ethics, suggests a very different place for practice from that in idealist models. First, practice comes to the fore because of the partiality and intimacy that define care ethics. We cannot think about material practice other than in particular, concrete ways, and more than any other ethical theory we have explored so far, care ethics is rooted in the concrete and particular. Second, the connection between the personal and the political demands attention to practices. Concrete activities are what mediate between the spheres and make values relevant in both. "The lived experience of feeling as well as thinking, of acting as well as receiving impressions, and of connectedness to other persons as well as the self" becomes the source for norms and goals, as Virginia Held explains.[45] Third, care approaches suggest a different approach to epistemology and thus to meta-ethics. Specific content emerges out of practices and experiences, but so do ways of knowing and reasoning. Ruddick calls this a "practicalist" view of reason, which arises out of distinctive practices.[46] This echoes some themes in pragmatism, as we will see in chapter 4, as well as virtue and Catholic approaches.

Contributions to a Practice-Based Ethics

Virtue, Catholic, and feminist ethics make important contributions both to the critique of idealist ethical theories and, more positively, to the development of a practice-based approach. A consideration of the five themes I have discussed in previous chapters can highlight some of the most significant features of these models and clarify the comparisons among models.

1. Virtue, Catholic, and feminist thinkers conceive of moral ideas in relation to, and as the product of, people's embodied experiences, emotional commitments, and social interactions. They challenge the Kantian conviction that ethics must stem from pure reason and be completely isolated from "empirical" matters, including both personal and social context. While Enlightenment thinkers feared that emotions would taint or bias moral decisions, alternative models understand personal relationships and loyalties as inevitable, and largely positive, components of both ethical theory and ordinary moral action. The critique of hyper-rationalism has been developed especially by feminists, who document the links between supposedly neutral reason and the privileged conditions and priorities of male thinkers. They argue that women's ties to domestic life and particularly to childrearing do not hamper moral reflection but rather enrich it and make it both more comprehensive and more useful. Virtue ethicists also insist that moral ideas must be, and always are, integrated into the whole of life and can be developed only as the result of continued effort, often understood as habituation. In this view, moral ideas cannot stand apart from the experiences and activities of moral actors.

2. These "alternative" models reject the proceduralist approach of many Enlightenment theories according to which morality is constituted by principles or rules that do not depend on, or change in response to, personal experiences, social and historical context, or substantive values. Like ideas in general, the structures of ethical theories are supposed to be independent of any particular content. Idealist ethics, in short, requires a degree of universality, objectivity, and generalizability that work against the thick details that provide concrete directions for action. In contrast, virtue, Catholic, liberationist, and feminist theories present "thick" ethics, with fleshed-out visions of good character, the good life for a person, and the shape of the common good. Theorizing then becomes an effort not to divide generalizations from particularities but rather to link them, to build larger structures from the complex, dense details of particular activities and lives.[47] They require content in a way that rationalist, universalist models do not. Virtue theories, for example, cannot be understood or even described, let alone followed, without knowing specific details about the character traits that a good person should possess, the ways these traits can be cultivated, and how they relate to each other. Catholic social thought, in turn, is grounded in Church traditions and theological claims that provide the necessary content for ethical thinking. Similarly, feminist ethics begins with the distinctive experiences of women, which pose a direct challenge not only to patriarchal power structures but also to the supposed thinness of masculinist theories posing as neutral.

3. One of the most important areas of agreement for the theories discussed in this chapter is their shared claim that humans are social animals and that, consequently, ethics must also always be social. Ethics is social in two senses. First, morality is the work of people who are shaped by their social histories and contexts and who cannot live good lives apart from social relationships, including those in the family as well as the public sphere. Second, the very subject of ethics is social life; moral decisions always affect and are affected by people and communities beyond the individual actor. All these models share the characteristic of feminist ethics described by Margaret Urban Walker: a view of moral life as "a continuing negotiation *among* people, a practice of mutually allotting, assuming, or deflecting responsibilities of important kinds, and understanding the implications of doing so."[48] Both Catholic and virtue models emphasize that moral action is directed to the common

good. They reject the methodological and normative individualism of liberal approaches such as Kantianism and social contract theory, in particular. Instead, they link morality to social relationships and connect both to larger social structures. People can become virtuous and happy, and can fulfill their various social roles, only by participating in the right kind of community, which may be the *polis*, the family, or the Church, among other options. This emphasis on sociability leads to norms related to communal life, such as mutual aid, willingness to compromise and sacrifice, and attention to the needs and interests of people who are dependent or marginalized. This membership is not merely a matter of attitude or identity but one of material practices and real relationships, supported by personal actions as well as social, political, and economic structures.

4. Another defining feature of these moral theories is an insistence that morality cannot be kept in a separate sphere of thought or action. It is woven throughout the whole of people's lives and of societies as a whole.[49] Because it is not the project of disembodied minds and isolated individual actors, ethics is inextricably tied up with all aspects of human thought and action. The models discussed here view ethics as an integral aspect of a whole life, including family, politics, and work. This is seen in the feminist insistence that what happens in domestic life and personal relationships matters for ethics, both because those are important spheres of moral action and because what happens there shapes who we are in all areas of life. Liberationist Catholics, in turn, link theological ethics to political and economic structures, insisting that we can only think morally and make moral decisions in light of social, as well as personal and religious, experiences.

5. The models discussed in this chapter contribute to an alternative view of the relations between intentions, actions, and consequences. They do not always include explicit rejections of linear models or explicit formulations of an alternative, but they assume a complex and mutual relationship between ideas and practices. Virtue theorists, for example, understand virtue not as something people can simply choose but as the product of repeated effort or habituation. In Catholicism, both personal works of charity and religious rituals not only inculcate moral dispositions but also help clarify the nature of the good that people should pursue. Care ethicists, in turn, look at practices of mothering and attentive love as both examples of ethical practice and ways to learn what ethics requires.

Conclusions

These themes show how the ethical approaches discussed in this chapter point us toward a different place for practice. They suggest that in everyday moral life and also in moral theory, it is not possible simply to identify or create an ethically correct attitude or intention. Such attitudes are often formed in and through practice, rather than apart from and prior to it. In addition, virtue, Catholic, and feminist approaches highlight the importance of relationships, emotions, and membership in concrete communities. This accords with their view of humans as social animals, who cannot act or think as isolated individuals, particularly in regard to morality. Humans are also "storytelling animals," as MacIntyre puts it, who develop and interpret ethical ideas in the context of narratives. These narratives are collective, part of the historical identity of moral communities. Only as members of such communities can people understand not just the right thing to do but who they are as moral actors and why these values are compelling for them. Another commonality between these traditions is a holistic view of ethics, most notably in virtue ethics, which emphasizes the cultivation of character over the whole of a person's life and in all types of action. Catholic and feminist thinkers, as well, approach ethics as not just a decision-making process but rather part of an integrated process involving all human capacities and spheres of life.

While most of these discussions do not involve explicit discussion of practices, they contribute to my critique of idealism and also, more important, begin laying the groundwork for a practice-based approach to ethical theory. For more explicit attention to practice and arguments about why this attention is necessary, I turn in chapter 4 to philosophical pragmatism, which, as its name implies, puts practice squarely at the center of moral thinking.

4

Pragmatism and Ethics

The Path of Inquiry

> To say that a man seeks health or justice is only to say that he seeks to
> live healthily or justly. These things, like truth, are adverbial.
>
> —John Dewey[1]

Introduction

Like health and justice, pragmatism itself is adverbial. It is, according to
William James, best defined "not as a philosophy but as a way of doing philosophy."[2] A contemporary interpreter makes a similar point: "Pragmatism,
in the most basic sense, is about how we think, not what we think."[3] As a way
of thinking, pragmatism rejects many features of dominant philosophical
and moral traditions, and especially universalism, abstraction, idealism, and
absolutism. In their place, pragmatism favors concreteness, open-endedness,
pluralism, and change. While pragmatism is not itself concerned primarily with ethics, it makes important contributions to the development of
a practice-based ethical theory. First, it insists on the connection between
theory and practice. This means that moral problems, like scientific ones,
cannot be solved in the abstract but must be approached in their concrete
reality. Second, pragmatism directs our attention to particular forms of practice, especially habit and problem-solving inquiry. Third and perhaps most
important, it underlines and examines the interconnections between means
and ends.

These features enable pragmatism to make distinctive contributions to
a practice-based ethical theory, while building on and moving beyond the
traditions discussed in chapter 3. Like virtue, Catholic, and feminist thinkers,
pragmatists assert that ideas are situated, humans are social by nature,
and morality is not separate from other forms of thought and action. Even
more than those traditions, pragmatists emphasize the complex, mutually

Works Righteousness. Anna L. Peterson, Oxford University Press (2021). © Oxford University Press.
DOI: 10.1093/oso/9780197532232.001.0001.

transformative interactions between ideas and practices. In short, they place practices at the center of moral knowledge and reflection and theorize practice explicitly—they think about what practice is, how and why people do particular things, and so forth. This makes pragmatism especially helpful in clarifying and highlighting the place of practice in ethical theory.

In this chapter, I focus on pragmatism's treatment of the relations between theory and practice, with particular attention to its approach to epistemology and also to habit. I also discuss practice theory, a contemporary approach that draws heavily on pragmatism. I highlight the similarities between the two in their treatment of practice and its central role in developing theory. While practice theorists do not make ethics a central concern, they help clarify the meaning and significance of material practices, for ethics and other forms of knowledge. Together, pragmatism and practice theory help us continue building the outline of an ethical theory in which practice plays a central role.

Theory and Practice

Pragmatism begins not with first principles or metaphysical foundations but with real-world problems that need solutions. In this perspective, theory and practice are never separate activities but always two sides of the same process of problem-solving. As John Dewey explains in an 1891 article on moral theory and practice, "Theory is the cross-section of the given state of action in order to know the conduct that should be; practice is the realization of the idea thus gained: it is theory in action."[4] Dewey's understanding of practice encompasses people's mental processes as well as physical and social actions. Theory and practice, like means and ends, only make sense in mutual interaction.

This is spelled out in pragmatist approaches to a variety of philosophical topics, including epistemology and education, as well as ethics. Moral theory, according to Dewey, is "all one with moral insight, and moral insight is the recognition of the relationships in hand."[5] Attention to relationships in hand will provide both necessary understanding of what is at stake and practical tools to address issues effectively. This concrete, problem-solving orientation contrasts sharply with the usual philosophical preference for universalist or abstract perspectives. Those theoretical models, according to pragmatists, lead to mistaken accounts of the world and unhelpful solutions to real-life problems. A pragmatist approach would resolve these issues and help people think more clearly about the challenges and puzzles they face and pursue solutions in an open-ended way that is oriented to problem-solving.

Problem-solving and practical effects are at the heart of the "pragmatist principle," proposed by Charles Sanders Peirce in 1878: "a conception, that is, the rational purport of a word or other expression, lies exclusively in its conceivable bearing upon the conduct of life."[6] In slightly more detail, Peirce proposed this guiding rule: "Consider what effects which might conceivably have practical bearings we conceive the object of our conception to have. Then, our conception of these effects is the whole of our conception of the object."[7] In other words, the practical effects of ideas are their most important aspect, as Dewey affirms: "Confirmation, corroboration, verification lie in works, consequences. Handsome is that handsome does. By their fruits shall ye *know* them."[8] Despite some similarities in the language, this is very different from Luther's claim that the good tree will bear good fruit. Luther believes that moral actors must become good internally, and then, as a consequence of their exemplary faith, they will perform good deeds. Dewey, however, does not conceive of moral goodness (or any quality) as something that can be achieved or even defined outside of practices. Bearing good fruit, or performing good deeds, tells us that the tree or the moral actor is good.

This emphasis on the practical effects of ideas was reiterated by William James, who, like Dewey and Peirce, conceived of pragmatism not as a particular theory but rather as a way of approaching almost any topic, "a method of settling metaphysical disputes that otherwise might be interminable." Facing such questions, James wrote, the pragmatic method tries "to interpret each notion by tracing its respective practical consequences. What difference would it practically make to anyone if this notion rather than that notion were true?"[9] This is where James's often quoted, often misunderstood phrase "cash value" emerges. "If you follow the pragmatic method," he explained, "you cannot look on any . . . word as closing your quest. You must bring out of each word its practical cash value, set it at work within the stream of your experience. It appears less as a solution, then, than as a program for more work, and more particularly as an indication of the ways in which existing realities may be changed."[10]

"Practical cash value," then, is not a crudely utilitarian calculation. Unlike utilitarians, pragmatists do not aggregate the predicted good and bad effects of a moral decision. Instead, they seek to learn how particular conceptions of the world can help improve people's lives. It is the real-world effect of believing one notion or the other. Pragmatists also believe, as Dewey put it, that "The hypothesis that works is the *true* one."[11] James also applied this to religion—the faith that works, that helps believers in the real world, is correct.[12]

The emphasis on practical consequences is well illustrated in the pragmatist approach to applied ethics. Most ethical theories focus on meta-ethics and normative concerns, often treating applied ethics as an entirely separate undertaking, of interest mainly to people focused on specific real-life issues such as medical or legal ethics. In pragmatism, however, applied ethics "becomes the principal phase of the enterprise of ethical philosophy," as Andrew Altman writes, "for, from a pragmatic perspective, it is only by judging the consequence of attempting to embody certain ethical principles in our lives and social arrangements that those principles can be justified or refuted. This is in direct contradiction to the traditional approach, which treats the consequences of commitment to a principle as irrelevant to its justifiability."[13] Pragmatists turn this traditional approach around, treating the practical cash value of a principle as central to its theoretical and moral strength.

A good example of this approach to applied ethics, and to ethics generally, can be seen in the work of environmental pragmatists. While most environmental ethicists begin with questions about the kind of value nature has and the reasons for this valuation, environmental pragmatists focus on the ways ethical thinking can contribute to solving environmental problems. The strength of an environmental ethic thus rests not on its internal consistency or theoretical sophistication but on its usefulness in real-world contexts—its cash value. Anthony Weston illustrates this pragmatist approach in his analysis of the process of gaining government protection for a wilderness area. Weston argues that we can appreciate and protect nature without the support of first principles or metaphysical groundings. A consensus may be rooted, rather, in an expansive, pluralistic search for common ground, in which all interested groups can talk about their experiences in and appreciation for nature. Practices thus ground value claims in two ways—the active dialogue that seeks consensus and the reflection on experiences that awakens respect and appreciation for the value of nature. This type of pragmatist approach is not, for Weston, "'second best,' 'weak' anthropocentric substitutes for the intrinsic values that many philosophers desire."[14] The diversity of concrete experiences in and with nature does not weaken but rather strengthens environmental ethics, by explaining the real value of nature and guiding correct behavior toward it.

Weston's discussion of environmental pragmatism illustrates how attention to what people actually do can help us think about practices in ethical theory, including normative and meta-ethics as well as applied ethics. A focus on practices can show us what people value and also that they have many different reasons for this valuation. It is not necessary for ethical theory, or helpful in real life, to pin down a single ultimate source for the value of nature or any other good. Thus, the task of moral philosophy is not to distinguish between "true" and "false" claims but rather to distinguish between helpful and unhelpful ways of thinking about a particular problem.

This approach to applied ethics reflects the pragmatist conviction that there is no absolute, universal moral goodness, any more than there is an absolute, universal truth, "out there" waiting to be discovered. Instead, goodness, like truth, emerges in and through human activity and experience. The moral principle that works is the good one. The question is what it means to "work," in a moral sense or by any other standard of judgment. This emphasis on functionality is tied to the pragmatist view of truth as an effort to solve practical problems, reflecting the close link between ethics and epistemology in pragmatist thought.

Epistemology and Ethics in Pragmatist Thought

Knowledge, for pragmatists, is provisional, collective, and never purely abstract; it is always tied to moral and practical concerns. The provisional character of knowledge rests on the pragmatist insistence that there is no transcendent source of objective knowledge outside human experience. This is particularly true for experimental inquiry, but all kinds of active operations teach us about ourselves, others, and the world. This is one of the most important claims of pragmatism: all human knowledge—scientific, social, and moral—emerges in the course of active, open-ended engagement with the world. Further, all these types of knowledge are experimental, in the sense that they are valid temporarily, until a better version emerges.

Every truth is a temporary way station on a continuing path of improvement made possible by rational inquiry and collective discernment. We cannot assume that a solution that worked once will work in a different setting, and thus, we must be open to new forms of knowledge and diverse perspectives that present novel options. The goal, in ethics as in science, is not to acquire some permanent and transcendent truth but rather to solve concrete problems. Problem-solving is central to pragmatism in all areas, and ethics is no exception. Problems are solved not by applying predetermined forms of knowledge but rather by gathering concrete, detailed information about the particulars of the case and reflecting on this knowledge collectively.

Here Dewey's concept of ends-in-view is helpful. An end-in-view, for Dewey, is a goal understood in relation to the means that are judged to be most likely to achieve the desired goal, which itself becomes a means toward a future goal. Being a "means" or an "end" is thus not a permanent condition but a relational quality. Ends-in-view serve as "means for directing action," guiding practical responses to a given problem.[15] Rather than starting with a fixed preconception of the best means for achieving a particular goal, Dewey insists, we must examine all means that are likely to attain the desired end and be willing to make corrections and adjustments in the course of pursuing ends. These adjustments are necessary because the ends we can perceive change as we act—thus, the ends that are "in view" at the beginning of a course of action will not be the same as those we view later. Here pragmatist fallibilism and experimentalism come to bear directly on ethics.

The notion of ends-in-view also draws on pragmatism's social understanding of human nature. Moral means and ends depend on "relationships in hand," the concrete interactions and experiences of people in a particular situation, which for Dewey constitute the defining concern of moral theory. This means that grand moral concerns, such as justice, can and should be resolved into specific relations among people. If the moral actor cannot "translate justice into actual relations," Dewey explains, "it becomes a generality, and can lead to bitterness of feeling which leads astray, to a blind feeling that things should be overturned because they are not what they should be."[16] Moral objectives, like truths, are steps in open-ended, constantly unfolding paths. The role of a good end-in-view, as Erin McKenna explains, is to "open up possibilities rather than close them off."[17] Virtuous persons should actively pursue knowledge about and from multiple perspectives, with an emphasis on the connections among diverse experiences and people.[18]

This points to the collective character of the acquisition of knowledge and also of knowledge itself. The process of learning must be shared, because it is necessary to have a community of inquirers that can uncover the errors in presumed truths and point toward better ways of understanding. This requires a social norm of widespread participation in democratic processes and conversations about moral issues. Good communities, good people, and good ends-in-view all promote widespread, free, and informed participation. This benefits both the community as a whole and the individual members, who improve their own "critical and flexible habits of mind" in and through their involvement in democratic processes, as McKenna puts it.[19] Political processes, like moral education, should focus not on specific desired ends but rather on "developing abilities that allow for multiple ends to be realistically possible."[20]

The goal of pragmatist knowledge is not just to learn how the world works but also to consider what people ought to do. Pragmatism rejects the kind of utopianism that presents unachievable ideals as guides for behavior. Through the application of critical intelligence, people can learn about the constraints they face as well as the prospects for positive change. Ends-in-view must emerge out of the present situation and be based on an accurate assessment both of what is already going on and of what changes might be achievable.[21] Thus, we should avoid predetermined goals that do not account for actual circumstances and that are not open to change. We return, then, to the guiding pragmatist values of flexibility, openness, and fallibilism. People must always be prepared for changes in the world and, equally important, for their own errors. We cannot become too attached to our own assessment of a situation or our ability to affect it in specific ways. Fallibilism is both the most moral and the most realistic stance toward the world.

The active, practical, and "adverbial" character of truth and goodness reflects the ways pragmatists connect theory and practice. Most Western philosophical traditions assert that knowledge, understood as true beliefs, comes from outside human sensory experience, rests on fixed ends, and is eternal and abstract. In contrast, pragmatists believe that knowledge is gained through active, ongoing, sensory exploration of the world, "the ongoing transaction of organism and environment" which is both the subject and the environment.[22] These transactions also constitute both the knower and what is known. Knowledge is not prior to activity but gained in and through human practices, and it must continually be tested and altered as needed.

Resting on this understanding of knowledge and inquiry, pragmatists emphasize the experimental and problem-solving nature of theory. The best knowledge, not just scientific but also moral, emerges through experimentation. This is how we know which idea "works." Theory is a tool for practice, not something prior to practice that can be "applied" and dropped down from heaven. In this perspective, as James put it, "Theories thus become instruments, not answers to enigmas, in which we can rest."[23] Sociological and even moral theories are akin to scientific hypotheses, always subject to ongoing investigation and continual testing. Neither truth nor goodness can ever be defined or located in a universal, objective, and final sense. They always remain provisional, subject to inquiry and testing as well as to the influence of social and historical context.

One important method of testing was Dewey's concept of "dramatic rehearsal," in which "possible avenues for acting are rehearsed before trying them out." This process "opens up a situation so it is perceived in a new way."[24] Dramatic rehearsal, for Dewey, is not simply thinking about possible future outcomes in a utilitarian way but "trying out" an act in imagination, to understand its meaning, implications, and force more fully. Dramatic rehearsal underlines the power of practice as a way to gain the knowledge and critical understanding that are vital for ethical action. In imaginative as well as physical practices, we learn about what we value and why, as well as considering the potential "cash value" of different courses of action in the real world.

Dramatic rehearsal also underlines the fallibilism that is central to pragmatism. We try things out because we are not sure if we are right, and we want to explore different options, testing them in relation to both the concrete situation and our goals. Fallibilism is especially associated with the work of Peirce, who understood it as a multilayered philosophical principle. It begins with "the thesis that, with regard to *any* proposition, it is humanly possible to hold a mistaken belief," as Joseph Margolis explains. Some thinkers propose this as an exhaustive definition of fallibilism. For pragmatists, however, fallibilism is not merely a rejection of the possibility of perfect knowledge but also an embrace of self-corrective inquiry, the conviction that "it is both possible and likely that, for any mistaken belief, a society of inquirers can, in a pertinently finite interval of time, discern its own mistakes and progress toward discovering the true state of affairs."[25] This true state of affairs, of course, is always an end-in-view, a temporary truth that will change in response to further inquiry and testing.

Fallibilism is relevant for ethical theory in at least two ways. It supports moral pluralism, since it challenges mainstream assumptions that moral claims have objective foundations, that norms are fixed, and that values have universal applicability. It also leads to distinctive claims about the relations between ideas, actions, and consequences. What Dewey called "the precariousness of existence"[26] means that we cannot control or even predict the effects of our moral ideas or actions. This contradicts linear views of the relations between intentions, actions, and consequences, which presume control of individual actors and also a predictable situation with no outside influences.

Habit and Practice

For pragmatists, practice is not a distinct, specific type of activity, as is action for analytic philosophy, but rather an expansive category that encompasses many forms of action, both ordinary and exceptional. Practices include all sorts of "active operations," the ways people not only express but construct themselves. There is no autonomous, self-contained actor who can think, intend, or make decisions outside of practice, because thinking, intending, and deciding are all practices. This accords with the pragmatist rejection of the supposed divisions between theory and practice, intentions and actions, or minds and bodies. This is evident in pragmatist approaches to habit, which is a central concept for pragmatism, as for virtue ethics.

Everyday usage often defines habit as repetitive, perhaps unthinking behavior. Dewey disagrees: "Repetition is in no sense the essence of habit," he writes. "Tendency to repeat acts is an incident of many habits but not of all."[27] If repetition does not define habit, what does? Most simply, pragmatists understand habit as "an ongoing set of activities that achieves some purpose."[28] Habits have roots in past behavior, but they are not outside of the critical processes of inquiry and reconstruction. They can be worthwhile or destructive, and it is possible for us to change them when needed. This is because they are not unconscious or mindless but rather a particular kind of consciousness. Their most characteristic quality is that they involve "the establishment in our nature of a rule of action," as Peirce put it.[29] These rules link thought and action, so that a habit is a way beliefs are hitched to characteristic forms of action, as Dewey explains, "an acquired predisposition to ways or modes of response" or the practical inculcation of ways of thinking and feeling. Dewey continues: "Habit means special sensitiveness or accessibility to certain classes of stimuli, standing predilections and aversions, rather than bare recurrence of specific acts. It means will."[30]

The pragmatist understanding of habit as will challenges Kantian, Lutheran, and other conceptions that define the will as an autonomous, disembodied capacity. Rather than separating actions and mental attitudes, as idealist philosophers do, Dewey links the two ever more firmly. Habit, he writes, is "that kind of human activity which is influenced by prior activity and in that sense acquired; which contains within itself a certain ordering or systematization of minor elements of action; which is projective, dynamic in quality, ready for overt manifestation; and which is operative in some subdued subordinate form even when not obviously dominant."[31] This echoes Aristotelian notions of habituation as the way people learn and inculcate virtue.

Dewey further joins habit to an understanding of will and moral agency by using it as the basis for his definition of character. Character, according to Dewey, is "the interpenetration of habits."[32] For pragmatists, as Elena Cuffari writes, "We are what we do, and our doing is a result of previous actions and of the environment in which we act. Yet our ways of acting in, through, and with an environment are always changing. Neither the organism nor the environment is ever the same twice. Ideally one's habits enable one to be responsive to new situations and adaptive to varying conditions."[33] Habit and practice create dispositions, which not only are mental attitudes but also involve an inclination to act in a particular way. There are no intentions or will apart from what people do and have done. Because they are rooted in practices, past and present habits are social. Habit encompasses "not only private behavioral patterns but also heritable interpretive structures, such as symbol systems, stories, beliefs, myths, virtues, gestures, prejudices, etc."[34] Habits provide the context for people's responses to different situations, not just because personal habits shape how individuals respond but also because collectively, habits create cultural patterns and structures that further condition people's actions. They mediate between our intentions and ideas and between everyday lives and their social contexts.

This conception of habit helps explain why pragmatists reject the idealist notion that moral conduct can be changed simply by an act of disembodied will. Rather, moral ideas and conduct are both part of habits, and they can only be altered alongside, and in mutual interaction with, larger changes in the actor's social context. Just as we cannot put out a fire by effort of will but only by changing objective conditions, Dewey asserts, the same holds for ethics.[35] This is not a reductive materialism but one in which the relations between objective conditions and ethics are dynamic and mutual. Material forces are not the only thing that matters, but they are as necessary as attitudes or efforts of will.

Dewey's understanding of habit grounds his critique of Kantian and utilitarian ethical theories, both of which wrongly separate character and conduct, motive and act, will and deed. This division takes different forms, but the underlying problem remains the same. Kantianism, according to Dewey, asserts "that only will, disposition, motive counts morally; that acts are external, physical, accidental; that moral good is different from goodness in act since the latter is measured by consequences, while moral good or virtue is intrinsic, complete in itself, a jewel shining by its own light." In contrast, utilitarians believe "that such a view is equivalent to saying that all that is necessary to be virtuous is to cultivate states of feeling; that a premium is put on disregard of the actual consequences of conduct, and agents are deprived of any objective criterion for the rightness and wrongness of acts, being thrown back on their own whims, prejudices and private peculiarities."[36] Dewey has sympathy with the utilitarian critique of Kant's focus on the individual will and disregard of consequences.

While he is more critical of Kantianism than of utilitarianism, Dewey insists that the two theoretical approaches "suffer from a common mistake. Both of them ignore the projective force of habit and the implication of habits in one another."[37] This weakness rests in no small part on a misunderstanding of the significance of practice. According to Dewey, both Kantians and utilitarians "separate a unified deed into two disjoined parts, an inner called motive and an outer called act."[38] Kant conflates will and deed, and utilitarians conflate acts and consequences, but both are equally wrong. "The utilitarian theory of equation of acts with consequences is as much a fiction of self-conceit as is the [Kantian] assumption of a fixed transcendental world wherein moral ideals are eternally and immutably real."[39] The problem with both is that they separate things that should not be separated, create abstractions and reified categories where they should see experience and fluid practices.[40] The particular type of practice that is habit helps Dewey explain both where other theories go wrong and how pragmatism addresses this error by uniting actions and motives. This lays the groundwork for important moral claims, including the unity of means and ends, as I discuss later in this chapter.

Practice Theory

A study of practice in ethics would not be complete without discussing practice theory, a contemporary approach in social theory that draws heavily on pragmatism, as well as Marxist, post-structuralist, feminist, and post-humanist perspectives. Core thinkers include Ludwig Wittgenstein, Pierre Bourdieu, Anthony Giddens, Sherry Ortner, and Michel Foucault, as well as pragmatists like Dewey and George Herbert Mead. The different forms of practice theory are held together less by a common method than by a shared conviction that "the status of human beings as 'subjects' (and 'agents') is bound to practices," in the words of Theodore Schatzki. According to this perspective, practices "displace mind as the central phenomenon in human life."[41] This parallels the arguments I make for displacing will as the central phenomenon in moral life. Practice theory, however, rarely addresses ethics in detail. It is, furthermore, generally rather abstract, interested in the way we think about practices more than about particular practices and their contexts.

One of the helpful contributions of practice theory is its definition of practices as the socially conditioned ways in which people construct their identities, relate to other people, and shape their societies. This echoes pragmatist understandings and provides a helpful grounding for thinking about practice in ethics. Practice theory also echoes pragmatism in its rejection of dualisms between mind and body, self and world, theory and practice, and agent and structure and its denial of the existence of mental states independent of embodied practices. Agency and will depend more on our actions than on interior attitudes, and both attitudes and actions, in turn, are shaped by many factors outside our control. We have agency, but we exercise it in relation to and under the constraints of objective conditions, other actors, and nature. In all these respects, practice theory sounds much like pragmatism.

The most significant differences, especially in relation to ethics, stem from the sociological grounding of most practice thinkers. In particular, practice theory gives more emphasis to the interactions between actors and institutions, the determining role of structures, and the relations between different scales of action. Here practice theory's affinities with Marxism are evident. Practice theory sees practices as constructing each scale, from the local to the global, and also mediating between them. Pragmatists might not disagree with any of these points, but they do not stress them. The differences are not only of emphasis, however. Pragmatism's emphasis on inquiry, experience, and ends-in-view give it a more consistent methodological identity than practice theory.

For my purposes, practice theory makes several contributions to thinking about ethical theory. First, it reinforces the pragmatist claim that there are no disembodied mental states independent of embodied practices. Attitudes, intentions, and faith do not emerge from within the isolated individual but rather are shaped in and through material actions.[42] Corresponding to this, practice theorists also agree with pragmatists that we must rethink the relationship between ideas and actions. If the will is no longer a disembodied internal attitude but rather part of ever-changing, open-ended interactions between people and their worlds, then the line from intentions to actions cannot be as direct and simple as idealist models propose. From a practice-centered perspective, what we think of as our autonomous free will or intentions are in fact themselves the products of interactions with experiences and activities. Thus, we cannot simply apply values or impose our will on the world or even on ourselves.

Because it pays more attention to structural and sociological factors than pragmatism, practice theory attends to the ways economic and political institutions, artifacts, and technology shape our practices and thus our beliefs and values. This marks perhaps the most important innovation of practice theory over pragmatism, at least for ethics. One implication of this is that we need to rethink the relations between different social scales. Just as structures and agents are connected in mutually influencing rather than dualistic ways, so are the various scales of human activity, from the most personal and local contexts through middle and global levels. Practices both define and connect these different scales, from the household to nation-states and beyond. These are crucial for ethical theory, because it is concerned about moral action, which is always situated in complex social settings and relationships. Few moral philosophers, however, draw on these sociological insights, especially in regard to the relations among social spheres. Here the tradition of social ethics, as I discussed in chapter 1, provides a valuable model for integrating social sciences, policy, applied ethics, and normative theory.

One of the most important contributions that practice theory makes to rethinking pragmatism and its cash value for ethics lies in its attention to the ways human practices and their consequences shape and are shaped by material forces. Like Marxists, practice theorists emphasize the ways both ideas and actions are conditioned by forces beyond individuals, including economic and political structures, formal and informal institutions, technology and land-use decisions, and culture and religion.[43] In all these contexts, practice theory insists, people construct themselves and act in the world in and through practices. Different technologies, structures, and institutions demand that we act in certain ways, and those actions have various moral implications—in their consequences for social and ecological welfare and also in how they teach us to think, feel, and act. A good example of this is the effects of engineering and design on human behavior, which I discuss more fully in chapter 9. Practice theory thus integrates core pragmatist concerns with insights from contemporary social theory, illuminating the ways technologies, land-use decisions, and institutional structures both enable and constrain moral action.

Pragmatism and Ethical Theory

At the start of this chapter, I noted that pragmatism is less a philosophy than a way to do philosophy. The same can be said for the moral implications of pragmatism: it is not an ethical theory as much as a way of thinking about ethics. We gain knowledge about right and wrong and express ideas about right and wrong in and through concrete practices. This in turn undergirds the pragmatist insistence on the unity of theory and practice. These emphases provide the context for thinking about more specific characteristics of a pragmatist ethic. These qualities reinforce and build on themes I have already discussed regarding the place of practice in ethical theory, including an insistence that ideas are always situated, a social definition of human nature, and a rejection of the separation of ethics from other spheres of life. Pragmatism also underlines new themes that both put practice at the forefront and carve out a distinctive place for it, especially the emphases on an open-ended problem-solving approach, value pluralism, anti-foundationalism, and, perhaps above all, the intimate connection between means and ends.

1. Pragmatists insist that ideas cannot be understood, and in fact do not exist, apart from concrete situations and human activities. This is a necessary implication of pragmatist epistemology. If knowledge is a human product, and people are always conditioned by social context and their own activities, then ideas can never have an abstract, independent existence. This leaves no room for ethical theories based on eternal foundations, universal law, or any metaphysics removed from real life. The rejection of foundations makes the justification of normative claims problematic, since if all value claims are socially constructed, there seems to be no reason to commit to one rather than another. Some critics believe that pragmatism is therefore incapable of offering moral guidance; it is "a philosophy which forever teases us about being on our way without ever telling us whither we should be going," as a critic wrote in 1923.[44] Because there are no transcendent moral ideas or absolute truths , there can be no predetermined answers that apply to every situation. This can make pragmatism seem either hopelessly vague and noncommittal or excessively relativist, especially in moral terms. There are no absolute standards to tell us "whither," to ground judgments or to guide theorizing.

The pragmatist response is to insist that moral value lies in the process of inquiry and change itself. It is not that pragmatists make no value claims but rather that those claims inhere in practices of inquiry, experimentation, critical reflection, and expansion of perspective. Dewey's normative principles focus, therefore, on process and growth, rather than the achievement of a fixed end: "Not perfecting as a final goal, but the ever-enduring process of perfecting, maturing, refining is the aim in living. Honesty, industry, temperance, justice, like health, wealth and learning, are not goods to be possessed as they would be if they expressed fixed ends to be attained. They are directions of change in the quality of experience. Growth itself is the only moral 'end.' "[45] For pragmatism, moral qualities such as virtues, norms, or ideals are never autonomous abstractions, universal foundations, or absolute goals. Rather, they are always ends-in-view, qualities of particular situations and activities that will—and should—change as practices and circumstances change.

Since there is no absolute or permanent standard of value, our choice is not between good and bad but rather between better and worse ends-in-view. The better option, for Dewey, constitutes the good in any given situation. It is always relative to the available possibilities and thus can never be defined outside a particular concrete setting.[46] This is not simply relativism, because there are standards, but the standards are based on empirical investigation and experience, gained through practices of inquiry. Standards will change, further, as our knowledge and ends-in-view change, in the course of our ongoing active operations in the world. Moral qualities cannot be known prior to action and reflection in concrete situations: "There is no such thing possible as an ethical philosophy dogmatically made up in advance," as James asserted.[47] Pragmatism thus stands against established moral theories, including both deontological and consequentialist versions, which believe that it is possible and desirable to attain a final end, "a completed activity, a static perfection," as Dewey wrote.[48] Ethics, like all intellectual and practical activities, can never rest as though it had achieved a final truth. The notion that a definitive end can be reached contradicts Dewey's central moral claim: "the end is growth itself."[49]

2. Even though pragmatists insist that moral ideas are always provisional, they do not think that they can ever be extracted or separated from the "thick" details of everyday life. There is no division between form and content, for

pragmatists, because ethics cannot be defined or articulated apart from actual human practices and experiences. Thus, a "thin" ethic, empty of content,
is impossible. If there is a way to identify particular moral values, principles,
or virtues for pragmatists, it is only by examining the practices that mediate
between people and their natural and social environments. As Dewey puts
it, "Honesty, chastity, malice, peevishness, courage, triviality, industry, ir-
responsibility are not private possessions of a person. They are working
adaptations of personal capacities with environing forces."[50] They are, in his
phrase, "adverbial," qualities that describe actions and not abstract principles
or essences separate from everyday life. The mundaneness of ethics is captured in the pragmatist understanding of habit as a source of "rules of action"
in human character, in Peirce's phrase.[51]

3. Pragmatists affirm that human beings are social creatures, with no autonomous identity or abstract essence that can be identified apart from social practices and experiences. Pragmatism's social view of human nature
shares with virtue and feminist ethics a rejection of the Enlightenment notion that people are innately rational and individualistic. Pragmatists view
human nature as characterized not by essences or fixed traits but rather by
active, problem-solving, and highly social interactions with the world—by
practices. These activities, and thus human nature itself, are thoroughly social. People do not think or act outside social interactions, morally or any
other way. Practices mediate the relations between persons and their environments, both social and natural.[52] Mental processes are not disembodied
inner states but physical activities, involving the whole historically, socially
situated body. We cannot get away from the fact that we are formed, and always think and act, in a social context. As Because we think as social beings,
minds are not only embodied but also extended, involved with forces and
processes outside the individual.[53] Practices are the way people construct
themselves in meaningful interaction with others and with the world in
which they live. These interactions shape both larger communities and individual actions, including those understood as mundane and habitual.
This social, relational approach means that people are characterized not by
essences or fixed traits but rather by active, problem-solving, and highly social interactions with the world. We cannot get away from the fact that we are
formed, and always think and act, in a social context.

This means that ethics is invariably concerned with social interactions. As
Dewey writes, "It is not an ethical 'ought' that conduct *should* be social. It *is*
social, whether bad or good."[54] If conduct is necessarily social, then ethics,

which is about human practice, is also always social. This is both a descriptive and a normative claim. Problem-solving, like all forms of knowledge and moral reflection, must be collective, because all forms of human acting and thinking are social. For pragmatists, therefore, "social ethics is not a subset of ethics, but ethics itself."[55] This means that apparently personal moral questions always have a social dimension, because we understand and respond in these situations based on our histories, context, and interactions as social beings. Not only are ethical actors always social actors, but ethics itself is first and foremost about social life. Ethical theory is also a social practice, in at least two senses. First, what we perceive to be good and valuable is the product of our social identities and experiences. Further, our deliberations about what to do are enhanced by our interactions with others.[56]

4. Pragmatists insist that ethics cannot be separated from other spheres of life or from other kinds of thought and action. Moral knowledge and action are not qualitatively different from other kinds of knowledge and action. Dewey makes this clear in his reflection on the nature of moral theory, which he defines, as I noted earlier, as "recognition of the relationships in hand." He adds: "This is a very tame and prosaic conception. It makes moral insight, and therefore moral theory, consist simply in the every-day workings of the same ordinary intelligence that measures dry-goods, drives nails, sells wheat, and invents the telephone. There is no more halo about the insight that determines what I should do in this catastrophe of life when the foundations are upheaving and my bent for eternity lies waiting to be fixed, than in that which determines whether commercial conditions favor heavy or light purchases."[57]

Moral values are deeply enlaced with what we know (or think we know) about the world and even with how we think we can have knowledge at all. As Sami Pihlström writes, "Our living in a world deeply structured by values is . . . a fact about the kind of lives we lead."[58] More simply, "All facts are value-laden."[59] It is an error, Dewey argues, to think that there exists "a separate non-natural faculty of moral knowledge because the things to be known, the matters of right and wrong, good and evil, obligation and responsibility, form a separate domain, separate that is from that of ordinary action in its usual human and social significance."[60] Instead, these moral themes are part of ordinary action and thought. They involve the same kinds of thinking and practice as other areas of our life, such as inquiry, habit, and so forth.

This is related to the idea that values cannot be separated from each other. Perhaps the most important normative value for pragmatists, and the one that holds the rest together, can be described as integrity. This is part of pragmatism's larger rejection of separations and dualisms of all sorts. Just as it insists on the ultimate unity of theory and practice and of means and ends, it understands individual virtues "as parts of a larger whole that must be brought into unity and harmony." Even though virtues such as justice, courage, wisdom, and temperance can be analyzed separately, "they cannot exist in separation from one another," as Marvin Kanne explains, because "we cannot be temperate without also being courageous, just, and wise; courageous without also being just, wise, and temperate; just without also being courageous, wise, and temperate; and wise without being temperate, courageous, and just."[61] This echoes the notion of the unity of the virtues in Aristotelian ethics. People who would become virtuous must take up practices and cultivate dispositions that support all the virtues. Pragmatists insist, in particular, that a person who pursues just one quality will lose both personal balance and the expansive vision that true virtue requires. Different ends-in-view should be integrated with each other within the individual moral actor, just as different perspectives must be understood and integrated within the larger society.

This challenges the concept of applied ethics, a category that makes sense only if ethics is something that exists apart from the rest of our lives, and especially from everyday practices, so that we need to develop procedures and rules according to which it can be used in real-life problems. Most work in applied ethics employs utilitarian or Kantian models, in which this approach makes perfect sense. These ethics begin with universal principles and from there deduce "the logical consequences of specified principles for particular empirical situations."[62] The applied part, in other words, is completely separate from the meta-ethical and normative dimensions. Only after the values at stake are specified can they be converted into concrete rules that can be applied in the situation at hand. Pragmatists insist, to the contrary, that values cannot be specified until they become known in action, and further that concrete rules must be specific to particular situations or practices. This means that normative, applied, and meta-ethics all refer to the same processes and cannot be isolated from each other.

5. Pragmatists conceive of the relationship between ideas and actions as complex, fluid, and mutually constitutive. It is impossible, in this perspective, to separate ideas and practices and thus simply enact ideas in concrete situations. In particular, pragmatists link means and ends. This means that ethics cannot be "applied" to concrete problems but only "done" in the course of

problem-solving. The relationship between means and ends provides a lens for examining the connections between ethics and other kinds of thinking, social forces, and concrete practice. In many approaches to ethics, both abstract and applied, means and ends are clearly distinguished from each other and related in only instrumental ways. In this model, practices are means in a purely instrumental sense, an application of intentions with the goal of achieving ends that have intrinsic value. The pragmatist critique of this approach is rooted in its rejection of fixed standards that divide things that have value in themselves from those that have subordinate value as means to achieve an end with intrinsic value.[63] Without this notion of permanent value, nothing is ever just a means or an end. Instead, there are only ends-in-view, which are ever-changing.

Pragmatists understand means and ends as "two names for the same reality," in Dewey's words.[64] They do not differ in quality or kind but because they are different points in a process. The difference between them depends not on their internal qualities but rather on their temporal order. This eliminates the usual distinction between ends as things with intrinsic value and means as things with instrumental value. What we call an end, as Dewey explains, "is merely a series of acts viewed at a remote stage; and a means is merely the series viewed at an earlier one. The distinction of means and end arises in surveying the *course* of a proposed *line* of action, a connected series in time."[65] What is at one moment a desired end—an end-in-view—becomes, in the next moment, a means to reaching new ends. This is an endless process, since new ends-in-view always emerge as we strive to satisfy current ones.[66] Ends-in-view are both ends, insofar as they can finish a conflict or a process of inquiry, and means, insofar as they are the activities by which we constitute our lives.[67] There is no disjuncture between means and ends, either conceptually or practically. "As the present carries us forward to some end-in-view, that future end-in-view will become, itself, a present, which will be carried forward to another end-in view, and so on," explains McKenna.[68] This relationship goes both ways, further: an end-in-view may become a means to a new end, but at the same time, "Every tool we use for the attainment of our purposes, every means we select to reach our ends, every instrumental good, may become an end which has intrinsic qualities, which is desirable or undesirable on its own account, which thus makes a difference apart from the future to which it serves to lead."[69]

From a pragmatist perspective, means and ends are both practices. For Dewey, "the 'end' is the last act thought of; the means are the acts to be

performed prior to it in time."[70] When we put practices first, we must recon-
figure both the meaning and the relationship between means and ends, and,
with that, notions about causes and effects, intrinsic and instrumental value,
intentions and consequences, and a host of other central aspects of ethical
theory.

Conclusions

Pragmatism has much to offer a practice-based approach to ethical theory.
More than the traditions of thought discussed in chapter 3, pragmatism
puts practices at the heart of theorizing. It does so in part through a commitment to open-ended and fallibilistic pursuit of knowledge, including
moral knowledge. We gain knowledge in and through practices of inquiry
and experimentation, and we must test ideas about goodness in and through
these practices and revise them on the basis of this experience. Pragmatism's
rejection of final ends and transcendent truths undergirds its emphasis on
ends-in-view, provisional goods, and goals that are worth pursuing but not
absolutizing. Practices play a central role throughout, in the processes of
gaining knowledge, articulating ends-in-view, and revising them in light of
additional information and experience.

Pragmatism also offers a distinctive approach to moral judgment, sum-
marized in James's notion of cash value. This points not to crude monetary
or instrumental evaluations but rather to an interest in the real-world usefulness of knowledge and concepts. People do not have access to any objective
truths outside the world of experience by which to judge ethical value; the
only way to evaluate is by looking at the difference information or principles
make in practice—in the way people live their lives. This is also reflected in
Dewey's conception of moral qualities as "adverbial," meaning they modify
active processes and practices.

As significant as these themes are, pragmatism's most important contribution to practice-based ethics probably lies in its reconception of the relationship between means and ends. Dewey's category of ends-in-view reflects
the pragmatist insistence that there can be no objective, lasting distinction
between means—what we do to pursue goods—and the goods themselves,
as goals of action. They are, in fact, "two names for the same reality,"[71] distinguished only by their temporal location. This foreshadows Gandhi's argument that means and ends are "convertible." For both pragmatists and

Gandhi, what makes means and ends convertible is the fact that both are practices. Today's means are things people do, in the process of pursuing ends; they become tomorrow's ends-in-view, which turn out to be practices as well—ways of living that eventually become means to the next end-in-view. This complex, fluid, and intimate relationship between means and ends, and the identity of both with practices, is central to the approach I continue fleshing out in subsequent chapters.

5

Material Practice and Morality in the Marxist Tradition

> The premises from which we begin are not arbitrary ones, not dogmas, but real premises from which abstraction can only be made in the imagination. They are the real individuals, their activity and the material conditions under which they live, both those which they find already existing and those produced by their activity.
>
> —Karl Marx[1]

Introduction

Even more than pragmatism, Karl Marx and the Marxist tradition put practice front and center and integrate it into all aspects of theory. Marxism is the "philosophy of praxis," in Antonio Gramsci's shorthand.[2] This philosophy, he wrote, is not the specialized pursuit of professionals but something in which every person can and does participate. In this perspective, Marxism can ground a fruitful approach to ethical theory, as a way to identify and clarify the forms of moral evaluation, reflection, and action in which everyone already participates.[3] This approach, however, is challenged by some Marxist thinkers, who assert that, at least in his mature writings, Marx had no interest in ethics, religion, and other "cultural" issues but only in political economy.[4]

Without arguing that Marx himself is a moral philosopher, I believe that his thought can contribute a great deal to an understanding of ethical theory in general and the ethical dimensions of practice in particular. Like other alternative streams discussed in previous chapters, Marxism has a social view of humans, emphasizes relationships (and explores them in contrast to alienation), and rejects the separation between thinking and action or between minds and bodies. In addition, Marx raises new themes and arguments, especially in his attention to the relations between ideas and structures and the ways material forces shape moral thought, both popular and academic.

Works Righteousness. Anna L. Peterson, Oxford University Press (2021). © Oxford University Press.
DOI: 10.1093/oso/9780197532232.001.0001.

Two questions loom over any study of Marx and ethics. First, is a Marxist ethic even possible? That is, is it possible to develop a Marxist ethical theory, or is Marx helpful primarily as an analytic resource for understanding and criticizing mainstream theories and their gaps, without necessarily being able to fill those gaps with a constructive ethic? This is an important question, but it is one that is primarily significant for studies of Marxism per se, rather than projects like mine that use Marxism as one among various resources for thinking about a particular problem. Thus, I do not spend too much time on this issue, although it is worth some attention, as it helps us understand Marx's own attitude toward morality, its place in his larger intellectual system, and the arguments among his various interpreters about what he really thought about a host of issues.

The second question is more directly relevant for my project: in constructing some sort of Marxist ethical theory, where do we focus—the few places where Marx pays explicit attention to ethics or the contribution to ethical theory made by his thought more broadly? I believe the latter tack is more fruitful, particularly in relation to practice. Thus, I begin this chapter with a discussion of the aspects of his thought that are most relevant to understanding his views on practice, ethics, and the relations between them. I first offer an introduction to aspects of Marx's thought that are most relevant for ethics, including his thinking about materialism, the relations between ideas and structures, practice, alienation, relationships, and labor. I look not only at the normative implications of his thought (e.g., his critique of exploitation) but also at what it might mean for ethics broadly, including meta-ethical questions about the structure of moral theory and its relation to other forms of thought. I explore these questions in Marx's own writings and in the work of several later Marxist thinkers.

Marx's Thought

In order to explore Marxism's contributions to a practice-based ethical theory, we must understand certain key themes in Marx's thought generally. These themes include his conception of an active materialism, his insistence on the mutual shaping of ideas and structures, his critique of alienation, and his emphasis on social relationships. A distinctive understanding of practice runs throughout and connects these.

Active Materialism

A common shorthand description of Marxist thought is "dialectical materialism," reflecting Marx's effort to synthesize the materialism of Ludwig Feuerbach with the dialecticism of Georg Wilhelm Friedrich Hegel. As a materialist, Marx rejects the idealism of dominant German philosophies, not only Hegelian but also Kantian, according to which ideas exist independently and take primacy over concrete experiences, objects, and structures. He elaborates his critique of idealism and articulated his own materialist approach in several of his early works, most fully in *The German Ideology*. In particular, Marx attacks the "young Hegelian" claim that consciousness is independent of and more important than material existence.

While affirming the superiority of materialism over idealism as a way to understand human experience, Marx also rejects Feuerbach's mechanistic materialism. In his brief, crucial, and sometimes cryptic "Theses on Feuerbach," Marx defines his own materialist philosophy, in contrast to Feuerbach's, as dynamic, active, and historical. As the first thesis asserts, "The chief defect of all hitherto existing materialism—that of Feuerbach included—is that the thing, reality, sensuousness, is conceived only in the form of the object or of *contemplation*, but not as *human sensuous activity*, *practice*, not subjectively." Here Marx explicitly identifies practice as his starting point and chief subject. This affirmation begins as a rejection of Hegel's idealism, which developed "the active side" but only "abstractly," because it "does not know real, sensuous activity as such."[5] This is the heart of Marx's approach for the remainder of his life: a combination of the active, fluid character of ideas for Hegel with the material concreteness of Feuerbach.

From his earliest writings, practice (praxis) is "the central concept in Marx's outlook—the key to understanding his early philosophic speculations and his detailed analysis of the structure of capitalism," as Richard Bernstein contends.[6] Practice is crucial for grasping Marx's conception of human nature, his theory of labor and production, and his vision of how social revolution can occur. Practice means different things to Marx, encompassing "human activity, production, labor, alienation, relentless criticism, and revolutionary practice."[7] Despite its range, praxis does not describe everything that humans do. Marx uses it primarily to describe activities that are connected both to larger social structures, on the one hand, and to ideologies, on the other. Like Alasdair MacIntyre, Marx probably would not consider kicking a ball or solving a math problem to be praxis, although these activities have a place in larger ideological and structural forms that he might analyze. We might say that for Marx, praxis is informed and conditioned activity, with some degree of intentionality—what Bernstein calls "labor directed by purposes."[8]

Because it focuses on practice, Marx's active materialism must take seriously the power of human agency and will. As Marx explains in his third thesis, elaborating his critique of Feuerbach: "The materialist doctrine that men are products of circumstances and upbringing, and that, therefore, changed men are products of other circumstances and changed upbringing, forgets that it is men who change circumstances, and that it is essential to educate the educator himself."[9] In other words, Feuerbach is correct in asserting that people are products of their social circumstances and history but wrong in failing to see the ways these social conditions interact with human agency and, crucially, the extent to which the latter influences the course of history. Marx offers another classic formulation of this position in *The German Ideology*: "Circumstances make men just as much as men make circumstances."[10] Again and again, Marx asserts as his "first premise" not structures or objects but "the existence of living human individuals."[11] His materialism is always active, never static or passive; it is regulated not by mechanical laws but by human practices.

Describing practice as informed by purpose or will might suggest that it can be separated from physical activities, but this would be to misread Marx. For Marx, consciousness cannot be viewed as "something other than 'sensuous human activity' or *praxis*." Rather, it must be "understood as an aspect or moment of *praxis* itself."[12] The relationship between physical activities and mental attitudes, like the link between structures and ideas, is a dynamic, fluid, and mutual interchange between aspects that cannot be understood separately. This is true not just of practice in general but also of specific kinds of activity. Perhaps the most important of these, for Marx, is labor or work, which Marx defines in *Capital* as "purposive activity . . . for the fitting of natural substances to human wants."[13] This transformation engages the whole person, and work is in fact as central to personal identity as it is to material production. In labor, and practice in general, people create themselves as well as the objects of their "sensuous activities."

Marx's focus on praxis provides methodology as well as content for his social theory. This method is bottom-up, grounded in thick, concrete details. "In direct contrast to German philosophy which descends from heaven to earth, here we ascend from earth to heaven," Marx writes. "That is to say, we do not set out from what men say, imagine, conceive, nor from men as narrated, thought of, imagined, conceived, in order to arrive at men in the flesh. We set out from real, active men, and on the basis of their real life-process we demonstrate the development of the ideological reflexes and echoes of this life-process."[14] The central role of "real, active men" for Marx is the centrality of practice: what is important about human beings in history is what they do with their bodies. Their actions both take place within and generate social relationships, material structures, and ideological systems.

Ideas and Structures

One of the most important implications of Marx's approach to Hegel and Feuerbach—his rejection of their overarching philosophies while adopting certain key themes—was a complete rethinking of the relations between ideas and structures. Whereas Hegel saw ideas as the drivers of history and society, Feuerbach began with material structures and objects, of which ideas are mere reflections. Marx saw both models as crudely essentialist. He sought to understand the interactions between ideas and structures in a more nuanced and dynamic way, which required serious engagement with the ideas of both thinkers.

The dialectic that Marx took from Hegel led him to understand the relationship between ideas and structures as one of constant mutual shaping. However, Hegel believed that this movement was driven by a spirit (*Geist*) moving autonomously through history, to which humans are connected only in the most general and abstract ways. Because Hegel understood human essence not as active flesh and blood but rather as self-consciousness, according to Marx, Hegel's philosophy made "man . . . into an abstraction of man."[15] Marx rejects the idealist conviction that mental states have an autonomous existence apart from living persons. All belief systems, attitudes, and ideologies emerge from continuous interaction between human agency and structural, historical conditions, mediated by human activity. "Morality, religion, metaphysics, all the rest of ideology and their corresponding forms of consciousness, thus no longer retain the semblance of independence," he argues. "They have no history, no development; but men, developing their material production and their material intercourse, alter, along with this, their real existence, their thinking and the products of their thinking." This nuanced understanding of the interaction between ideas and structures is undermined by the punchline with which Marx ends this passage: "Life is not determined by consciousness, but consciousness by life."[16] The last sentence, when quoted in isolation, suggests a more reductive and deterministic approach than that which characterizes Marx's thought overall.

He does not mean, as is often assumed, that consciousness or ideas are mere reflections (superstructure) of material conditions. Rather, he wants to emphasize the way life—meaning human sensuous activity, material existence—is the source of all human products, including mental products. The structural conditions that create religion and all cultural forms are no more or no less than the practices of real people: "*man* is not an abstract being, squatting outside the world. Man is *the human world*, the state, society."[17] Thus, "consciousness is never anything else than conscious existence, and the existence of men is their actual life-process."[18] Both structures and ideas, in other words, are forms of practice, products of human practice, united in their relationship to sensuous human activity in the world. This is the necessary background for understanding the connection between "base and superstructure," a common framing for the relations between economic and political structures, on the one hand, and culture, art, religion, and ideologies, on the other. The notion that the material base mechanistically determines or produces the ideological or cultural superstructure reflects an erroneous interpretation of Marx's understanding of both terms as well as the relationship between them. Both Marxists and critics alike sometimes assert that Marx saw superstructure as a mere reflection of the base, in some direct, linear, predictable way. This interpretation ignores Marx's own emphasis on the active, willful, creative nature of human practice, which, again, is the source of both base and superstructure.

The relationship between base and superstructure is crucial to Marx's understanding of ideology, particularly his notion that ideologies will reflect the material situation and interests of the people who articulate them. Marx famously asserted that "The ideas of the ruling class are in every epoch the ruling ideas."[19] Behind this claim is a critique of the idealist belief in the independence of ideas, their autonomy as free-floating intellectual atoms. This presentation serves the dominant class by removing ideas from their actual historical origins and making them appear universal.[20] Because the relationship between ideas and material structure is so crucial to Marx's thinking, he returns to it frequently in various contexts, which can lead to apparent contradictions if different statements are read in isolation. The best way to understand Marx's views on this issue is to look at his writings as a whole, where continuities and core principles emerge. A holistic view also makes it possible to appreciate the passages that capture Marx's nuanced understanding of the relationship between ideas and structures. He expresses this complex view most famously in *The Eighteenth Brumaire of Louis Bonaparte*: "Men make their own history, but they do not make it just as they please; they do not make it under circumstances chosen by themselves, but under circumstances directly found, given and transmitted from the past."[21] At the forefront here are practices: the human process of finding, making, changing, and transmitting, always constrained by circumstances but never fully determined by them.

Alienation

Alienation or estrangement is one of the most important themes in Marx's work, from his earliest philosophical writings to his later work. It not only appears throughout Marx's opus but is one of the threads unifying his diverse writings. The theory of alienation describes relations between persons, their activity, its products, other people, nonhuman nature, and the human species—thus, it is "a grand summing up of Marx's conception of man in capitalist society," in Bertell Ollman's words.[22] Marx's arguments about alienation involve descriptive, normative, and methodological claims about human nature, society, capitalism, work, religion, ideology, and more, and practice is at the heart of them all.

The simplest way to define alienation for Marx might be as the division of things that should be united. The concept of estrangement, as Paul Tillich puts it, "presupposes original oneness."[23] What happens in alienation is that people believe or feel themselves to be separate from something to which they are really connected—labor, the products of labor, other people, and even their own identity. These things that appear (falsely) to be separate take on a life of their own and come to stand over and against the people who created them in and through their practice.

Marx worked out his conception of alienation through his analysis of religion. "The criticism of religion," for him, was "the basis of all criticism."[24] This criticism begins with Feuerbach's notion of religion as what Marx calls an "*inverted world consciousness*," produced by an "*inverted world*." Because the root problem is the material conditions that generate religious illusions, the way to combat religion is to "struggle against that world whose spiritual aroma is religion."[25] There is no point in fighting ideas when their causal conditions continue. While much of Marx's analysis of religion closely follows Feuerbach, he emphasizes the active character of materialism, in contract to Feuerbach's mechanistic approach. This dynamic understanding and the nuances it makes possible are evident in Marx's most famous passage regarding religion:

> Religious suffering is at the same time an expression of real suffering and a protest against real suffering. Religion is the sigh of the oppressed creature, the sentiment of a heartless world, and the soul of soulless conditions. It is the opium of the people. The abolition of religion as the illusory happiness of men is a demand for their real happiness. The call to abandon their illusions about their conditions is a call to abandon a condition which requires illusions. The criticism of religion is, therefore, the embryonic criticism of this vale of tears of which religion is the halo.... Religion is only the illusory sun about which man revolves so long as he does not revolve about himself.[26]

Religion is an opiate, but it is also much more. It not only comforts those who are suffering but also expresses their suffering and protests against it. Religion, in Marx's view, reveals problems that it cannot solve. This is because religion is fundamentally the product of alienation. Human power, sociability, and creativity are projected onto an imagined deity, who comes to stand over and against his human inventors. "The basis of religious criticism is this," Marx declares: "*man makes religion*; religion does not make man." Because people fail to understand that ideas are social products, they mistakenly believe that ideas themselves have independent existence. And indeed, this false conviction takes reality in distorted, alienating social conditions. Thus, Marx concedes that "Religion is indeed man's self-consciousness and awareness so long as he has not found himself or has lost himself again."[27]

This dynamic, Marx came to understand, also operates in other forms of alienation, most specifically in those caused by the division of labor in capitalism, which gives each person a specific kind of activity from which she cannot escape and which defines her in a static, confining way. The division of labor and capitalism in general generate four kinds of alienation from which workers suffer: from the products of their labor, from the process of labor itself, from other people, and from their deepest nature, or "species being." These oppressive features of capitalism turn practices that should be joyful and creative into torment. In possessing the products of workers' labor, what the capitalist owns "is *not* something 'merely' external to and indifferent to the nature of the producer. It is his activity in an objectified and congealed form."[28] Marx does not mean that simply objectifying oneself in the production of objects is necessarily alienating; this is in fact the distinctive human capacity and activity. This process is alienating only under certain conditions, when human products become hostile to the producer because they enrich others at the cost of negating and dehumanizing the producer.[29] This dehumanization is part of what Marx understands as the alienation of people from their "species being" (*Gattungswesen*), what people are meant to be and would be in non-exploitative conditions.[30]

One of the most diabolical aspects of capitalism is that it stifles people's ability to recognize this good. Both capitalist ideology and their own alienated existence lead people to desire false goods, to think that they will become happy and fulfilled not by changing the structural conditions of their lives but rather by pursuing superficial, temporary sources of comfort. This is the context for Marx's assertion that religion is the opium of the people. It dulls their pain so that they are not able to see and eliminate the true causes of that pain. Religion and other social opiates thus represent the illusory happiness of suffering people, and its pervasiveness should be read as "a demand for their real happiness."[31] This clearly normative claim involves a substantive notion of happiness, linking Marx's thought to more explicitly moral theories, from Aristotle to utilitarianism.

Marx is also an ethical thinker insofar as he presents a vision of a good society, which he describes as one in which "the objects that a man produces are no longer the chains for alienating him, but the means by which there is a free, social, and human expression of him in the very activity he performs and in the products that he produces."[32] Instead of being controlled by the process of production, people would control it. They would overturn the division of labor that stunts their capacity for free and full development of their human capacities. In a non-alienated society, what is restored above all is correct relationships between people, between people and their work, and between people and their species being. This vision of what human life should be undergirds Marx's critique of the way things currently are.

Relationships

Alienation provides Marx with a way of thinking about relationships—their breach and the possibility of repairing them. One reason capitalism is so dehumanizing is that it keeps people divided, rather than freely collaborating. This enforced separation is especially harmful because people are innately social, according to Marx, and it is wrong for them to be pitted against one another.

This sociality is not simply a trait of human nature, though it is that, but also an ontological reality. For Marx, every social factor or aspect, as Ollman argues, is itself a relation, even "things" like the products of labor.[33] This is because for Marx, "the basic unit of reality is not a thing but a Relation."[34] Relationships define the thing itself; they do not come after the fact. This echoes an internal view of relations that is also found in other theoretical frameworks, notably Buddhism and deep ecology. It stands in contrast to the decidedly external view of relationships that is common in most modern Western thought, both secular and religious, according to which there are essences that define things, persons, or ideas before those things enter into relationships. Marx puts relationships first, to "interiorize" the interdependence among different social factors as part of the definition of "the thing itself," in Ollman's words.[35]

Because relationships are so epistemologically and ontologically fundamental to Marx, other key concepts in his thought can be understood by reference to this concept. A good example of this is social class, as analyzed by the British Marxist historian E. P. Thompson. Class is not an abstract or mechanistic category for Thompson but rather "something which in fact happens . . . in human relationships." It happens when, "as a result of common experiences, people feel and articulate the identity of their interests as between themselves, and as against other men whose interests are different from (and usually opposed to) theirs."[36] Social practices create this shared identity and relationships, so that "class is defined by men as they live their own history."[37]

For Marx, practices are relationships, and vice versa. In practices, we express and develop our relationships to others, to our work, and to our own capacities and identity. These practices and relationships, further, constitute persons and continue to constitute them throughout their lives. This is particularly the case for labor, the main kind of practice Marx writes about, which is especially subject to alienation. Work should be the fulfillment of human capacities, an exercise of creativity, and the motor of social relationships, so it is an end in itself as well as a means to an end. We become alienated and oppressed in capitalist organization of production precisely because work becomes only a means to the end of making a living. Marx's arguments about alienation and relationships include both implicit and explicit normative claims—about human nature, human activity, and social organization. Thus, these discussions provide a foundation for thinking about the larger intellectual tradition of Marxist scholarship on ethics.

Perspectives on Marx and Ethics

There are not many systematic, full-length reflections on Marxist thought in relation to ethics. In this section, I explore three of the most important, each of which raises different issues and highlights distinctive themes, although practice plays a role in all.

Steven Lukes, *Marxism and Morality*

Steven Lukes's *Marxism and Morality* is organized around a central tension, which he sums up thus:

> On the one hand, it is claimed that morality is a form of ideology, and thus social in origin, illusory in content, and serving class interests; that any given morality arises out of a particular stage in the development of the productive forces and relations and is relative to a particular mode of production and particular class interests; that there are no objective truths or eternal principles of morality. . . . On the other hand, no one can fail to notice that Marx's and Marxist writings abound in moral judgements, implicit and explicit.[38]

The paradox, in sum, is that Marx both denies and embraces ethics. On one hand, Marx often appears to reject the idea of a normative ethic as contrary to his theoretical system, because morality, like religion, will wither away when we organize the means of production correctly, or because morality is a bourgeois concept not just in its particular manifestations but as a general category, or because Marxism is about describing and analyzing reality accurately and not about prescribing norms. On the other hand, and despite his apparent dismissal of moral philosophy and moralism, Marx's work is driven, from start to finish, by what can only be called ethical concerns with oppression, justice, freedom, and human fulfillment.

Lukes believes the paradox can be resolved if we distinguish between two different meanings of morality: "the morality of *Recht*" and "the morality of emancipation." Marx sees *Recht* as a bourgeois framing of moral obligation, a way to preserve private property and class distinctions and mask the oppressive nature of capitalism's organization of production with abstract talk of individual rights and dignity. On the other hand, the morality of emancipation is intrinsic to Marx's vision of communism. This is not just distinct from the morality of *Recht* but entails liberation from it and from the conditions that created it.[39] Just as people in an unalienated society will not need religion, they will not need individualistic, alienated forms of morality.

In light of this paradox, Lukes asks how we can assess Marx's contribution to ethics and in particular to the construction of an ethical theory that guides action. He highlights both important weaknesses and some valuable strengths of Marxism. The first defect is the "generation of illusions regarding the ways particular actions can contribute to long-range goals.[40] In other words, Marxism makes a faulty diagnosis of the proper connection between means and ends, based on a false "certainty that its end-in-view was indeed in prospect, and certainty about which means were required, and thus permitted, to bring it into being."[41] By questioning the grounds for this certainty and its usefulness, Lukes makes a pragmatist, and specifically Deweyan, critique. One of the core differences between pragmatist and Marxist approaches to ethics is that pragmatism never suspends its radical contingency for long enough to assert the kind of certainty about ultimate goals that characterize Marx's vision of communist society. This becomes important in Cornel West's critique of Marx, as I discuss later.

This leads to the second main weakness that Lukes sees in Marx's morality, which he calls "moral blindness." Lukes believes that Marx and the Marxist tradition too often hold the interests of persons in the here and now to be irrelevant to the project of human emancipation.[42] Here Lukes addresses "the Gulag question" posed by Michel Foucault, which asks what in Marx's own thought made possible the abuses committed under Stalin and other modern socialist states and the justification of them.[43] This responds to the claim by many socialists that the Soviet system was not truly Marxist but rather distorted, manipulated, and abandoned Marxist principles and pursued self-interest and power for its own sake. While there is clearly some truth in these claims, they avoid the question of whether socialism, and Marxism in particular, includes elements that led, however unintentionally, to the abuses of "really existing socialism." Lukes believes that it does, and specifically that the Marxist theoretical tradition lacks resources to resist evils done in its name. We can think about this problem, he says, as a form of "disablement." What this means is that "despite its many strengths, the theory of the founders was blind and deaf to, and silent about, certain ranges of moral questions—roughly, those concerning justice and rights, which set constraints on how people are to be treated in the here and now, and in the immediate future."[44] Because of Marx's overriding concern with social, historical, and political questions, he devalues the sphere of personal morality and interpersonal relationships, which traditional ethical theories generally see as the heart of morality.[45] This emphasis on structures generates both the most significant weaknesses but also the greatest strengths of Marx's contributions to ethical theory.

The first major contribution that Lukes identifies is that Marx offers a conception of freedom and of the constraints upon it that is far deeper and richer than classical liberal views. This is related to Marx's critique of *Recht*, which asserts that emancipation comes not through the separation of individuals from the larger society but rather in and through relationships. Second, Marx challenges us to ask about the grounding for the abstractions of *Recht*: "What *are* the generically human interests that underpin talk of human rights? Why should they have more than merely local standing?"[46] The abstract idealism of the liberal philosophical tradition, especially in its Kantian versions, takes for granted a universal foundation for its claims, but Marx points out the historically, socially specific nature of all ideas. His challenge implies a meta-ethical claim that morality depends upon social relations, as part of the larger links between base and superstructure. Marx's general philosophical thought has much to offer in thinking about these relations, as I elaborate later. First, though, I turn to two other systematic treatments of Marx and ethics in order to tease out other issues that need further discussion.

Cornel West, *The Ethical Dimensions of Marxist Thought*

The chief value of Lukes's work is to help us sort out what Marx and Marxism have to say about philosophical ethics. It is not, however, a systematic analysis of Marx's thought about ethical issues, and even less is it a constructive ethic based on Marxist themes. As Lukes himself makes clear, this is not his task. A more detailed discussion of the ethical themes in Marx's work and that of several important Marxist theorists appears in Cornel West's book *The Ethical Dimensions of Marxist Thought*. West offers a close reading of some of Marx's most important works, grounded in his view of Marx as a "radical historicist," who both critiques mainstream philosophical ethics and offers an alternative.

While Lukes focuses on Marx's paradoxical attitude toward ethics, West develops the promise and limitations of Marxism as a source of moral theory. He sees Marxism's primary shortcoming as its failure to address existential questions and its main contribution as its grounding of ethics in a larger materialist theory that is committed both to systematic sociological analysis and to human liberation. For West, the core of Marxist theory in regard to ethics is "the discrepancy between moral ideals and moral practice—or more specifically, the way in which systems of production have hitherto seemed to require a discrepancy between particular interests of a specific class and the claims of universal interests by ideologues of that class."[47] This discrepancy leads to what Lukes calls the morality of *Recht*—supposedly abstract, universal values that in fact serve the material interests of a ruling class.

West argues that Marx's "radical historicist metaphilosophical vision" calls not for a new version of philosophy but rather for the end of philosophy as it has been defined. The core of the Western philosophical tradition has been a quest for certainty and foundations that, according to Marx, is misguided and ultimately doomed to failure. It is doomed, West contends, because there is no philosophical "last court of appeals" that is above contingent and variable morals. Liberal philosophy—the abstraction of *Recht*—tries to lift itself "out of the flux of history—an impossible task." Instead, West says, the source of morals must come from "consciously identifying with—and digesting *critically* the values of—a particular community or tradition."[48]

West's reading of Marx is strongly influenced by pragmatism. Truth-searching, he writes, "is not a quest for necessary and universal forms, essences, substances, categories, or grounds, but rather a perennial activity of solving problems, responding to dilemmas, or overcoming quagmires."[49] His pragmatist critique of Marx hints at a new paradox, distinct from the one Lukes identifies. On the one hand, Marx embraces "the anti-foundationalist arguments of the American pragmatists." On the other hand, he "wants to retain a warranted-assertability status for social explanatory claims in order to understand and change the world."[50] In short, according to West, Marx did not follow through on the radical historicism of his own system.

For West, pragmatism is more radical than Marxism, at least in its commitment to a thoroughgoing historicism. A comparable historicism within Marxism, according to West, would make it possible to bring content to Marx's implicit normative claims. This content could come in part by exploring "the oppositional cultures" and lived experience of oppressed people. This approach prioritizes "the distinctive elements of the structures of feeling, structures of meaning, ways of life and struggle under dynamic circumstances not of people's own choosing."[51] Here West echoes Raymond Williams, the British cultural critic, whose phrase "structures of feeling" indicated a desire for historical rootedness and substantive content.[52] Such attention to the lives and practices of real people would make for better understanding, but more important, it would contribute to social change. Like pragmatists, Marx is interested in a fundamentally practical quest, in which the point of knowledge and theories is, as the eleventh thesis on Feuerbach asserted, to change the world. West appreciates this but also pushes Marx to follow through on the practical and normative implications of his own thought. The search for philosophical understanding or truth, in this view, is not about representing objectives but about transforming circumstances and conditions.

Paul Blackledge, *Marxism and Ethics: Freedom, Desire, and Revolution*

Paul Blackledge's account of Marxism and ethics shares commonalities with those of both Lukes and West. Like Lukes, Blackledge emphasizes Marx's claim that most ethical theories reflect the class interests of dominant groups. Blackledge highlights in particular Marx's critique of liberal philosophers, especially Kant, for their atomistic understanding of human nature, their assumption that competition is inevitable, and their belief that morality must be based on "a disembodied conception of reason."[53] In addition to this negative or critical aspect of Marx's moral thought, Blackledge argues that it can make many positive contributions to ethical theory. Whereas West emphasizes Marx's radical historicism, Blackledge views Marx through an Aristotelian lens. Marx's ethics, in his view, "amounts to a modern version of Aristotle's account of those practices underpinning the virtues through which individuals are able to flourish within communities."[54] Marx and Aristotle share a highly social view of human nature and a conviction that ethics must make concrete practical contributions to the good life for persons and communities.

Of the three interpreters of Marx considered here, Blackledge offers the most expansive analysis of moral themes in Marxist thought and of Marx's potential contributions to ethical theory. He also embraces Marxism the most fully. Although he is not uncritical, he does not follow Lukes's suggestion that elements in Marx's own thought contributed to the development of Stalinism. Instead, Blackledge asserts that "classical Marxism" can be "reconstructed and disentangled from its Stalinist caricature" to offer a truer picture of Marx's own thought. This reconstructed model has great potential, for Blackledge, not just to criticize capitalism and other forms of oppression but also to build a positive theoretical and practical alternative to capitalism.[55]

Practice is at the heart of this alternative. Blackledge points out that for Marx, practice comes first, as a source of knowledge that informs both theorizing and political activism. "By contrast with the liberal myth that we first judge a situation before acting upon it," he writes, "Marx illuminated the assumed forms of practice that underpin this ideological way of conceiving the problem of choice and agency." Blackledge hints at a pragmatist streak when he adds that Marx's way to overcome the presumed contradiction between understanding and acting is "by reinterpreting the 'is' and 'ought' as two sides to the same practice."[56] This means that the "is"—a critique of the problems of capitalist society—points within itself, simultaneously, to the "ought"—the revolutionary goal of a free, democratic society. This reflects the implicit normative content in Marx's thought, leading us back to Lukes's paradox and the larger question about the possibility of a Marxist approach to ethical theory.

Marxism and Ethical Theory

Building on the discussions of Marx and other scholars' approaches to Marxist ethics, I now look at how practice can serve as a connecting theme in the development of a Marxian approach to ethical theory. Drawing on the work of Marx and other socialist thinkers, I discuss several key themes and issues discussed earlier, now put directly in the context of ethical theory.

1. Marx and the Marxist tradition insist that ideas are always created by people in particular material and historical circumstances, influenced by these forces and by the interests of the moral agents involved. Thus, there are no autonomous moral ideas, and ethics can never be an application of neutral reason to isolated problems. Like feminists, pragmatists, and other critics of universalizing approaches to social thought, Marx insists that moral ideas, like all other forms of thought, are always partial, provisional, and situated. There are no absolute answers, no fixed foundations, and no final solutions. Marx's distinctive contribution to this critique is to insist that people are the products of societies and practices and that their positions in the relations of production shape their knowledge and values. There is no "abstract being, squatting outside the world," as Marx puts it.[57] Because people develop ideas with the world, in light of their particular histories, relationships, and interests, ideas are always to some extent an expression of material relations. "The ideas of the ruling class are in every epoch the ruling ideas."[58] They are the idealized expression of dominant material relations, This does not mean that ideas are mere reflexes of material conditions; Marx consistently criticizes this kind simple determinism. As he notes in his third thesis on Feuerbach, "The materialist doctrine that men are products of circumstances and upbringing, and that, therefore, changed men are products of other circumstances and changed upbringing, forgets that it is men who change circumstances, and that it is essential to educate the educator himself."[59] What is most important is the mutually constitutive relationship between people and circumstances, ideas and structures, rather than a crude focus on one or the other.

2. In a Marxist model, ethics is thick and substantive. Marx critiques the empty formalism of idealism. First, it is impossible to separate the structure of ethical theory from its content. This is a pragmatist point as well and an important meta-ethical claim for both traditions. In both, but especially for Marx, ethics is internal to other forms of thinking and practice, so moral evaluation is already included in all kinds of thinking. For Marx, " 'facts' contain their own condemnation and a call to do something about them."[60]

An example of this can be seen in his analysis of religion, which is both descriptive and prescriptive. As Ollman writes, this analysis "does not prepare us for an evaluation but includes it."[61] There are no thin, formal theories, for Marx, because all statements about the world, including normative ones, entail evaluations, echoes of the practices and relationships that created them. The claim that there can be no morally neutral, non-situated description of the world provides a context for a further exploration of ethical themes in Marx's work.[62]

3. Marx's view of human nature and reason means that ethics is always social; people have no way of thinking about the good, or about anything else, except as social beings. In addition, normative claims are, first and foremost, about the life of people in community with others. Humans' cooperative, social nature demands a cooperative, sociable form of living. Capitalism makes this impossible, although life under capitalist regimes can show people what they are missing and thus reveals, in a backhanded way, the values that they hold most dear. As MacIntyre writes, in capitalism, people discover, above all, "that what they want most is what they want in common with others; and more than this that a sharing of human life is not just a means to the accomplishment of what they desire, but that certain ways of sharing human life are indeed what they most desire."[63] In living out a particular mode of life, we can discover goals and values that we may not have recognized otherwise. The means—the practices that come from living in a certain way—reveal ends, including both practical and normative goals. This may be because we realize important values that are inherent in our current situations, or it may be because real life contrasts so sharply with what we come to realize we value. The latter occurs in Marx's criticisms of what is wrong about the division of labor, the stultifying role of dominant ideologies, and other negative aspects of capitalism, Marx puts forth, at least implicitly, a positive vision of what a good human life and a good society should be.

Alienation is the way Marx understands the contrast between current life and a normative good and also the factors that thwart the realization of that good. Alienation, again, represents the division of things that should be united: people from one another, from the process and products of their work, and from their own intrinsic nature or species being. In capitalism, as Marx puts it, a person "is a hunter, a fisherman, a shepherd, or a critical critic, and must remain so if he does not want to lose his means of livelihood." In the unalienated existence of communist society, in contrast, "nobody has one exclusive sphere of activity but each can become accomplished in any branch he wishes, society regulates the general production and thus makes it possible for me to do one thing today and another tomorrow, to hunt in the morning, fish in the afternoon, rear cattle in the evening, criticise after dinner, just as I have a mind, without ever becoming hunter, fisherman, shepherd, or critic."[64] Although Marx frames this as a description of a future society, it is obviously a prescription as well. The good for humans is to be free to develop all their capacities and powers, to control the products and process of their own labor, and to live in solidarity with other humans.

The context for these moral claims is Marx's social understanding of human nature. Like Aristotle, pragmatists, and some Christian thinkers, Marx insists that humans are by nature social animals. This descriptive *is* leads to a normative *ought*: people can only live good lives and achieve happiness in community with others. Thus, for Marx, as for Aristotle, to be good is to desire what is right for the human person. As MacIntyre puts it, ethics and desire are united. What humans naturally desire, if their desires are not distorted by the oppressions of capitalism, is what will lead to their free development in the context of united communities. MacIntyre calls these "shared desires" a moral "absolute" which provides a normative ground for condemning a range of social practices and institutions that deny our "common humanity with others." This absolute normative grounding, he asserts, is the "reason that the Marxist condemns the H-bomb. Anyone who would use this has contracted out of common humanity. So with the denial of racial equality, so with the rigged trial."[65] Practices of solidarity are both means to achieve a better society and ends in themselves. The affirmation of common humanity is a practice, a norm, and a concrete social good.

4. Marx does not permit any split between ethics and other kinds of thought and action. Just as ethics cannot be separated from historical, material conditions, it cannot be divided from other forms of thought. From a Marxist perspective, as Agnes Heller explains, "Morals have no separate sphere of their own, but are present in all spheres."[66] Moral systems will reflect their historical circumstances and above all the conditions and experiences of the people who articulate and live them. "Morals in an alienated world are themselves always alienated," Heller writes, emphasizing that normative claims are inextricably shaped by the conditions of the people who articulate them.[67] This explains the religious worldviews of the working classes, for example, which reflect the proletariat's miserable conditions and impossible hopes. Economic and political context also explains liberal theories of *Recht*, which Marx criticizes as "rights of the egoistic man, of man separated from other men and from the community," and its practical application is the right to private property.[68] The morality of *Recht*, therefore, reinforces the "egoism" of the dominant classes. It cannot be emancipatory, as Lukes points out, because of its relation to material conditions, which shapes the content and the impact of all ideas.

5. Ideas and practices are always connected. This is a central claim for Marxists, not only in regard to ethics but in all areas of inquiry. "The central thrust of Marxism is the connection of theory and practice," as Williams asserts.[69] Ideas are formed in and through practices, never prior to or apart from them, and practices and ideas alike are always conditioned by the material base. Thus, we can only understand ideas, including moral ones, in relation to economic, political, and social processes and structures. "Creating the basis, you create the superstructure," affirms MacIntyre. "There are not two activities, but one."[70] The activity that creates both ideas and material structures is sensuous human practice.

Marx's approach to ethics is embedded within his larger philosophical arguments, particularly regarding the relations between ideas and structures or between superstructure and base. We can only understand the nature and meaning of ideas, including moral ones, by probing their relations with material forces. These structures provide a framework for the emergence of ideas and other aspects of the material relations "around which the human relations can entwine themselves, a kernel of human relationship from which all else grows," as MacIntyre writes. "All else" includes moral claims, but there are more specific implications for ethical theory: moral ideas not only cannot be understood apart from social structures, but they cannot emerge outside them. Their development is simultaneous and mutually dependent.

The link between base and superstructure is necessary, but it is never a simple, predictable, or linear relationship between causes and effects. There is no general formula that we can apply to different settings and societies, because "the difference between one form of society and another is not just a difference in basis, and a corresponding basis in superstructure, but a difference also in the way basis is related to superstructure."[71] Although structures influence ideas in every society, they do so in distinctive ways, because human agency shapes and is shaped by the practices that create both structures and ideas. Thus, in every case, we cannot understand base, superstructure, or their connections without studying the particular historical and material conditions, ideas and other cultural expressions, and the particular human activities involved. There is nothing abstract or universal involved, only human sensuous activity. The material base, explains Williams, is not "a fixed economic or technological abstraction" but rather is rooted in "the specific activities of men in real social and economic relationships, containing fundamental contradictions and variations and therefore always in a state of dynamic process."[72] This is a central Marxist theme: in and through practices, real human individuals create both base and superstructure. For ethical theory, this means not only that practices shape how we think about value but also that ethical thinking is itself a practice.

Conclusions

Marxism has much to offer to a practice-based approach to ethics, beginning with the question, framed by Lukes, of whether morality is merely a form of ideology, a reflection of the material interests of particular classes. If we want to understand ethics as more than a mere reflex of the base, Lukes's question offers a critical awareness that all thought is not just socially constructed but inextricably linked to the material conditions and experiences of the thinkers. In order to reflect on and understand the nature of ethical ideas, therefore, we have to understand their historical and social context and the material interests they advance or hinder. For Marx, as for pragmatists, ethical ideas cannot be understood apart from these larger contexts; they are not a separate category of thought, such as *Recht*, but rather a dimension or type of practice connected in multiple ways to other forms of human activity.

Marx insists that the material base is not mysterious, static, or abstract; it is the process and result of human practices. This is the heart of his critique of Feuerbach's materialism, to which Marx contrasted his own active, practice-centered materialism, because the material base—the world—is nothing other than the result of human practices. Again, we can recall Marx's affirmation that people make their own history, even though they never make it in circumstances of their own choosing. Practices are everything to Marx; they are relationships, structures, ideas, and life itself.

Marx also contributes to a practice-based ethics an insistence on the real-life impact of ideas, as his eleventh thesis on Feuerbach makes plain: "The philosophers have only interpreted the world, in various ways; the point, however, is to change it."[73] In this as in several other points, Marxism aligns with pragmatism. Both give practice a privileged epistemological and methodological significance. They posit practices as the way we experience, know, understand, and evaluate our experiences and the world. Marx, however, also assigns to practice a generative or ontological force that seems lacking in pragmatism. In Marx's thought, "human sensuous activity" creates everything, in both society's material base and in superstructural elements such as values, ideas, culture, and knowledge. This is a description of how things work, for Marx, but it also entails a normative, or at least crypto-normative, claim about the value of practices. This can be seen, for example, in the labor theory of value, according to which human work, not capital, is responsible for the worth of products. More broadly, Marx's arguments against the division of labor, alienation, and other oppressive aspects of capitalist society rely on assumptions about the normative value of practice. Human activity has an intrinsic value, as the expression of human creativity, sociability, and will. These claims extend far beyond pragmatist arguments about the importance of practice.

Together, pragmatism and Marxism advance us considerably in thinking about the place of practice in ethical theory. However, we still need a fuller understanding of the relations between means and ends, which lie at the heart of ethical theory, at least when we think about the place of practice. The only means we have are practices, and the ends we seek are our ethical goals or values. The link between means and ends, in this light, is the relationship between practice and ethics. Ultimately, however, even this distinction is tenuous, since ethical reflection itself is a practice, and means and ends are continually becoming each other, as Dewey's notion of ends-in-view makes clear. In order to unpack this more fully, I turn in chapter 6 to religious pacifism, which includes a more extensive and explicit treatment of the means-ends relationship than any of the other ethical theories discussed so far.

6

Religious Pacifism

Peace as Means and End

Means are after all everything. As the means, so the end. . . .
There is no wall of separation between means and end.

—Mohandas K. Gandhi[1]

Introduction

Pacifism is commonly defined as opposition to war, and it is usually counterposed to just war theory, which articulates the conditions under which war might be justified. I argue that both pacifism and just war theory are not narrow or strictly applied approaches to the morality of violence but rather comprehensive ethical theories, with implications about normative and meta-ethical issues beyond war. This is because positions on violence are tied to foundational moral and theological questions, such as what is the good, how we should determine the moral course of action, what an ethical community looks like, and more. I argue, similarly, that just war theory is a much more wide-ranging approach to moral problems than its usual portrayal.

While just war theory has been the subject of countless scholarly books and articles, far fewer philosophers and theologians devote serious attention to pacifism. This dismissal has several sources, including a common conception of pacifists as unrealistic extremists, outside the mainstream of their traditions, and also perhaps a notion that pacifism is a spiritual practice without serious intellectual dimensions. When analyzed as an ethical theory, however, religious pacifism provides important grounds for critique and constructive insights and in particular for understanding practice's roles in ethical theory. In this chapter, I argue that practice is at the center of a holistic and innovative ethical theory, defined by but not limited to a pacifist position regarding political violence.

Works Righteousness. Anna L. Peterson, Oxford University Press (2021). © Oxford University Press.
DOI: 10.1093/oso/9780197532232.001.0001.

I begin with a discussion of pacifism and just war theory as approaches to war and peace. Next, I turn to the development of Christian pacifism as a comprehensive religious ethic, beginning with its origins in the early Church, through its development in the Anabaptist tradition and the thought of Martin Luther King Jr. Building on this discussion, I look at the theory of nonviolence developed by Mohandas K. Gandhi, a major influence on King and contemporary pacifist thinkers. Gandhi and King point to the ways pacifism and nonviolence can open up our thinking about ethical issues far beyond war and peace.

War, Peace, and Ethics

Both scholars and laypeople often view pacifism as a rigid opposition to the use of violence, in war and perhaps in all aspects of life. They challenge pacifists with questions such as what a pacifist "would do if England were invaded and a Storm Trooper tried to rape his mother," as A. A. Milne wrote.[2] This assumes that pacifism is both inflexible and narrow, a strict prohibition against using any kind of violence, with no connection to other aspects of morality or life in general. It also conceives of pacifism as highly individualistic, a choice made by isolated moral actors without consideration for context, history, or relationships. Both assumptions prove false when we look carefully at the history of pacifism and the ideas and practices of actual pacifists. Some pacifists object to all violence, in all settings, but many distinguish between personal protection, for example, from Milne's Storm Trooper, and the institutionalized use of violence in war.

Objection to this institutionalized use of violence—what Anabaptist Christians call "the sword"—is the defining trait of pacifism as a moral stance. For pacifists, violence is the use of force, coercion, or threat of such to achieve a goal. In particular, for discussions of the ethics of war, violence refers to the use of institutionalized violence to achieve ideological or political goals. This kind of violence is found most obviously in war, but many pacifists do not limit their philosophical and ethical reflection to this context. War provides a dramatic illustration of the reasons to oppose violence, but the structural use of violence extends throughout many other parts of our lives and communities.

Nonviolence, in contrast, is the refusal to use these means to achieve goals. Thus, as the Mennonite theologian J. Denny Weaver explains, for pacifists, "nonviolence informs the entire theological program."[3] Thus, pacifists refuse to use violence as part of any struggle to achieve moral, religious, or political goals. Taking violence off the table has inspired many pacifists to search for peaceful methods of achieving their goals, which might include broad social change or simply the right to live according to their principles. Conversely, I argue, the fact that violence—the use or threatened use of force—remains available as a way to pursue moral and political goals informs the entire program of just war theorists. The acceptance of violence as a legitimate and even inevitable method of pursuing political, religious, and social goals seems so normal or realistic that just war arguments rarely receive the kind of scrutiny that pacifism receives. One of the contributions of an investigation of pacifism as an ethical theory, in fact, is its ability to illuminate the far-reaching consequences of the just war acceptance of violence.

The core of pacifist moral theory is thus not the simple claim that war is wrong or that individuals should not defend themselves, but rather that violence is wrong when it is used by those with power to enforce their interests or goals, material or ideological. It is wrong because it causes harm to its victims and its perpetrators alike, and it is also wrong because it is ultimately counterproductive. In a nutshell, pacifists argue, violent means cannot lead to peaceful ends, and more broadly, immoral practices cannot bring about ethically sound results.

Just War Theory

Pacifism is often defined in relationship to just war theory, the dominant approach to military and political violence among both religious and secular ethicists. Just war theory proposes, in brief, that war can be morally justified under certain circumstances, if a series of conditions are met. This issue arose for Christians after the conversion of Constantine, which transformed Christianity from a persecuted minority religion, firmly pacifist and nonconforming, to the religion of the Roman Empire. In this new context, Christians had to ask whether a Christian empire could justify waging war, if Christians could or should participate, and how the damage and brutality of war could be constrained.[4] The just war tradition is rooted in Augustine's efforts to answer these questions. He concluded that Christian love need not be incompatible with the use of violent force. Augustine and other post-Constantinian thinkers articulated a conditional acceptance of war that broke decisively with the pacifism of the earliest Church. Christians can serve Caesar, they argued, as long as they do so with the proper attitudes. Moral quality lies in intentions and the will, so fighting can be acceptable as long as it is done with love.

Almost a millennium later, Thomas Aquinas added a crucial new principle: only a war declared by a legitimate ruler, which for Thomas meant a Christian monarch, could be just. Thomas's addition to Augustine's thought provided the core for the classic model of just war theory. This model divides just war criteria into two categories. The first, *jus ad bellum*, considers the justice *of* the war, meaning the justification of a decision to go to war in the first place. *Jus ad bellum* conditions include the justice of the cause, the exhaustion of peaceful ways to resolve the conflict, legitimate authority, and likelihood of success. The second category of just war criteria, *jus in bello*, addresses the manner of waging the war. The most important *jus in bello* rule is noncombatant immunity, which asserts that combatants may not target civilians, captives, or wounded soldiers. *Jus in bello* rules are meant to keep war confined to the battlefield, a limitation that has rarely been maintained, especially in modern warfare.

Most just war theorists contend that *jus ad bellum* and *jus in bello* do not depend on each other and can be evaluated separately. This assumes, as Robert Holmes puts it, "that one can justify the resort to war independently of, and antecedently to, justifying both the necessary means to conducting it and the acts constitutive of it."[5] The separation between the morality of the decision to go to war and the morality of fighting it removes material practices—the acts of threatening, harming, destroying, and killing that constitute war—from ethical reflection about going to war. This separation reflects the consequentialist question that lies at the heart of just war theory: will the war's expected benefits outweigh its costs, generating more good than bad effects? Can it be acceptable, in other words, to use evil means to pursue a good end?[6]

These questions come to the fore in the doctrine of the double effect (DDE). While DDE is discussed in other contexts, including bioethics, it was first developed in relation to war. It asserts that soldiers may perform acts likely to have evil results if the directly intended effects are morally acceptable, if the intention of the actors is good, and if the positive effect is sufficiently good to compensate for the evil effects. Double effect makes it possible to reconcile the usual just war prohibition against attacking civilians with the need for exceptions in pursuit of military and political goals.

We can explore the application of DDE in Michael Walzer's concept of su-preme emergency, a phrase he borrowed from Winston Churchill to describe a situation in which extraordinary, overwhelming goods are at stake.[7] Walzer agrees with Churchill's claim that the risk of an Axis victory in World War II threatened the survival of foundational goods of Western culture such as democratic governance, human rights, and the rule of law. The "immeasur-able evil" of Nazism, according to this logic, gave the Allies the right to decide when to follow the rules of war and when to disregard them, for example, in bombing civilian areas of German cities.

While Walzer poses this as an extreme and unusual threat, it becomes hard to distinguish from his general arguments in support of war as a method of resolving political conflict. The discussion too easily slides into a ver-sion of "just necessity," or the notion that "whatever justifies resorting to war in the first place justifies the means necessary to winning it," as Holmes explains.[8] This appears similar to precisely the kind of consequentialist arguments that Walzer himself rejects, as Alex Bellamy notes: "it contradicts Walzer's own deontological account of the just war tradition. It flirts with realism and succumbs to utilitarianism, both perspectives that Walzer him-self denounces."[9] When appeals are made to just necessity, "there are no in-dependent moral constraints upon the conduct of the war."[10] Because this presumes that just cause overrides the rules of war outlined in *jus in bello*, it belies the supposed separation of *jus ad bellum* and *jus in bello*. This justi-fication rests on what Holmes calls an internalist model, which asserts that once just cause has been established, there is no need or possibility for ad-ditional critique. There is no outsider position from which to criticize par-ticular practices, because the war itself is just. Double effect exemplifies this fundamentally consequentialist logic: because I have good intentions, I can do bad things that will further the good goals I seek.

In similar fashion, the condition of legitimate authority overrides many other criteria. Authorizing the sovereign or the state to declare war entails giving them the power to decide if all the other criteria are met, which means that the different just war criteria are not, in practice, truly separate from each other. Because the leader has the power to interpret the *jus ad bellum* criteria, as Laurie Calhoun explains, "decree by a legitimate au-thority can transform an impermissible act of homicide into a permissible act of killing during wartime."[11] Like just necessity, legitimate authority becomes a meta-criterion that subsumes all other justifying conditions.

The internalist model thus subordinates other moral conditions to the determination of just cause and legitimate authority.

In contrast, an externalist model asserts that standards for judging the practice of the war are independent of the cause that justified going to war in the first place. In theory, at least, just cause does not offer the state a blank check for any and all practices, and double effect cannot open a wide door for exceptions to the prohibition on targeting civilians. In the real practice of war, however, there is rarely, if ever, an independent authority that can exercise these checks on the power of the sovereign to decide what is both "just" and "necessary."

A pacifist criticism of just war theory argues against both the internalist idea that just cause legitimizes all actions done in its name and also the externalist idea that the means and ends of war are independent of each other. Pacifists insist that in thinking about the justification of the cause or "end" of war, the means—the practice of war—must be front and center. This approach acknowledges, as Holmes writes, that

> One does not just go to war. One goes to war for certain reasons, to achieve certain ends or objectives. The very act of embarking upon war presupposes them, as does the selection of certain means by which to try to achieve them. This means that to justify going to war requires justifying the selection of means from the outset. There are not two separate acts here, the embarking upon war and the implementation of chosen means. To embark upon war *is* to implement the chosen means.[12]

This view puts practices front and center in moral theorizing and points to the interconnection of means and ends that is at the heart of pacifist thought. Just war theory, in contrast, requires the theoretical separation of means and ends. The starting point of just war theory is a taken-for-granted assumption that it is morally acceptable, even necessary, to use evil means to bring about a good end. This approach to ethical reflection on war does not ask *if* the practice of war can ever be justified, which ought to be the first and most important question on the table. Instead, just war theory is predicated on the assumption that war can be justified, and thus wrestles only with questions about when and under what conditions it can be justified.

The Convergence of Pacifism and Just War Theory?

One common philosophical interpretation of pacifism defines it as structurally similar to just war theory, differing only in the final conclusion about whether war can be justified sometimes or never. This perspective is codified in the "convergence" model, which asserts that pacifism and just war theory both start with a prima facie objection to war, and the only meaningful difference between them is that pacifists never lift that objection, while just war advocates sometimes do.

The convergence or prima facie model sees just war theory and pacifism as united on the really important principles and divergent only on relatively minor details about specific cases. This approach presupposes a positive answer to the crucial question of whether war can ever be justified. With this taken for granted, the purpose of theorizing about war is to articulate whether a particular war can be justified or, more precisely, to identify the conditions that might justify overriding the prima facie duty not to kill other people. It is not surprising that just war theorists would find the convergence model appealing, since it presents their views on war as essentially peaceable and characterizes pacifism as a stream within just war theory rather than a fundamental challenge to it.

From a pacifist perspective, the convergence model profoundly misunderstands pacifism by portraying it as merely a variation on the just war theme. This comparison begins with the assumption that war is an acceptable means to pursue desirable ends, which is precisely the claim that pacifists reject. Thus, pacifist and just war theories have fundamentally different starting places, not the shared common ground assumed by convergence advocates.

I experienced this disjuncture several years ago, while presenting a paper on another issue. Almost in passing, I used Mennonite theologian John Howard Yoder's description of war as "killing people on purpose."[13] My use of the phrase prompted a heated response from an ethicist in the audience who contended that I was mistaken not about the morality of war but about what it involved—its practices, in short. He insisted that war does *not* involve killing people on purpose. What I had seen as a simple statement of fact struck him as a pointed attack on his own values. He was not persuaded when I said that my comment was descriptive rather than normative, that is, that war might be killing people on purpose and still be justifiable. The exchange ended with a mutual agreement to disagree. We did not take it up again later, so I am not precisely sure why he rejected so strongly, but I suspect it is because he believes that deliberately killing people is wrong and at the same time that just war theory is right. To reconcile these two moral stances, he must deny that supporting just war theory entails accepting deliberate killing. This claim is clearly absurd; war is nothing if not killing people on purpose. To describe war in this way is neither a falsehood nor a pacifist slur. Any ethical reflection about war must come to grips with the fact that deliberate killing is the defining practice of war. There are countless moral arguments about the circumstances in which generally harmful acts, such as war, euthanasia, capital punishment, or imprisonment, can be justified. These arguments will not succeed if they do not start with an accurate understanding of what is being done. In the case of war, practices of killing are at the heart of what is being argued about; to remove that reality makes theorizing meaningless.

Beginning with those defining practices underlines the inadequacy of the convergence model. It rests on narrow definitions of both models and unites them as a set of rules about whether to justify a particular war, rather than as wide-ranging, complex ways of thinking not just about war but about moral thought and action generally. The convergence model assumes that pacifists and just war advocates will rarely have reason to disagree, since there will be few efforts by the state or other powerful groups to use violence as a political tool. In reality, the practice of war is far from exceptional—it is "politics by other means," a constant for as long as people have recorded history. Military violence is a factor even when a country is technically at peace, due to the costs and social effects of maintaining an army.

Just war theory is embedded within a larger ethic resting on cost-benefit calculations and the regular use of force to achieve political goals, "an underlying political theory that understands power as essential to political order, as necessarily forceful, but also to be placed at the service of genuine goods."[14] Pacifism, in contrast, is rooted in an underlying political ethic that says coercive power cannot be used even in the pursuit of genuine goods. This is a fundamental meta-ethical and normative difference, not merely a variation in applied conclusions. To understand pacifism as a comprehensive ethical theory more fully, I turn to the origins and historical development of Christian pacifism.

Christian Pacifism

Pacifism and War in Early Christianity

The historical, symbolic, and intellectual origins of Christian pacifism lie in the life of Jesus as described in the Synoptic Gospels (Matthew, Mark, and Luke). Christian pacifists read these accounts not just as an inspiration but as a literal guide to right living, defined by imitation of Jesus, *imitatio Christi*. Jesus's humanity is central to pacifist theology and ethics, because through his actions, Jesus revealed himself as "the bearer of a new possibility of human, social, and therefore political relationships."[15] This new possibility calls to Christians to follow Jesus's model in concrete ways, by practicing *imitatio Christi* in every aspect of their lives.

This vision of Christianity is rooted in biblical passages such as the story of the final judgment in Matthew 25:31–46, sometimes called the parable of the sheep and the goats, because it declares that the Son of Man "will separate the people one from another as a shepherd separates the sheep from the goats." To the sheep, or true Christians, he will say,

"Come, you who are blessed by my Father; take your inheritance, the kingdom prepared for you since the creation of the world. For I was hungry and you gave me something to eat, I was thirsty and you gave me something to drink, I was a stranger and you invited me in, I needed clothes and you clothed me, I was sick and you looked after me, I was in prison and you came to visit me." Then the righteous will answer him, "Lord, when did we see you hungry and feed you, or thirsty and give you something to drink? When did we see you a stranger and invite you in, or needing clothes and clothe you? When did we see you sick or in prison and go to visit you?" The King will reply, "Truly I tell you, whatever you did for one of the least of these brothers and sisters of mine, you did for me." Then he will say to those on his left, "Depart from me, you who are cursed, into the eternal fire prepared for the devil and his angels. For I was hungry and you gave me nothing to eat, I was thirsty and you gave me nothing to drink, I was a stranger and you did not invite me in, I needed clothes and you did not clothe me, I was sick and in prison and you did not look after me." They also will answer, "Lord, when did we see you hungry or thirsty or a stranger or needing clothes or sick or in prison, and did not help you?" He will reply,

"Truly I tell you, whatever you did not do for one of the least of these, you did not do for me."

This familiar tale presents an ethic that is not just about specific actions such as feeding the hungry, welcoming the stranger, caring for the sick, or visiting those in prison, important as these deeds are. Behind these moral imperatives lies a meta-ethical framework in which pursuing the good means putting practice first; those who do not help "the least of these" are not true Christians.

The same vision is expressed in the Book of James, which begins with a question about the meaning of faith as an internal state: "What does it profit, my brethren, if someone says he has faith but does not have works? Can faith save him?" (James 2:14). James gives a negative answer to these questions: faith cannot, in fact, save someone who does not practice good works.

> What good is it, my brothers and sisters, if you say you have faith but do not have works? Can faith save you? If a brother or sister is naked and lacks daily food, and one of you says to them, "Go in peace; keep warm and eat your fill," and yet you do not supply their bodily needs, what is the good of that? So faith by itself, if it has no works, is dead.

> But someone will say, "You have faith and I have works." Show me your faith apart from your works, and I by my works will show you my faith. (James 2:14–18)

The heart of this moral vision is the unity of values and practice. This union precludes other kinds of divisions, particularly the split, central for Augustine and Luther, between two contrasting types of moral citizenship. The theological model that nurtures pacifism permits only one citizenship, in the reign of God which Christians are called to construct here and now, however partially and fallibly. As true discipleship, this citizenship includes nonviolence and a willingness to challenge the dominant culture, as a concrete expression of *imitatio Christi*. The rejection of violence is linked to the mutual love that, as Tertullian wrote, "brands" Christians in the eyes of outsiders: " 'See,' they say, 'how they love one another'; (for they hate one another), 'and how ready they are to die for each other.' (They themselves would be more ready to kill each other.)"[16] Like later Christian pacifists, Tertullian argued that

Christians must obey the highest moral standards and serve as a model of discipline, sacrifice, and altruistic love. These qualities lead naturally to pacifism, which is not a separate principle but an expression of an overall vision of the Christian life. And pacifism, like Christian love, must be practiced; it is never simply an interior attitude.

As noted in chapter 2, however, Christian ethics became increasingly interiorized after the conversion of Constantine, the Edict of Toleration, and the establishment of Christianity as the official religion of the Roman Empire in the early fourth century. This theological and moral shift corresponded with dramatic changes in the Church's relationship to the larger society and government. It was no longer a radical minority opposed to the core values of the majority but the official faith of the empire. This made pacifism problematic, because it posed questions about Christian support for Roman military actions and Christian participation in the army. Some Christians, notably Augustine, argued that once the empire became officially Christian, church members could and even should serve in its army. More generally, the post-Constantinian Church adopted a worldview that was consistent with the cultural, institutional, and political, as well as moral, priorities of the empire; it was no longer an oppositional minority but rather a bastion of the status quo.

Pacifism in the Radical Reformation

The intertwining of Christianity and the dominant culture grew into what historians call Christendom, a society with the Church at the center of almost every sphere of activity, including education, art, family life, economics, and politics. This intermingling, and the corruption it sometimes enabled, prompted Luther's break with the Catholic Church in 1517. The Lutheran Reformation opened the floodgates to additional divisions, and various groups began claiming authority for their particular visions of Christianity. Among the earliest and most distinctive movements was the Radical Reformation, which began in Switzerland around 1524. Two residents of Zurich, Conrad Grebel and Felix Manz, rejected infant baptism on the grounds that only persons old enough to make a conscious decision to accept Christ should join the Church. They became known as Anabaptists, or "rebaptizers," due to their practice of adult baptism. Several Anabaptist groups quickly emerged, the largest of which was the Mennonites, named after Dutch reformer Menno Simons.

Anabaptists diverged not only from the "popish" errors of the Catholic Church but also from Lutheran and, later, Calvinist Protestantism. Their rejection of infant baptism—"the first and greatest abomination of the pope"—gave the movement its name, but a commitment to pacifism was equally central to Anabaptist identity. Radical Reformers agreed with Luther that institutionalized violence, or "the sword," was necessary in the larger world to protect the good and punish the wicked. They disagreed, however, about what this meant for Christian ethics. Luther insisted that while the sword had no place within the community of true believers, Christians could and must wield it on behalf of the state, as hangmen or soldiers.

"There must be those who arrest, accuse, slay and destroy the wicked, and protect, acquit, defend and save the good," he wrote, and Christians must be willing to take up these tasks. When a Christian does so "not with the intention of seeking one's own ends, but only of helping to maintain the laws and the State, so that the wicked may be restrained, there is no peril in them and they may be followed like any other pursuit and be used as one's means of support."[17] While Luther declared Christians to be citizens of two kingdoms, Anabaptists insisted that true Christians could not serve this world or use any violence, including legal coercion or threats, even in self-defense. They also could not act as magistrates, participate in the legal and political mechanisms of the state, or even swear oaths.

Anabaptists radicalized many of Luther's principles, particularly regarding the question of how Christians might relate their faith to membership in the larger society. For early Christians, who lived under Roman rule, allegiance to God and Caesar clearly conflicted, but for the post-Constantinian Church, the lines blurred. The Church and civil society, or faith and citizenship, did not seem to impose conflicting demands or identities. Medieval Christendom took the union of worldly and Christian identity to an extreme, at least in the eyes of reformers. Rejecting this integration between Church and world, Luther insisted that human society would always fall far short of Christian ideals. Christians thus belonged to two kingdoms, that of the world and that of God, which imposed very different obligations. Christians should try to fulfill both, rejecting worldly demands only if they conflicted directly with the Bible, on explicitly religious matters.

The Anabaptists agreed with Luther that human society as a whole would never be fully Christian, but they rejected the possibility of dual citizenship and insisted that true Christians had only one authority, God. Their vision is presented in the Schleitheim Confession, also known as "The Brotherly

Union of a Number of Children of God Concerning Seven Articles," produced in 1527 by Swiss Anabaptists. The Schleitheim Confession spells out core values that still guide Anabaptist theology and practice on a number of issues, including the need for true Christians to be united with one another and to live as true disciples, which meant imitating Jesus's model:

> the rule of the government is according to the flesh, that of the Christians according to the Spirit. Their houses and dwelling remain in this world, that of the Christians is in heaven. Their citizenship is in this world, that of the Christians is in heaven. . . . In sum: as Christ our Head is minded, so also must be minded the members of the body of Christ through Him, so that there be no division in the body, through which it would be destroyed. Since then Christ is as is written of Him, so must His members also be the same, so that His body may remain whole and unified for its own advancement and upbuilding.[18]

While remaining unified among themselves, Christians must separate from the inevitable violence and corruption of the worldly realm, because "everything which has not been united with our God in Christ is nothing but an abomination which we should shun."[19]

Central to this model is an understanding of the sword as a shorthand for the violence and corruption of the world. As the Schleitheim Confession explains, "many, who do not understand Christ's will for us, will ask whether a Christian may or should use the sword against the wicked for the protection and defense of the good, or for the sake of love. The answer is unanimously revealed: Christ teaches and commands us to learn from Him, for He is meek and lowly of heart and thus we shall find rest for our souls."[20] The sword symbolizes not just military violence but all forms of coercion and pursuit of power. Christians must forswear the sword in every aspect of their lives, keeping themselves apart from the corrupt institutions and practices of the secular world. Thus, pacifism, as rejection of the sword, is not simply an applied ethic regarding war but a comprehensive way of life.

Rather than a divided citizenship in the life of a single Christian, Anabaptists asserted a division between Christians and the world. As the Schleitheim Confession explains, "All those who have fellowship with the dead works of darkness have no part in the light. Thus all those who follow the devil and the world, have no part with those who have been called out of the world unto God. All those who lie in evil have no part in the good."[21]

Resistance to the darkness of the world is possible only in the context of a community of true believers as pure and harmonious as the reign of God announced by Jesus. Practices are not just a way of pursuing or accessing the good but in themselves make the good possible. In the Anabaptist vision of how Christians ought to live, correct action (orthopraxy) takes precedence over correct belief (orthodoxy). The core of this vision remains the same for contemporary Anabaptists as well: it is a "theology for living," as the Amish farmer and writer David Kline puts it.[22] Within this practice-centered ethic, the core substantive values remain nonresistance and nonviolence. Both are rooted in the concept of *Gelassenheit*, usually translated as nonresistance but sometimes as yieldedness, submission, resignation, surrender, detachment, selflessness, and tranquility.[23] Nonresistance combines Christian neighbor love, humility, and peaceableness with a stubborn refusal to conform to the dominant society.

In addition to nonresistance, Anabaptists value nonconformity to the world, although different groups interpret this principle in varied ways. Old Order Anabaptists, including the Amish, Hutterites, Swiss Brethren, and Old Order Mennonites, express their nonconformity through physical separation and the rejection of various aspects of contemporary life. More liberal or "mainstream" Mennonites, most of whom belong to the Mennonite Church USA, express their nonconformity through pacifism, some occupational restrictions, and a distinctive understanding of what it means to be a Christian and a member of the church. According to the Mennonite *Confession of Faith*, "Conformity to Christ necessarily implies nonconformity to the world."[24] What this means for ethics and daily life is that

> True faith in Christ means willingness to do the will of God, rather than willful pursuit of individual happiness. True faith means seeking first the reign of God in simplicity, rather than pursuing materialism. True faith means acting in peace and justice, rather than with violence or military means. True faith means giving first loyalty to God's kingdom, rather than to any nation-state or ethnic group that claims our allegiance. True faith means honest affirmation of the truth, rather than reliance on oaths to guarantee our truth telling.[25]

This statement is notable for the centrality of practices rather than ideas in the definition of true faith. Faith is not a mental attitude, or at least not only that, but a set of practices: doing the will of God, seeking the reign of God, acting in peace and justice, affirming the truth. These practices not only express individual faith but create and hold together the believing community.

Martin Luther King Jr. and the Beloved Community

While the Radical Reformation tradition kept pacifism alive for centuries as a minority stream within Christianity, the most prominent modern Christian advocate of nonviolence was a Baptist, Martin Luther King Jr. (Dorothy Day, another prominent twentieth-century Christian pacifist, was Catholic.) At the start of his civil rights career, King's embrace of nonviolence was largely pragmatic. He believed that it would be suicidal for African Americans to use violent methods, given the disparity in power and resources and the demonstrated willingness of racist officials to use deadly violence. As the movement developed, King incorporated Gandhian ideas about nonviolence more fully, as James Cone explains, so desegregation became not the final goal but a means to achieve the higher end of the beloved community.[26] Eventually, King articulated a far-reaching, principled embrace of pacifism as not just a strategy for the civil rights movement but a vision of what Christianity and a good community should be.

One of the most significant expressions of King's evolving understanding of the philosophy of nonviolence, especially as it relates to his Christian faith, is his "Letter from a Birmingham Jail," written after his arrest for participating in protests in 1963. The letter responded to a message sent to King by eight white Christian leaders, who called his participation in the protests in Birmingham "unwise and untimely" and questioned his presence there. King related his situation to the original Christians' existence as a persecuted minority under Roman rule. "The early Christians rejoiced when they were deemed worthy to suffer for what they believed. In those days the church was not merely a thermometer that recorded the ideas and principles of popular opinion; it was the thermostat that transformed the mores of society."[27] Practices are not just a reflection of the world but an active force that changes the world. In contrast to the practices of early Christians, King critiques the comparative weakness of the contemporary Church, which sanctions the status quo rather than disturbing it.

In response to his correspondents' praise for the behavior of police officers at the protests, he writes, "It is true that they have been rather disciplined in their public handling of the demonstrators. In this sense they have been publicly 'nonviolent.' But for what purpose? To preserve the evil system of segregation." Here King makes a point about the complex meta-ethics of nonviolence: the intertwining of means and ends applies not only to attempts to pursue desirable ends through violent means but also to the inverse situation. Thus, his insistence that "the means we use must be as pure as the ends we seek" does not only mean that "it is wrong to use immoral means to attain moral ends" but also "that it is just as wrong, or even more, to use moral means to preserve immoral ends."[28] Racists' individual practices cannot be separated from their motivations and their place in larger social structure. Rather than affirming either intentions or practices alone as the determinant of moral quality, King insisted on the unity both of ideas and practices and of means and ends.

King expanded his commitment to nonviolence in his 1967 "Declaration of Independence from the War in Vietnam," which offered a more global, holistic, and explicitly political approach. The "Declaration" listed King's reasons for opposing the war, beginning with the fact that it was draining resources that could be used to improve social conditions for the poor in the United States. In addition, African Americans were disproportionately represented in the army, sent to fight and die for a nation that did not treat them as first-class citizens: "We were taking the young black men who had been crippled by our society and sending them 8000 miles away to guarantee liberties in Southeast Asia which they had not found in Southwest Georgia and East Harlem."[29]

Perhaps most important, King described his opposition to US involvement in Vietnam as an expression of consistent nonviolent principles. If his rejection of violence as a method of political change was to have force at home, he reflected, he had to apply it globally as well. He recalls his conversations with angry, desperate young African American men and his assertions that "Molotov cocktails and rifles would not solve their problems" and that "social change comes most meaningfully through nonviolent action." This message, he writes, was undercut by their questions about Vietnam. "They asked if our own nation wasn't using massive doses of violence to solve its problems, to bring about the changes it wanted. Their questions hit home, and I knew that I could never again raise my voice against the violence of the oppressed in the ghettos without having first spoken clearly to the greatest purveyor of violence in the world today—my own government."[30] Nonviolent direct action to challenge racism at home must be partnered with nonviolent direct action to challenge unjust military action in Vietnam.

King's commitment to nonviolence demands consistency, in theory and in practice. This moral vision is rooted in a Christian community that can nurture discipleship. Like the Anabaptists, King believes that collective practices and mutual support create this community and also enable Christians to pursue a shared vision of a good society. King differs from the Anabaptist tradition in the explicitly political nature of his pacifism and his Christian commitment in general. In contrast with the Anabaptist emphasis on separation from the world, King insists on engagement and active struggle, echoing the thought of Gandhi, a major influence on his work.

Gandhian Nonviolence

The embodiment of values in practice, even while pursuing larger goals, is central to the thought and work of Mohandas K. Gandhi. Gandhian thought draws on a variety of sources, including Hinduism and Henry David Thoreau. Gandhi focuses less on pacifism in the familiar sense, as opposition to war, than on nonviolence as a principle for guiding all forms of political action.

Gandhi defines his central principle, satyagraha, as "holding on to Truth," or Truth-force.[31] Satyagraha describes "the process of looking for the truthful aspects of each side's position, trying to find a broad resolution that includes them all, and clinging to it."[32] The notion of clinging may suggest too static a position, since Gandhi admits that conflicts always include multiple points of view, each of which may have some claim to truth. Even more than the goal of achieving truth, satyagraha describes the process of struggling to find the truth. There is a pragmatist dimension, as Mark Juergensmeyer notes, in the way satyagraha "encourages one to engage in conflict in order to find a solution to it."[33] There are pragmatist echoes as well in the notion that sometimes we enter fights "not so much to defend the truth as to discover it."[34] The struggle itself brings out the truth and the deception of both sides, just as the pragmatist process of inquiry, exploring and weighing diverse evidence and points of view, makes possible a fuller and more accurate—though never final—answer to pressing questions. This open-ended, pluralistic, and respectful approach to seeking truth reflects Gandhi's commitment to nonviolent methods of change. "Pursuit of truth," in his view, "did not admit of violence being inflicted on one's opponent." Instead, adversaries "must be weaned from error by patience and sympathy. For what appears to be truth to the one may appear to be error to the other."[35]

Gandhi's most distinctive contribution both to political strategies of non-violence and to ethical theory is the intertwining of means and ends. A famous phrase attributed to Gandhi summarizes his position: "The ends are the means in the process of becoming."[36] In some circumstances, it is possible to use the desired end as a practical means. If, as Juergensmeyer notes, "your opponent has not totally limited your options, then you can fight in the most direct way a Gandhian can: you can simply start carrying out your alternative to the conflict as if you had already won the right to do so."[37] Thus, the means to achieving one's ultimate goal becomes the implementation of that goal as a practice and a way of life. This is evident in many of Gandhi's tactics, such as the salt march and his use of the spinning wheel as a method of protest. Independence activists began carrying out their goals, such as economic self-sufficiency, "and the very act of doing it became a prime weapon in their struggle to resist the British. The goal was the means."[38]

For Gandhi, the intertwining of means and ends is not just a political strategy but a comprehensive ethical theory. This theory is often described in relation to nonviolence, a principle that, more clearly than pacifism, is not limited to military conflicts but addresses a wide range of real-life moral problems. Gandhi's ethical approach is rooted not so much in an aversion to violence as in a commitment to the interconnection between means and ends. His chief normative claim, in its simplest form, is that "Fair means alone can produce fair results."[39] However, this suggests an instrumentalism that is belied by Gandhi's assertion that means and ends are "convertible terms." It is not just that good means lead to good ends but rather that the two are inextricably connected. Thus, a person "cannot do right in one department of life whilst he is occupied in doing wrong in any other department. Life is one indivisible whole."[40] The seamless connection between different spheres of action underlies Gandhi's assertion that "pure motives can never justify impure or violent action."[41] This holistic vision is the mirror opposite of Kant's willingness to let the world perish if that is the price of acting from a pure will.

Gandhi's emphasis on practical integrity requires that nonviolence and other core principles be practiced not just in political conflicts but in everyday life, in social interactions, production, and labor. Personal actions must enact the same values that Gandhians hope to see realized in the larger society, because "larger social changes must stem from individual transformation."[42] This unity of individual and social practice also characterizes Christian pacifists, who reject the Lutheran conviction that religious and social actions can be judged differently. Because human lives are integrated wholes, actions in every sphere of our lives are means toward the same end. Just as there is no division between means and ends, there can be no separation between the personal and the political. Gandhi rejects Kant's desire to maintain clean hands even at the cost of world destruction and also the consequentialist separation between means and ends, reflected in the just war argument that immoral actions can be justified in the pursuit of desirable goals. In contrast to both these positions, Gandhi insists that the means shape not just the likelihood of achieving intended goals but the character of the end itself.

Pacifism, Nonviolence, and Ethical Theory

Pacifism and just war theory are comprehensive ethical theories, not just applied ethics that are relevant to a particular political problem. Both make meta-ethical and normative claims that again extend far beyond questions of war and peace. In order to explore these claims and the ways pacifism can support the development of a practice-based ethics, I return to the themes I have highlighted in preceding chapters.

1. Pacifists agree that ideas are not autonomous and that ethics cannot be an application of neutral reason. This affirmation appears more complicated for pacifists than for pragmatists or Marxists, since religious pacifists, in particular, appeal to divine truths, such as the command to do no harm or to shun the sword. However, these ethical and theological ideas are at once both transcendent and immanent. Even though they originate with God or scripture, they cannot be fully expressed or fully known except in collective practices. This is the meaning of Gandhi's insistence that moral principles are "enunciated in the action itself."[43] Acts contain their ends, as Gandhi insisted, so that there are no ends outside human practices and the world of experience. The Anabaptist conviction that faith without works is dead makes a similar claim about the dependence of mental states—ideas, intentions, faith—upon practical embodiment in the world. There is no inner attitude, existing in some spiritual or ideal world, that can make actions good or bad. The actions themselves carry their own moral interpretation.

2. Because the pacifist good consists of particular practices rather than rules, attitudes, or consequences, ethics must be substantive. Norms have meaning only as a way of life; formalist procedures cannot capture what is required. For Christian pacifists, the most important substantive norm is that people are to live in community, and they are not to coerce or violently force other people. Yoder's notion of the kingdom as social ethic[44] and King's vision of the beloved community serve as concrete examples of this conception of ethics, as do the movements and institutions that Gandhi created during the Indian independence struggle. The characteristics of these communities flesh out the normative ethics of religious pacifism. Their members abstain from using violence as a means to pursue objectives, they commit to mutual aid, and on important matters they subordinate their self-interest to the common good.

Just war theory also illuminates the tensions between formal and substantive ethical theories. The convergence model presents a fundamentally formalist conception of just war theory, which must be "empty and vacuous," in Childress's words. It has no thick content but is merely a structure that organizes how ethical reflection unfolds. Childress and other advocates of the convergence model see pacifism as a formalist model; this is what makes possible agreement not only among different just war theorists but also between just war advocates and pacifists.[45] Further, according to Childress, there is no single substantive theory of just war, because a pluralistic society cannot reach consensus about core values. In this context, the convergence approach offers a framework for debating which wars, if any, can be morally justified.[46]

I argue that the very formalism of the prima facie model, however, makes such debates impossible, because we cannot identify and assess the real values and costs at stake. Focusing on practice can bring substance into our reflections on right and wrong. In both pacifism and just war theory, the substantive claim involves the practice of war. As Yoder puts it, regardless of the abstract principles or cost-benefit calculations involved, "the activity being discussed is still killing people on purpose."[47] This concreteness is what gets lost in formalist versions of just war theory and the supposed convergence between it and pacifism. Instead of focusing on abstractions such as just cause or proportionality, Yoder contends, we must look at the value of the concrete lives at stake. "To evaluate violence morally," he writes, "is to evaluate the worth of the value violated."[48] In war, the value violated is not an abstraction but human lives and communities, as well as natural environments.

3. Like most of the other "alternative" ethical theories I have discussed, religious pacifists assume that human nature is social and that ethics is about the realization of social goods. The specifically pacifist version of this

position insists that humans are called to live in a beloved community, characterized by peace and solidarity, which they must construct on earth. Loving relationships between people are not just a moral ideal but a reality, because of the way God created humans. Social structures play a role in advancing or discouraging moral behavior, which led both Gandhi and King to advocate socialism as an important normative value. Gandhi understood socialism as a doctrine of equality that could end the brutality of India's caste system, under which people suffered not only from exploitation and deprivation but also from isolation. Gandhi took the same approach to building socialism as he did to achieving economic autonomy, racial equality, and national liberation: through material practices. Thus, he wrote, "The first step in the practice of socialism is to learn to use your hands and feet. It is the only sure way to eradicate violence and exploitation from society."[49]

Toward the end of his life, King also came to believe that racial equality and the end of poverty required radical economic restructuring toward a form of democratic socialism. In August 1967, King's address to the Southern Christian Leadership Conference directly challenged capitalism. "Why are there 40 million poor people in America?" he asked. That question led to further questions about the ownership of the means of production and ultimately about the moral legitimacy of capitalism:

> When you begin to ask that question, you are raising questions about the economic system, about a broader distribution of wealth. When you ask that question, you begin to question the capitalistic economy. And I'm simply saying that more and more, we've got to begin to ask questions about the whole society. We are called upon to help the discouraged beggars in life's market place. But one day we must come to see that an edifice which produces beggars needs restructuring. . . . You see, my friends, when you deal with this, you begin to ask the question, "Who owns the oil?" You begin to ask the question, "Who owns the iron ore?"[50]

King and Gandhi shared a normative commitment not only to nonviolence and egalitarianism but also to significant economic restructuring. While the Anabaptist stream in Christian pacifism rarely engages in explicitly political critiques, the substantive content of Anabaptist ethics includes a commitment to democratic, egalitarian, and communitarian principles, especially mutual aid, which do not conflict with King's or Gandhi's values. In all these cases, the normative ethic associated with religious pacifism is not simply a set of strictures about the use of military violence but a comprehensive guide to practice and collective life.

4. Another theme common to the ethical theories I have been discussing is the refusal to make morality into a separate type or realm of decision-making. If ethics must be practiced, it is part of all spheres of life. The moral life, for both Christian and Gandhian pacifists, is an integrated whole. Christians are not citizens of two spheres, subject to competing loyalties, as Augustine and Luther proposed. Rather, they are citizens of the reign of God, full stop. This unites their loyalties, their ideas, and their actions and makes it impossible to separate ethical ways of thinking or acting from other aspects of one's life.

Weaver argues that what makes Anabaptists distinctive is not their theology but "the lived dimension of their faith."[51] The content that lived dimension is found in *imitatio Christi*, as the Mennonite *Confession of Faith* explains: "We witness to the nations by being that 'city on a hill' which demonstrates the way of Christ."[52] Christians can discern this way with the help of the Church, which can guide them to be in the world without belonging to the world. This "in but not of" can be achieved only within a community that imitates and embodies the reign of God. "We believe that the church is called to live now according to the model of the future reign of God," continues the *Confession of Faith*. "Thus, we are given a foretaste of the kingdom that God will one day establish in full. The church is to be a spiritual, social, and economic reality, demonstrating now the justice righteousness, love, and peace of the age to come."[53] Values like nonviolence are not limited to extreme situations like war but are woven into every part of personal and social life. Day in and day out, what a person does, how a community lives, is an ethic.

5. Perhaps most important, religious pacifists reject linear models of moral action in favor of a unity between means and ends. A linear view of the relationship between intentions and actions suggests that there is just one decision to be made, or perhaps a series of decisions, each made one at a time, by a single actor who can clearly predict the consequences of each action. The assumption that certain actions will lead inevitably to the expected consequences rests on a mechanical view of relationships between people, as Yoder writes: "If I turn the machine one way it will follow one course inevitably, if I push a different set of buttons the machine will clearly operate in another direction."[54] People (and other sentient beings) obviously are not as simple or predictable as this model assumes, and further, they never act in a social vacuum.

This linear model fails obviously when applied to complex situations in which many people are making decisions at the same time and acting at the same time, "changing by their actions the situation upon which the decisions of each agent will impinge."[55] War is clearly this kind of situation, one in which no individual actor can have full control or foresee what is actually going to happen; no one is omniscient or even in possession of full and reliable information.[56] This challenges core assumptions of just war theory, which presumes complete knowledge of all variables, predictable actors, and a straightforward link among intentions, actions, and consequences. The contrast with just war theory illuminates pacifism's comprehensive challenge not just to military violence but to conventional ways of thinking about morality. Because just war theory assumes a separation of means and ends, it permits the use of lethal violence to pursue political goals. The core of just war logic, that the end justifies the means, presumes that the cause and conduct of the war are independent of each other and can be evaluated and justified separately. According to this logic, it is possible to fight a just war immorally and, possibly, to fight an unjust war morally.

Pacifism sidesteps this logic by asserting that to justify a war "requires establishing antecedently that those means are permissible."[57] This does not simply invert the hierarchy of value so that means take priority over ends but rather reframes the relation between them so that ends and means cannot be separated, conceptually or in real life. Pacifists reject linearity and put in its place a complex, fluid vision of the unity—or "convertibility," as Gandhi put it—of means and ends. The unity of means and ends makes sense in a larger religious worldview, as Yoder frames it: "To say that 'the means are the ends in process of becoming' is a cosmological or an eschatological statement. It presupposes a *cosmos*—a world with some kind of discernible moral cause-effect coherence." In this world, suffering is redemptive, a view that both Yoder and King inherit from the Christian tradition.[58] Yoder quotes King's assertion that "there is something in the universe that unfolds for justice" and interprets this to mean that "In the final analysis, means and ends must cohere because the end is preexistent in the means, and, ultimately, destructive means cannot bring about constructive ends."[59]

This conviction that the universe "bends toward justice," as King also proclaimed, has a religious foundation. "The triumph of the right" is assured, Yoder explains, "because of the power of the resurrection and not because of any calculation of causes and effects, nor because of the inherently greater strength of the good guys. The relationship between the obedience of God's people and the triumph of God's cause is not a relationship of cause and effect but one of cross and resurrection."[60] This rejects both the instrumental rationality of consequentialism and the dismissal of consequences in Kantianism. Consequences matter, but only as part of an integral process in which means and ends cohere and even become each other. This echoes also the pragmatist idea of ends-in-view.

Because the separation between ends and means is necessary not only for just war theory but for many influential approaches to ethics, the normative, meta-ethical, and applied implications of pacifism and nonviolence go far beyond war. This is the larger significance of Yoder's assertion that "Actions proclaim. The medium and the message are inseparable. *What* God is doing is bringing into existence a new historic reality, a community constituted by the flowing together of two histories, one with the law and one without. *How* God is doing it is not indistinguishable from *what* God is doing, and *how the world can know* about it is one and the same thing."[61] The meta-ethical logic that describes God's actions also characterizes human practices. Even for secular pacifists, the medium and the message are inseparable, because what we are doing cannot be distinguished from how we do it. Morality in this view is "adverbial," to use the phrase Dewey applied to truth; it is a quality of human actions and not an essence that exists independently of them.

Conclusions

Because the core of religious pacifism is lived practice, it comes closer to a comprehensive practice-focused ethical theory than the other models I have explored. Pacifism is the "practical embodiment of a religious conversion experience," as Lisa Sowle Cahill puts it, as much or more a way of life than a theory.[62] While embodying their values in concrete practices, pacifists must avoid violent or coercive pressure as a method for pursuing desired goals. The means and the ends must cohere, not out of a desire for deontological consistency but because they are not essentially different things; they are convertible, in Gandhi's phrase, or as Dewey might point out, they are different stages in the same process. Practices are at the heart of this ethical theory, because they are the only means we have for pursuing ends or enacting values.

The convertibility of means and ends suggests, further, that moral goals are themselves practices. This is seen in the Anabaptist notion of the kingdom as social ethic, which asserts that a particular kind of practice, *imitatio Christi*, is both the goal and the way to achieve the goal. A similar logic shapes King's vision of the beloved community, which is not just a future goal to be constructed but also the way Christians are to live here and now.

The scope of pacifism as a moral theory is lost in conventional conceptions of it as an applied ethic, confined to thinking about war. Understood more broadly, it is not only relevant to real-life problems other than war but also, unlike most moral theories, actually "applied" in real life. In particular, we can consider the nonviolent movements for civil rights and national liberation in South Africa, India, and the United States led by Gandhi and King. These experiences show the application of nonviolent and pacifist principles in settings other than military violence. Another interesting practical example is the rise of intentional communities that strive to follow Gandhian principles by committing "to practice nonviolence in virtually all facets of life, from agriculture to constructing buildings to interpersonal communication," as Whitney Sanford explains.[63] A similar approach marks Catholic Worker communities, which, like the Gandhian groups, view nonviolence as an expansive ethos that shapes everyday practices such as interpersonal relationships, eating, and work, as well as positions on social and political issues. Food choices, in particular, can "demonstrate possibilities for living out sets of values" while also creating tensions, particularly around meat eating.[64]

We can see the broad scope of pacifism and nonviolence by looking at another common problem for applied ethics: environmental protection and sustainability. Mennonite theologians have proposed understanding violence against nature in terms of their tradition of "living without weapons," as Walter Klaasen writes.[65] Klaasen relates this to the specifically Anabaptist concept of *Gelassenheit*, or "letting go." In this view, "true nonresistance" consists in letting go of the illusion of complete control, including "the idea that we build the kingdom, that we must in our generation bring it to its completion."[66] While giving up the conceit that fulfillment of the reign of God is in our hands, Klaasen asserts that we should take the biblical visions of perfect peace and harmony literally: "We live in God's kingdom now; we are its citizens now. We ourselves participate in fulfilling the hope and the vision by seeing and hearing and doing like the citizens of God's kingdom now. So we do not hurt or destroy in God's holy mountain, the whole creation." Nonviolence here is a living guide to social relations not just with people but with nonhuman creatures, "because we share the same breath of life with them. . . . We are not private individuals; we are part of the whole."[67]

This glimpse into Anabaptist applied ethics provides a bridge into the next three chapters, which explore real-life problems in three important areas of applied ethics: law, medicine, and environmental protection. In all of these cases, I explore the ways a practice-based approach can contribute to better understanding of what is at stake as well as to constructive solutions.

7

The Lives That Matter

Racism, Free Speech, and Moral Dilemmas

The constitutional right of free expression is powerful medicine in a
society as diverse and populous as ours. It is designed and intended
to remove governmental restraints from the arena of public discussion, putting the decision as to what views shall be voiced largely
into the hands of each of us, in the hope that use of such freedom will
ultimately produce a more capable citizenry and more perfect polity
and in the belief that no other approach would comport with the
premise of individual dignity and choice upon which our political
system rests.

—US Supreme Court decision, *Cohen v. California* (1971)[1]

Introduction

Richard Spencer is a deliberately controversial white nationalist who believes
that white people and European culture are superior to other groups and that
ethnic diversity is a threatening and destructive aspect of contemporary US
society. In recent years, one of his main strategies for promoting his views
has been to rent venues at public universities, which are prohibited by the
First Amendment from refusing him access. Spencer's campus events have
prompted lawsuits and sometimes violent demonstrations. They also spark
important and difficult ethical debates, which center on the tensions between
hate speech and free speech but also raise broad questions about the values
and practices of universities themselves and also larger communities.

Many public and scholarly discussions about hate speech describe the
problem as a choice between freedom of expression and racial equality. This
frames the debate as a moral dilemma, in which it is necessary to choose
between two important and mutually exclusive values. Thus, the choice
often appears binary, as Richard Delgado and Jean Stefancic point out: "If

Works Righteousness. Anna L. Peterson, Oxford University Press (2021). © Oxford University Press.
DOI: 10.1093/oso/9780197532232.001.0001.

minorities demand a speech code, we can either oblige them or not. If the ACLU challenges a speech code, we can strike it down, or not."[2] Philosophical and legal analyses of this issue often assume this polarized model, focusing on the question of when, if ever, it is acceptable to limit free speech. The possible answers are usually either a choice between a Kantian absolutism, which would never limit freedom of expression, and a utilitarian calculation, which might find that Spencer's appearances take too high a toll on values of social solidarity, racial justice, and civil peace. Looking at this real-life ethical conflict through the lens of practice sheds new light on questions about the values that are at stake, the options available to people involved, the role of context and structures, and the impact of moral choices. This raises the question of whether the dilemma model is the only or best way to frame the moral issues raised by Spencer's campus tour and hate speech more generally. A focus on practice also directs our attention to the relations between substantive values and the procedural principles that protect them. The tensions between substance and form are especially evident in appeals to moral equivalence by various parties involved in the Spencer conflicts. Spencer's campus tour thus offers a way to reflect on the contributions of practice-based ethical theory to real-life problems.

Richard Spencer and the Campus Tour

> We must give up the false dreams of equality and democracy—not so that we could "wake up" to reality; reality is boring—but so that we can take up the new dreams of channeling our energies and labor towards the exploration of our universe, towards the fostering of a new people, who are healthier, stronger, more intelligent, more beautiful, more athletic.
>
> —Richard Spencer[3]

Spencer is "one of the country's most successful young white nationalist leaders—a suit-and-tie version of the white supremacists of old, a kind of professional racist in khakis," as the Southern Poverty Law Center describes him.[4] He gained notoriety for his celebration of the November 2016 presidential election: "Hail Trump, hail our people, hail victory!"[5] Such barely veiled invocations of Nazi Germany appear frequently in Spencer's "identitarian" discourse, which also draws on the language and imagery of American white supremacist organizations such as the Ku Klux Klan. At the core of this discourse is a conviction that white people are threatened and must organize to preserve their "heritage, identity, and future," as Spencer's organization, the National Policy Institute (NPI), puts it.[6] Spencer does not call himself a white nationalist, but his goal is precisely that: the creation of a white "ethno-state" to overcome what he sees as the destructive effects of immigration, integration, and multiculturalism.

Spencer and the NPI have been active for years, but following Donald Trump's election, they raised their profile with a series of events at or near public universities. One of these events was a May 2017 march in Charlottesville, Virginia, to protest the planned removal of a statue of Robert E. Lee. Spencer led participants in chants such as "What brings us together is that we are white, we are a people, we will not be replaced!"[7] The same themes took center stage when Spencer returned to Charlottesville in August for an event titled "Unite the Right." Carrying tiki torches and chanting "Jews will not replace us," a few dozen white-shirted protesters marched to the Lee statue, where they encountered antiracist protesters. Spencer supporter James Fields drove a car into a group of protesters, killing one protester, Heather Heyer, and injuring twenty-eight others. (Two police officers died in a helicopter crash during the event as well.)[8] Unrepentant, Spencer returned to Charlottesville the following month for another rally, where he proposed global links for American white nationalism: "Russia is our friend. The South will rise again. Woo-hoo!" At that third Charlottesville event, Spencer reiterated his intent "to come back again and again and again."[9]

Spencer does not go to colleges because student groups invite him. Rather, he rents lecture halls at public universities because they are subject to the First Amendment and may not deny speakers on the basis of content. This protection rests on the Supreme Court's 1977 ruling that Skokie, Illinois, had to give the American Nazi Party a permit to march and more broadly that public entities may not limit extremists' freedom of speech or assembly.[10] Further decisions regarding the "heckler's veto" prevent institutions from using expectations of protest to refuse controversial speakers or force them to pay extra security costs.[11] These rulings make public universities affordable sites where Spencer can generate media coverage. Spencer himself insists that he targets universities in order to talk with young whites about the failures of multiculturalism and liberalism. Constructive conversations, however, rarely feature in Spencer's campus visits, which are characterized by conflict and drama rather than reasoned discussion.

After the disastrous August 2017 rally in Charlottesville, Spencer announced a "campus tour," starting with my employer, the University of Florida in Gainesville. Spencer first applied to speak at UF in September, but the university denied his request, citing fears of violence. Spencer threatened to sue, as he has successfully done at several other institutions. After lengthy deliberations, university administrators decided they could not prevail and turned to damage limitation. They developed a massive security plan which involved closing roads, barricading large sections of campus, requiring UF identification to enter many buildings, and banning a long list of items, from purses to tiki torches. Three days before Spencer's October visit, Florida governor Rick Scott declared a state of emergency, in order to facilitate the transfer of additional law-enforcement resources to Gainesville. The most recent reports show that various public agencies spent nearly $800,000 on security and planning for the visit.[12]

After UF leaders ended their efforts to keep Spencer away, conflicts flared over the proper response to his visit. The administration's approach was to move Spencer off center stage. Officials created a website that embedded Spencer's talk within a larger narrative about free speech and the university's mission as "a place where people from all walks of life come to debate, agree or disagree and express themselves without fear of censorship or reprisal."[13] The site did not discuss Spencer himself, apart from statements by UF president Kent Fuchs describing him as a racist with values diametrically opposed to those of the university. This official treatment of Spencer acknowledges the conflict: on the one hand, a democratic society must permit freedom of expression to all, regardless of their ideas; on the other hand, some ideas, including white supremacy, conflict with the core democratic value of equality.

While UF officials had to work within strict legal parameters, local activists were not so fettered. Nor were they united on the best way to respond. Everyone in Gainesville seemed to disapprove of Spencer, but there was little agreement on anything else. Some residents argued that the most effective way to undermine Spencer was to deny him the publicity he so obviously craved. Toward that goal, a local brewery offered free beer in exchange for event tickets. The aim was to encourage people who opposed Spencer to claim tickets (which were to be made available for free from the UF box office a few days prior to the event), trade them for beer, and leave Spencer with an empty hall. Other bars made the same offer, and the scheme went viral. Spencer learned of the plan and demanded that the university permit his organization to distribute the tickets privately, again threatening to sue.

Another effort to deny publicity was "Ignore Richard Spencer Day," whose logic (as someone wrote on the event's Facebook page) was that "You ignore toddlers having a tantrum. You ignore bullies trying to get a rise out of you. To respond is to reinforce bad behavior."[14] From this perspective, the best way to undercut Spencer is to avoid demonstrations that would generate more attention. This approach followed the advice of the Southern Poverty Law Center, which asserts that counter-protests create "spectacles" that "only serve to embolden the speakers and allow them to portray themselves as victims." The best way to protest Spencer "is not to show up at all."[15] Undoubtedly, white supremacists deliberately seek conflict both to increase media coverage and to frame themselves as victims of "political correctness." Shortly after Spencer's UF talk, for example, the Daily Stormer, a neo-Nazi website, boasted, "Mission accomplished," insisting that everything had gone according to plan: "Libshits freak out, university spends $600,000, we get mad media coverage, we look great in front of a bunch of apes."[16] This involves a great deal of spin; less partisan coverage called the UF visit a failure for Spencer, given that his audience included mainly protesters, he failed to finish his talk, and three of his supporters were arrested for attempted murder.

Against the ignorers, some people in Gainesville insisted that everyone who opposed Spencer should attend demonstrations. Their reasons were partly moral—Spencer's ideas are so dangerous that they must not be left unchallenged—and partly practical, since large protests have drowned out Spencer and his supporters at other events. The main protest organizers, No Nazis at UF, initially hoped to prevent Spencer's visit and were frustrated by the decision to rent him a hall. Some argued that university officials should have faced the inevitable lawsuit; some even claimed that UF leaders tacitly accepted his ideology.[17] One visitor to the Ignore Richard Spencer Day Facebook group wrote that anyone who does not attend the rally is "enabling and supporting a Nazi." Another charged that the group should "rename your event Good German's [sic] Day."[18] These critics saw a conflict not between white nationalists and those who oppose them but rather between people who actively protest and those who fail to confront moral evil. These activists saw no significant political or moral difference between UF administrators (including its Jewish president) who bowed to legal inevitability, Spencer opponents who decided to avoid the event in order to minimize publicity, and Spencer supporters. As pragmatists would point out, such attacks on potential allies who differ on tactics further polarize already divided communities and make it difficult to build strong coalitions and constructive solutions.

Despite the infighting, those who took to the streets kept their messages mainly positive, reiterating the community's commitment to racial justice, inclusion, and love. In the days leading up to the event, slogans such as "Gators, not haters" and "Gators chomp Nazis" appeared everywhere, from official communications to a concrete lion on fraternity row. On the day of the talk, a small plane flying over the campus towed a banner that read: "Love conquers hate! Love will prevail!" As Spencer's speech began, a music professor climbed eleven flights of stairs in the bell tower on campus and played "Lift Every Voice and Sing," also known as the black national anthem.[19]

Inside the auditorium, the audience included a few dozen Spencer supporters, most from out of town. They were vastly outnumbered by protesters, whose shouts drowned out most of Spencer's talk. He grew visibly frustrated, calling the audience "animals" and "babies." Outside, a rally of several thousand people was watched by hundreds of police officers. The only violence on campus occurred just after the talk, when a protester punched a man wearing a shirt covered with swastikas. The swastika-wearing Spencer supporter was later engaged by another protester, a young African American man who asked him, "Why do you hate me?" (and eventually convinced him to accept a hug). The most serious incident occurred off-campus a few hours later, when three of Spencer's supporters, all from Texas, were arrested for attempted homicide. They had driven past a group of protesters waiting at a bus stop, and after an exchange of insults, one shot at the group. The bullet went wide, fortunately; had it injured or killed someone, reflections on the event would be very different.[20]

Racism, Free Speech, and Moral Dilemmas

Spencer's visit to Gainesville raises a number of issues for ethical theory and analysis, focusing on the question of how a democratic society should respond to hate speech such as Spencer's white nationalist rhetoric. Public discussions about this issue usually focus on the supposed conflict between "two fundamental democratic principles that operate at cross purposes: freedom of expression, which implies support for racist speech, and racial equality, which implies the opposite."[21] These opposing values cannot be combined or integrated; thus, this appears to be a classic moral dilemma, in which we must choose one value at the cost of the other. Following the dilemma model, the Spencer case seems to pose two familiar options. On the one hand, we could affirm a universal right to freedom of speech regardless of content. In support of this position, historical and political evidence shows that exceptions can lead down dangerous paths of intolerance, political closure, and oppression. Silencing one group can establish a precedent for more general restrictions on freedom of expression and other democratic practices. Free speech is foundational to democratic processes of collective deliberation and citizen action and is also demanded by "the premise of individual dignity and choice upon which our political system rests," as the decision in *Cohen v. California* quoted in the epigraph to this chapter underlines.

On the other hand, racial insults and assertions that some groups are inferior to whites and do not "belong" in the United States oppose the assumptions about universal human dignity that free speech is supposed to reflect. Derogatory language about specific races and social groups, more broadly, "remains one of the most pervasive channels through which discriminatory attitudes are imparted," as legal scholar Richard Delgado argues. "Such language injures the dignity and self-regard of the person to whom it is addressed, communicating the message that distinctions of race are distinctions of merit, dignity, status, and personhood. Not only does the listener learn and internalize the messages contained in racial insults, these messages color our society's institutions and are transmitted to succeeding generations."[22] Racist taunts and other forms of hate speech cause real harm, emotional and political. It is hard to argue that allowing Spencer to talk about a white ethno-state will generate the greatest possible good for the greatest possible number. His words and his supporters cause emotional harm to individual members of targeted groups, make the larger culture less welcoming of diversity, and create a real threat of physical violence. As Delgado argues, "Racism and racial stigmatization harm not only the victim and the perpetrator of individual racist acts but also society as a whole. Racism is a breach of the ideal of egalitarianism, that 'all men are created equal' and each person is an equal moral agent, an ideal that is a cornerstone of the American moral and legal system."[23]

Questions about whether, when, and how to limit hate speech, then, seem to pose a forced choice between two foundational values: freedom of speech and respect for all persons. The actual legal resolution to this dilemma, in the United States, is a "free speech extremism," rooted in a Kantian insistence on the universality of moral laws, which do not admit of exceptions. On this view, the First Amendment grants a near-absolute right to speak at public venues.[24] This legal position is more extreme than popular opinion. Surveys show that most Americans are firmly committed to freedom of expression as an essential principle of our democracy, but they are more willing to limit racist speech than other kinds of expression. The General Social Survey tracks support for free speech with the question "Who should be allowed to give a speech in your community?" Over the past forty years, support for free speech by "marginal" or "extreme" groups has risen steadily, with one notable exception: "There's no greater support for the racist."[25] In the latest survey, about 60 percent of respondents said a racist should be permitted, significantly fewer than those who would permit speeches by a communist or atheist.[26] Racial equality is thus one of the few values that regularly override Americans' generally high commitment to civil liberties.[27]

The conflict between free speech and racial justice is about different kinds of equality: a formal equality that grants all individuals the right to speak and a substantive commitment to antiracial equality. One solution is what legal philosophers call "free speech consequentialism," which balances individual liberty with concern for consequences by setting legal boundaries to freedom of expression.[28] This approach guides the laws regarding hate speech in many western European nations. In France, for example, it is illegal to incite racial hatred; to use racially defamatory, contemptuous, or offensive language; or to deny publicly the Nazi Holocaust.[29] The primary objective of such laws is not to end racism or make societies more tolerant but rather "to diminish the presence of visible hatred in society and thus benefit members of visible minorities by protecting the public commitment to their equal standing in society against public denigration."[30] Tellingly, they aim not at intentions but rather at actual practices.

Free speech consequentialism requires identifying and justifying any limitations imposed on freedom of expression. One way to proceed is to look for qualitative differences in the speech we may limit. This is the approach taken by legal scholar Mari Matsuda, who argues that "racist speech is best treated as sui generis," that is, in a category of its own. Certain explicit expressions of racism present "an idea so historically untenable, so dangerous, and so tied to perpetuation of violence and degradation of the very classes of human beings who are least equipped to respond that it is properly treated as outside the realm of protected discourse."[31] This is the logic behind European laws limiting hate speech, which rest on "the conviction that speech of this sort—defaming vulnerable minorities and inciting hatred against them—[is]

sui generis, and that it [has] to be regulated if any speech was."[32] Treating white supremacy as uniquely dangerous is an effort to remove it from the category of protected speech without surrendering a general commitment to freedom of expression. Even in pluralistic societies, according to this perspective, certain ideologies are outside the realm of legitimate options that may be expressed publicly.

Free speech consequentialism provides an alternative to the stark choice between unrestricted individual liberty and draconian limitations on freedom of expression. Proposals such as Matsuda's offer constructive attempts to delineate the grounds on which certain expressions can be limited. However, these arguments still take place, for the most part, within the parameters and terms of debate established by the dilemmatic framework. They are camps within a hegemonic model, not a rejection of it. Looking at this issue from other perspectives, including moral theories beyond Kantianism and utilitarianism, can reveal other issues at stake and other ways of resolving them.

Richard Spencer and Ethical Theory

When we view the conflict over hate speech from a practice-centered approach, it does not look like a debate about abstract principles. Instead, cases like Spencer's concern the actions and experiences of concrete people, all socially situated and politically interested. Exploring the case from this perspective thus presents new ways of thinking about the ethical issues raised by hate speech. This examination also brings to the fore important elements of a practice-based ethical theory, especially the relations between form and content.

1. Ideas do not exist in a vacuum. Hate speech and free speech are not abstractions, and we cannot untangle the ethical issues they raise by looking at concepts alone. Ideas—about speech and anything else—exist because people have them, and we need to look at who holds these ideas, at their descriptive and normative content, and at their "cash value," particularly their real-life impact on affected communities. In pursuing these questions, we can draw on the pragmatist emphasis on shared processes of inquiry and conversations oriented toward practical problem-solving. These processes and conversations must keep in mind the value of democratic processes not

only in political institutions but "as a deep, substantive way of life, an ethical ideal requiring internal moral development."[33] This development takes
place in various sites, not only in formal institutions or philosophy but in and
through everyday experiences that serve as sources of critical reflection.[34]
These experiences include habits, which, as virtue ethicists argue, make us
into particular kinds of people.

The best way to view Spencer's campus tour is not a one-time crisis for
particular communities but rather part of an ongoing struggle to reflect and
work collectively on difficult issues. In particular, pragmatists would reject
assertions that there is only one morally correct answer to a complex problem
and that we can know in advance what the answer is. Only by talking and
working together can we develop solutions that do justice to the values that
are important to different participants.

2. The conflicts about Spencer's talks are especially instructive for thinking
about the problem form and content, and especially the distinction between
thick and thin moral reasoning. The dominant framing of free speech is as a
conflict between the thin, procedural norm of free speech and the thick, substantive value of racial equality. This contrast explains why it seems logically
coherent to defend the rights of people whose views we abhor, as expressed in
the classic formulation of principled abstraction, often attributed to Voltaire
but actually written by Beatrice Evelyn Hall: "I disapprove of what you say,
but I will defend to the death your right to say it."[35] This value undergirds the
free speech extremism that dominates discussions about hate speech in the
United States.

This ethical stance is part of the Enlightenment project of developing abstract general principles that apply to any individual in any time, at any place,
and in any particular situation. Kant's first formulation of the categorical imperative exemplifies this formalist model, dictating the way to proceed but
not the content of the universal law: "Act only on that maxim whereby thou
canst at the same time will that it should become a universal law."[36] Other
famous ethical generalizations, from the principle of utility to John Rawls's
veil of ignorance, reflect the same conviction that in a secular, enlightened
world, moral authority cannot rest on anything in particular. On this view,
legitimate principles are defined precisely by their thinness or lack of content—which means, of course, that there is no place for material practices in
legitimate ethical theories.

This prioritizing of thinness has a number of problems, which can both
illuminate and be illuminated by the conflicts over Spencer. One of the first

issues we encounter is that thinness and thickness are not always clear-cut; it is not always obvious which principles are more universal, which more parochial and content-filled. For example, we might define the Spencer case as a clash between the thick worldview of white supremacists and universal principles of human dignity. We could ask whether racial justice is an abstract principle—a formal equality that is color-blind—or a substantive value that is rooted in specific histories, communities, and practices. In other words, even if we wanted to retain the hierarchy in which thin norms always take precedence over content-filled ones, we may have trouble distinguishing which is which.

In addition, not all normative content fits equally well into the "empty vessels" provided by formalistic ethical models. For example, the supposedly neutral principle of free speech which seems to support Spencer's campus tour is challenged by the content of his speech, which rejects precisely the democratic universality that free speech is supposed to protect. Spencer's rejection of "false dreams of equality and democracy" in favor of creating a particular "new people" prioritizes substantive claims—the identity of a particular community—over formal rules that apply equally to everyone and privilege no one.

Another issue is that in attempting to present neutral, universally applicable principles, thin ethical theories reify complex relationships and experiences into simple, static formulations. They reduce "the social to fixed forms," as Raymond Williams writes, making the mistake of "taking terms of analysis as terms of substance."[37] Foregrounding "terms of analysis" is a mistake, in Williams's view, because it provides a false impression of neutrality. In this model, terms of substance—the concrete experiences, loyalties, interests, and histories that define moral commitments—do not disappear entirely but are often masked or redefined into supposedly neutral terms. This is why, as Marx noted, "The ideas of the ruling class are in every epoch the ruling ideas."[38] The dominant classes present their ideas not as reflections or justifications of their place in the world but rather as universal principles, valid for everyone. The formulation of thin ethical theories requires this separation of ideas from the individuals and classes that hold them; the theories then appear neutral, rational, and universally applicable.[39] The substance lurking beneath such presentations was captured by Anatole France: "The law, in its majestic equality, forbids rich and poor alike to sleep under bridges, to beg in the streets, and to steal their bread."[40]

A 1988 letter to the *New York Times* used this quote to underline an argument regarding a Supreme Court decision that "an indigent North Dakota child who lived 16 miles from the nearest school has no constitutional right to take a school bus without paying a fee." In the ruling, Justice Sandra Day O'Connor recognized that "genuine hardships were endured" by the child and her family but affirmed that "we have previously rejected the suggestion that statutes having different effects on the wealthy and the poor should on that account alone be subjected to strict equal protection scrutiny."[41] This is a thin reading of equal protection under the law, according to which equal access to public goods does not require the ability to obtain or use those goods. A thick ethical theory would critique the supposed universality of this position, noting that equality means nothing if it remains an abstraction. The Supreme Court, in O'Connor's reading, affirms a thin legal equivalence that is not affected by extreme differences in substantive equality, any more than the legal equivalence enshrined in the First Amendment is affected by substantive differences in the content of speech.

Free speech extremism gives equal status to vastly different claims and positions. This can lead to arguments that differing positions have not only equal legal status but also moral equality. When used in debates about hate speech, claims about moral equivalence reveal the inadequacy of the line between thin and thick ethical positions. The procedural norm of legal equality masks substantive claims about what is valuable, who can speak, and so forth. A common example of this in debates about hate speech is a leveling of "left" and "right" sides in the debate. Trump evoked this equivalence when he asserted that there were "fine people" among both the white nationalists and protesters in Charlottesville. Trump's implicit claim was simplistic, emotive, and individualized: what matters is the character of the people on different sides of the conflicts over racism, Confederate monuments, and Richard Spencer. By emphasizing the supposedly similar personal traits of the different actors, Trump simultaneously depoliticized the conflict and legitimized the political ideology of Spencer and his allies. He used the two groups' equal right to free expression, in other words, to justify substantive normative and political claims.

The same sort of equivalence was proposed by Ted Yoho, the Republican representative of Florida's third district, which includes Gainesville. In response to Spencer's visit to UF, Yoho described Spencer's critics as "Antifa, a so-called 'anti-fascist' group comprised of radical Marxists and anarchists."[42] Trump equates white supremacists and their critics by finding "fine people" in both groups; Yoho equates them by dismissing all groups as equally ex-treme and suggesting that only "radicals" oppose white nationalism. Both strategies legitimize positions on the moral and political fringe by placing antiracist activists and white nationalists in the same category. They define the problem not as a substantive disagreement between white supremacy and racial equality but as a procedural conflict between two comparable sets of individuals. They do not look at history, normative content, structures of power, or material practices.

These positions conflate legal and moral status by implying that the legal equality between Spencer and his critics makes the content of their speech morally equal. This constitutes a philosophical category mistake, but it is also a calculated political strategy that legitimizes white nationalists while delegitimizing those who protest them. A similar calculus lies behind attacks on the antiracist movement Black Lives Matter (BLM) that use counter-slogans such as "all lives matter" and "blue lives matter" to paint BLM as narrowly partisan and uninterested in the common good. To counter "black lives matter" with "all lives matter" suggests that there is no need to single out African Americans, to assert the value of their lives apart from the ge-neric value of all human lives. These statements make sense only in a con-text in which, as one Trump supporter put it, racism is a "leftist lie."[43] These responses deliberately ignore precisely the themes that a practice-based ethic highlights: power structures, historical context, and the actions and lives of real people. Instead, they employ the apparently neutral language of moral equality to dismiss BLM's substantive criticisms of police killings of unarmed African Americans. They are the equivalent, as some critics pointed out, of asserting that "all cities matter" while much of Houston was underwater due to Hurricane Harvey.[44]The generic moral claim that "all lives matter" turns the discussion from one about police brutality and racial profiling, a concrete and politically charged issue, into vacuous assertions of the equality of all life, removed from the actual social context in which some lives face far greater threats than others. This echoes the bourgeois morality of *Recht*, which Marx described as the rights "of egoistic man, of man separated from other men and from the community."[45] Asserting equal rights in forms such as "all lives matter" reflects this isolation, not just of people from each other but of ethical theory from real lives and practices. It reflects the appeal to neu-trality that France mocked with his reminder that the law prohibits rich and poor alike from sleeping under bridges. France's point, of course, was that the law's practical impact—its cash value—is highly unequal. In cases like this, appeals to the "majestic" neutrality of the law are at best disingenuous, at worst thin veneers over class interest. Similarly, in light of the undeniable fact that nonwhite lives do not matter as much to those in power, claims that "all lives matter" express the interests of certain groups—racists, the police, government officials—who want to minimize criticisms of their use of power.

The same is true of the more specific claim that "blue lives matter." To counterpose BLM's critique of police brutality with this assertion implies that police lives are threatened in similar ways and that affirming black lives somehow disrespects law officers. (Trump has recently gone farther, calling Black Lives Matter a "symbol of hate."[46]) To assert that "blue lives matter" uses an apparently neutral, inoffensive claim to dismiss what should be the equally inoffensive claim that African American lives are valuable. However, both assertions are in fact thick and full of history, content, and power inequalities. Some people may sincerely believe that police officers are at mortal risk and that this is a substantive fact that matters to normative claims. (In fact, however, killings of on-duty officers have declined in recent years, while killings *by* police officers have increased.)[47] Or they may think that holding up black lives in particular is an unusually and unwarrantedly content-filled claim and that moral debates should only involve neutral statements that apply equally to all. The intentions behind the slogans matter less than the practices in this case. Talking about "blue lives" or "all lives" is a practice of diversion and dismissal that harms already traumatized and victimized communities, prevents the hard conversations and material changes that are necessary to address systemic racism, and empowers white supremacists who hide behind an apparently neutral formalism to promote racist content.[48]

These critiques of BLM, and similar ones of antiracist activists such as Kaepernick, parallel the arguments about Spencer. Removing the content and thus the practices from these discussions makes it hard to understand the varying positions. An empty formalism focused on a neutral right to free speech would insist that both Spencer and Kaepernick are protected equally by the First Amendment and that neither should be restricted. Many people, on both right and left, are less consistent. They believe that one or the other should be restricted, on the basis of substantive differences not just in the values they prioritize but in the way they understand values such as free speech, racial equality, democracy, and more. Thus, some people think that public universities that do not want Spencer must still permit him to speak but that the NFL should be able to prohibit Kaepernick and other athletes from kneeling during the national anthem. This position is often based on a particular version of American patriotism, which understands freedom of speech as categorically different from protest focused on national symbols. Others think the reverse, that Spencer's hate speech should be banned, but Kaepernick should be allowed to wage his silent protest. This position understands Kaepernick as a straightforward case of freedom of expression but sees Spencer as not just an expresser of ideas but an active threat to the physical and psychic well-being of "non-European" people.

In other words, many people believe that certain substantive values—antiracism or respect for national symbols—can override First Amendment rights; the problem is that they disagree about which values take precedence. Both political conservatives and liberals support the First Amendment, but they define it very differently based on who is speaking, what the speaker says, and which norms are threatened by the speech in question. Liberals seek to limit speech when it expresses racism, anti-Semitism, or misogyny, while conservatives want to ban speech they find obscene or unpatriotic. This variation is not hypocrisy but rather a difference in interpretation that rests on substantive experiences, interests, and worldviews. Rights, as Joseph Mello points out, "are not disembodied entities which are applied to all individuals equally—their legitimacy is tied to the perceived legitimacy of the rights bearer advancing the claim."[49] Even supposedly "empty" or universal categories, in other words, are in fact filled with content from the beginning. The same principles mean different things to different people, in part because experiences of oppression or privilege shape how people understand and apply formal norms such as freedom of expression. The formalism of mainstream ethical thought cannot make sense of and assess these disagreements, other than to label them as inconsistent.

In contrast, most religious and virtue ethics embrace thick content. Their moral claims are non-abstract, non-universal, and grounded in the experiences and histories of concrete communities. These substantive ethics tell us not just what procedures to follow but what specifically we should do, which goals to seek, which virtues to embody, which deity to worship. Religious traditions offer obvious examples of specific, content-filled claims: existence is suffering, there is no God but Allah, Jesus is the son of God. Not all substantive ethics are religious, but most are rooted in specific cultures and often to "communities of memory," which provide a "second language" of tradition and commitment, in contrast to the formal emphasis on individual liberty that dominates mainstream US culture, as Robert Bellah and colleagues argue in *Habits of the Heart*.[50] Because substantive values are tied to particular cultures and communities, they are neither universal nor objective and thus are generally not expressed in law in pluralistic, secular, and democratic societies.

In such societies, it is common to believe that "the possibility of an emancipatory politics" requires transcending local cultural practices, as John O'Neill writes.[51] Cosmopolitan, democratic politics, in this view, entails a minimal moral language, with "thin" standards, detached from particular histories, commitments, and biases of local communities. O'Neill proposes that there need not be an incompatibility between "a universal and objective ethical reflection of the kind many philosophers aim for and the project of uncovering interpretative depth in ethical life of the kind anthropology offers." The connection between universalism and local detail, he explains, lies in "the possibility of conversation across the thick ethical vocabularies.[52] Such conversations can be the basis for a cosmopolitanism that is rooted in particular cultures and concrete experiences. This cosmopolitanism has the additional benefit of uncovering the ultimately local origin of all forms of thought. As O'Neill writes, "the mere fact that our attitudes, understandings and perceptions have some local cultural origin cannot matter as such. They could have no other origin."[53]

O'Neill is writing about environmental ethics and the valuation of nature in different cultures, but his insights are applicable to other kinds of moral discourse and thought. His point is that we do not need a thin or minimalist language to talk about values across cultures: "Greater depth need not be associated with a shift away from claims that make wider contributions to global conversations about value." Ethical arguments rooted in the thick details of particular experiences and communities, in other words, can contribute to broadly relevant moral theories and claims. The key, O'Neill adds, is to distinguish "between a good that is specific to a local culture and a local cultural specification of a good."[54] Many goods have universal or near-universal relevance; the fact that these are embedded in particular communities and described in locally specific terms does not mean that the values themselves are not important in wider contexts or that the local expressions cannot participate in and contribute to larger conversations about ethics. This can illuminate the arguments about free speech, hate speech, and racism. Moral critiques of hate speech, for example, may be rooted in the experiences of particular communities that have suffered concrete harms at the hands of racist individuals and institutions. Their perspective is no less valid, and no less relevant to cosmopolitan conversations, than the views of communities that have not suffered from systematic discrimination and thus approach hate speech in more abstract or formalistic ways.

This is a helpful context for thinking about the tensions between formal protections and substantive claims that are central to political and social struggles over hate speech. The guarantee of freedom of expression makes possible the public presence of racist ideologies, while the substantive consensus against these ideas ensures that these ideologies always meet with resistance. The arguments about Spencer in Gainesville, at every level from university administrators to community activists, were grounded not in rejections of free speech or racial equality but rather in negotiations about how to understand and embrace both and how to do so in relation to local culture and identity. Thus, UF's official response emphasized the university's distinctive identity, on the one hand, as a long-standing proponent of freedom of speech and, on the other hand, as "Gators, not haters." The active resistance to Spencer also took a local tone, as protesters shouted chants heard at UF sports events: "Orange, Blue!" and "Let's go, Gators, let's go!" These expressions, which infuriated Spencer, are clever and powerful ways to root a principled moral stance in content-filled identities and relationships. They point, further, to the possibility of connecting rather than divorcing form and substance in ethical theory.

3. Trying to clarify the moral conflicts raised by Spencer also underlines the social character of both human nature and ethical reflection. The dilemma model falsely suggests that individuals have the power to resolve ethical problems on their own. However, real ethical challenges involve multiple people and usually multiple communities, and it is impossible to understand, let alone resolve, the moral issues without learning from the interests and perspectives of different stakeholders. Further, ethical issues are always situated within particular historical and structural conditions, which shape the situation and the options for improvement. People trying to resolve real problems, in sum, must take into account a host of factors, many of them outside the control of any single individual. For example, and as Marx would emphasize, there are always material forces and interests involved in any moral conflict, even though these are often masked by abstract and idealist discussions. From a Marxist perspective, the only way to deal with the division and hate fomented by white nationalists like Spencer is to identify and alter the material factors that contribute to it. In the case of Spencer, we might ask who benefits from white supremacy, why certain people favor it, and how

economic and political structures are involved in its expansion—or might help to prevent it from spreading.

4. The Spencer case shows that productive reflection and action are impossible if we isolate ethical issues from other parts of life. Spencer's desire to express his controversial opinions at college campuses and his ability to do so are linked to a host of social, political, cultural, and economic factors. He does not speak in a vacuum, and we cannot think about the meaning of his speech in a vacuum. This underlines the problem of viewing a case like this as a parallel to hypothetical moral dilemmas. The frameworks that philosophers use to analyze dilemmas deliberately exclude context and empirical information; Kantians and utilitarians alike focus on "either-or" questions that must be decided in the abstract, without knowing gritty details. In a real-life case such as Spencer's visit to Gainesville, however, we need to think about moral questions and options in conjunction with thick details, such as the concrete effects of racism on the lives of real people and the past actions of white nationalists who attend Spencer's events. This makes it possible to consider Spencer's speech as a set of practices, embedded in larger structures and linked to the practices of other people.

Another helpful perspective comes from virtue ethics, with its focus on the necessity of an ongoing cultivation of character, rather than cut-and-dried single decisions. For virtue theorists, the ways people address racism in general, and Spencer in particular, are part of an integrated pursuit of moral good. Responses to such problems are, further, intertwined with other aspects of people's lives, since the development of character cannot be isolated from social and political factors. As Alasdair MacIntyre puts it, "Every action is the bearer and expression of more or less theory-laden beliefs and concepts; every piece of theorizing and every expression of belief is a political and moral action."[55] This might help us sort out the conflicts about different ways to express moral and political opinions, not just by Spencer but also by Colin Kaepernick and other athlete activists, among others who have been involved in recent controversies about free speech.

5. Like the relations between form and substance, the links between intentions, actions, and consequences are central to debates over hate speech. A speech act is not just the simple expression of an individual's ideas but a practice that both shapes and is shaped by other practices. Spencer may believe he is expressing ideas that he uniquely created, but he can think and speak them only because of historical, cultural, and material practices that support them. And he may intend only to express his sincere beliefs, without meaning to inflict emotional harm or incite violence. However, such harms are not just possible but likely. Further, they occur not only in obvious incidents, as in the immediate aftermath of a rally, but also in subtle and pervasive ways that strengthen racist structures and cultures and make future hate speech more likely. Attitudes are not simply "applied" in actions and structures, but rather are made possible and shaped by them. This is not a mysterious process, but a practical, "sensuous" one, as Marx would say. Racist statements both express a belief that some people do not deserve respectful, compassionate treatment and actively contribute to a world in which people are not treated that way.

Conclusions

All the players in the Richard Spencer drama affirmed the principle of free speech—including Spencer, the protesters, the ignorers, the university administration, and even Representative Yoho. What differentiated the groups and created conflicts was their varying understandings of the relations between free speech and other values. These understandings are rooted, in turn, in different practical experiences and contexts. In this situation, as in many other moral conflicts, we face not clear-cut choices that take place in a vacuum but instead messy entanglements of real people with disparate commitments and social locations. The actors often perceive not a forced choice between different principles but rather a clash between different understandings of the same principle. Instead of a single dilemmatic choice between two abstract ideals, the Spencer controversy involves multiple conflicts and divisions, unfolding not between abstract principles but rather between different groups of people. Even if we focus only on free speech and racial equality, the conflict was not between these principles in the abstract but between different ways of interpreting and prioritizing them in real life.

This helps us think about means and ends. Spencer's public speeches and rallies, which are his main means of pursuing his goals, express and also construct particular identities, his own as a "dissident intellectual" and that of his followers as disenfranchised victims fighting against a multiculturalist mainstream. The importance of his talks as practices is evident in the fact that many of the people who attend his talks do not live where he is speaking and travel significant distances—not so much for his lectures, which vary little in content, but for the experience of being with people who share their marginal views and engaging in collective practices such as torchlit marches, chants, and occasional brawls. The events are means that embody the ends that they pursue: white solidarity, the free expression of racist attitudes, and the intimidation of non-Europeans.

On the other hand, the people protesting Spencer, much like BLM and NFL protesters, also use practices to embody their goals of racial equality, black pride, and cultural transformation. The practices themselves—experiences of solidarity and defiance—can affect protesters' convictions about the rightness of their values and goals, about the moral significance of their opponents, or about the links between intentions and actions. An event like the killing of Heather Heyer, the protester run over by a Spencer supporter in Charlottesville, is especially powerful, revealing what the costs can be. As pragmatists would point out, ends may change as a result of such practices, and a means can become an end. For example, when protest becomes dangerous, just showing up takes on greater resonance. This has been true in historical struggles over civil rights, national liberation, women's suffrage, protection of native lands, and more.

Practice turns our attention to the people targeted by white nationalists: African Americans, Latinos, immigrants, Muslims, Jews, women, LGBTQ communities, and more. For them, the conflict is not an abstract choice between two competing values but rather a concrete challenge to the value of their lives. BLM makes this evident, beginning with the name: it is about lives. Life is nothing but practices, as Marx affirmed again and again: "As individuals express their life, so they are."[56] There is no empty essence of universal humanism that can be extracted from the substantive experiences and identities of actual people. To assert that these lives matter is a normative claim that makes sense only in a content-filled and practice-focused ethical theory. Such an approach is also necessary to understand the ethical meaning inherent in the practices associated with Spencer's visit, including not just engagement with ideas about free speech and race but also experiences of arguing about Spencer, of protesting, and of confronting the practices of white supremacy: the killing, deportations, beatings, and everyday degradations. Framing moral conflict as a dilemmatic choice between abstract goods leaves no room for any of these experiences.

Attention to practices fleshes out the substance of thick moral claims, undermines claims to neutrality and absence of content, and challenges the supposedly clear division between thick and thin ways of talking about ethics. If, as I contend, we cannot think about moral conflicts without attention to practices, then the case of Spencer suggests that when we do take practices seriously, it becomes impossible to think about ethics in neutral, abstract ways. There are always real people involved and real lives at stake, and their practices inevitably enter into the articulation of all moral claims.

8

Euthanasia, Human and Other

In a social and cultural context which makes it more difficult to
face and accept suffering, the temptation becomes all the greater
to resolve the problem of suffering by eliminating it at the root, by
hastening death so that it occurs at the moment considered most
suitable.

—John Paul II, The Gospel of Life[1]

Introduction

The lives that matter are not always human, as an op-ed in my local news-
paper a few years ago made clear. The writer asked, "Why do we expect
loved ones to endure lingering, miserable deaths while we [ensure] that our
pets . . . die as free from pain as possible?"[2] This question implies a comparison between human and nonhuman euthanasia that is rarely addressed
in academia or other public settings.[3] However, it is a fairly common theme
in everyday discussions about ending the lives of pets, where the taken-for-
granted option of humane euthanasia stands in stark contrast to the heated
arguments around human euthanasia and physician-assisted suicide (PAS).
The question underlying these debates is, as bioethicist Jessica Pierce puts it,
"Why is it that we have such a revulsion against euthanasia for human beings,
yet when it comes to animals this good death comes to feel almost obligatory?
If it is an act of such compassion, shouldn't we be more willing to provide this
assistance for our beloved human companions as well?"[4] Suggestions that
we are not as compassionate with humans as with pets imply that the rules
against assisted suicide prevent us from doing the right thing by our own
species. With nonhuman animals, we are morally and legally permitted to
weigh costs and benefits, because their lives do not have absolute value. We
can be utilitarians in regard to our animal companions, and thus, we need
not prolong lives that are dominated by negative experiences and feelings.[5]
This is perhaps the only time when not being human gives an individual an

Works Righteousness. Anna L. Peterson, Oxford University Press (2021). © Oxford University Press.
DOI: 10.1093/oso/9780197532232.001.0001.

advantage, expressed in familiar comments such as "I just wish we could be so compassionate with people."[6]

These sentiments include several interesting implicit ethical claims about human euthanasia, one of the most important and contentious issues in medical ethics. The comparisons to animal euthanasia assume that euthanasia is compassionate, that it is the right thing to do with dying pets, and that the laws regarding humans are sometimes cruelly restrictive. Less obvious, but perhaps just as important, is the implication that it is possible to compare the meaning of euthanasia for different species—but only obliquely. This comparison is risky because of the taboo against comparing the value of human and animal lives. It is valuable, however, because it helps us clarify what is at stake, especially the role of relationships and social structures in shaping the value of life.

At the heart of discussions about euthanasia is a particular kind of practice: deliberate killing. The question here, as in debates about the morality of war, is whether it can ever be morally justified to take a life. If so, what criteria or conditions can justify the act of killing? Can good intentions justify an otherwise impermissible act? How do material structures shape moral choices? Looking at euthanasia through the lens of practice helps us explore these questions and consider values, angles, and options that may not come to the surface otherwise.

In order to think through these problems, I begin with common definitions and central issues in scholarly treatments of the ethics of human euthanasia and PAS. I then look at these discussions in relation to the euthanasia of non-human animals, a comparison that clarifies key issues at stake in regard to human euthanasia, including the place of relationships and context in valuing different lives and the role of intentions in justifying deliberate killing.

Human Euthanasia and Assisted Suicide

Definitions

The English word *euthanasia* combines two Greek words—*eu* and *thanatos*—to describe a "good death." Euthanasia is usually defined as a painless death caused by another. However, lack of pain is not the only or the most important feature. If only the manner of death were at stake, as Philippa Foot points out, then "a murderer, careful to drug his victim, could claim that his act was an act of euthanasia. We find this ridiculous because we take it for granted that in euthanasia it is death itself, not just the manner of death, that must be kind to the one who dies."[7] A good death must be one that is intended for the patient's own good, rather than the benefit or convenience of others. The official definition of the American Medical Association (AMA) echoes this point, focusing on the person's physical suffering as what would make the fact of death good: "Euthanasia is the administration of a lethal agent by another person to a patient for the purpose of relieving the patient's intolerable and incurable suffering."[8] The conditions for a truly good death highlight both intentions and practices. The killing intends the alleviation of suffering, and it is achieved in a painless or humane way.

In all discussions of the morality of euthanasia, intentions are central. Euthanasia is defined by the desire of both patient and physician to end suffering. However, there are variations in how patients' intentions are known and their relations to the intentions of others. Some of these nuances are expressed in the distinctions among voluntary, non-voluntary, and involuntary euthanasia. Voluntary euthanasia occurs when a person has clearly indicated a wish to die, either in the moment or in a living will. Non-voluntary euthanasia describes circumstances when a person cannot express an opinion, as in cases of irreversible coma, and has left no advance directive. Involuntary euthanasia, when death is against the patient's wishes, appears to be a contradiction in terms, since, as Peter Singer points out, euthanasia by definition must be a good death, and "it is hard to see how killing a person who wants to go on living can be a good death."[9] However, some philosophers imagine specific circumstances in which this might be morally justified. For example, if soldiers cannot carry a gravely wounded comrade to safety, it may be kinder to kill him with a single gunshot rather than leave him to die slowly or be tortured by enemies. Involuntary euthanasia may also include the use of increasing doses of morphine to control pain, which eventually causes death.[10]

While intentions distinguish voluntary from non-voluntary euthanasia, practices generate another set of distinctions. This is the difference between active killing, usually by lethal injection, and passive euthanasia (or "letting die"), which is usually accomplished by the withdrawal of treatment or sustenance needed to maintain life. There are several kinds of passive euthanasia, all of which entail withholding life-saving measures. When the person has issued clear instructions, voluntary passive euthanasia is widely accepted, especially when there is a clear record of the patient's desire to avoid extraordinary measures. Non-voluntary passive euthanasia occurs when a person requires external resources such as a respirator or feeding tube to stay alive, is not able to communicate her wishes clearly, and has not completed an advance directive. This creates a difficult but not uncommon moral, emotional, and legal dilemma. A number of prominent court cases have addressed this issue, especially when relatives disagree about whether a person would have wanted to be kept alive in this condition. Given the widespread acceptance of voluntary passive euthanasia, the main issue here is discerning the patient's true will.

The distinction between letting die and killing foregrounds practice, since it hinges on the difference between actively assisting someone to die and failing to take extraordinary measures to save them. This line is very important to ethicists, policymakers, and physicians who see a qualitative difference between actively killing and causing death by withholding treatment. This assumption guides the AMA, which opposes active euthanasia because it is "fundamentally incompatible with the physician's role as healer, would be difficult or impossible to control, and would pose serious societal risks."[11] On the other hand, the AMA directs physicians to "respect the decision to forego life-sustaining treatment of a patient who possesses decision-making capacity."[12]

Many religious groups, similarly, accept the withholding or withdrawal of extraordinary measures to sustain life while opposing active euthanasia. This is consistent with a widespread religious opposition to suicide, based on the claim that human life is sacred and only God has power over life and death. In both the Jewish and Catholic traditions, as Aaron Mackler explains, "killing oneself or others violates God's plan. . . . Our lives ultimately belong not to us but to God."[13] This is the position of the Roman Catholic Church; most mainline, evangelical, and Anabaptist Protestants; most Jewish and Muslim authorities; and newer groups such as the Seventh-Day Adventists and Mormons.[14]

While many philosophers, theologians, and medical professionals share a consensus in favor of voluntary passive euthanasia, active euthanasia remains highly controversial. Material practices are at the heart of these debates. In voluntary active euthanasia, "the physician performs an act that is specifically intended to take the patient's life, through, for example, lethal injection."[15] This remains controversial with physicians, courts, and many religious groups. Closely related to voluntary active euthanasia is PAS, in which "medical help is provided to enable a patient to perform an act that is specifically intended to take his or her own life, for example, overdosing on pills as prescribed by the physician for that purpose."[16] In PAS, the patient performs the action that ends life, and the physician helps by providing drugs, setting up the method of delivery, and so forth, but does not do the deed, as in active euthanasia.

Some philosophers and a few liberal religious traditions, such as the United Church of Christ and the Unitarian Universalists, officially support the legalization of PAS. Their position rests mainly on respect for patient autonomy. Some philosophers argue that once the patient has decided to seek death, the most humane means should be employed, which does not always favor "passive" means. "Rightness and wrongness depend exclusively on the merit of the justification underlying the action, not on the type of action it is," as Tom Beauchamp puts it. "A judgment that an act of either killing or letting-die is justified or unjustified therefore entails that something else be known about the act besides its being an instance of killing or an instance of letting die."[17] For example, active euthanasia may be justified in the case of a suffering, terminally ill person who requests a lethal injection, while passive euthanasia may be clearly immoral in cases such as a refusal to perform a surgery that will cure an otherwise healthy person. James Rachels also argues that the distinction between passive and active euthanasia should not be the main consideration: "Once the initial decision not to prolong [a suffering person's] agony has been made, active euthanasia is actually preferable to passive euthanasia, rather than the reverse. To say otherwise is to endorse the option that leads to more suffering, not less."[18] Letting a person die slowly from starvation or dehydration, for example, may be far less kind than actively providing an overdose of morphine. This recalls the comparison to pet euthanasia, in which "letting die" is seen as more painful and cruel than active euthanasia.

Moral Arguments

Several themes dominate arguments about euthanasia and assisted suicide: quality of life, individual autonomy, the value of human life, and the problem of the slippery slope. Quality of life refers to the question of whether a life that is dominated by physical suffering, with no hope of relief, is worth living. Those who support legalized euthanasia or assisted suicide often assert that some things are worse than death, including a lingering, painful process of dying. The principle of autonomy arises in relation to the claim that persons should be able to make decisions about whether to continue a life in conditions they find unbearable. This opposes the common religious argument that only God has the right to take life. Apart from this religious objection, Foot contends, "there seems to be no case to be made out for an infringement of rights if a man who wishes to die is allowed to die or even killed."[19] The right to take one's own life when it is no longer bearable is the flip side of the right to continue living even if one's life is inconvenient or burdensome to others. Both are expressions of autonomy, or the patient's capacity to do what she wants and intends to do—to enact certain practices, in other words.

While the desires of the patient are foremost, the attitudes of physicians and medical professionals are also important. It is unproblematic to assert that medical personnel have a moral duty to respect patients' wishes and that they should intend to relieve suffering. The problem arises when relieving pain or following the patient's wishes causes death. Here the doctrine of double effect (DDE) is often invoked. I discussed DDE earlier in relation to the ethics of war and peace, its first philosophical context. In reflections on euthanasia and assisted suicide, philosophers and theologians invoke DDE to distinguish between the direct, morally permissible effect of reducing pain, on the one hand, and the indirect, morally prohibited consequence of ending life, on the other. Bioethicists or physicians might employ DDE to argue that increasing doses of morphine are being used primarily to control a patient's pain. Even if the dose eventually becomes high enough to kill the patient, the primary intention was to relieve pain. Double effect permits the same action—an overdose of sedative—to be first-degree murder, criminally negligible accident, or justifiable euthanasia, depending on the intentions of the person who administers it.

This seems to reaffirm that it really is the thought that counts in determining when a life is good or evil to a person. However, the distinction between active and passive euthanasia also foregrounds practice, because it concerns the actions or inaction of medical professionals. In both killing and letting die, the physician's intentions are the same, to ease suffering and respect the patient's wishes, which makes euthanasia potentially justifiable. The debate hinges on the moral difference between acting and not acting. However, this line is not always clear. As Singer notes, it requires effort to turn off a ventilator or withdraw a feeding tube, and this may count as a positive action.[20] The distinction between acting and not acting thus does not always describe what happens actually, and it does not change the consequences of the decision. The main benefits of this distinction may be to reduce guilt felt by the physician, even though the prolonged dying caused by passive euthanasia can be worse for patients and their loved ones.

While autonomy is most often involved in arguments favoring PAS, those against it frequently cite the value of human life, which is so sacred or absolute, in their view, that it is never acceptable to take an innocent human life. Their arguments may rest on religious grounds: because God gives life, only God should be able to decide when life ends. Even when the religious language is not explicit, the underlying assumption is that human life has a unique value which may be violated only under the most extreme and exceptional conditions. The human person is not "his own rule and measure," as Pope John Paul II put it.[21] According to this perspective, medical professionals should relieve pain but not actively hasten death.

Opponents of PAS also cite the social risk of permitting physicians to kill their patients. If people are permitted to choose death and physicians are permitted to assist them, some argue, we face dire consequences, including pressure on sick people to end their lives prematurely and, in the worst case, instances of euthanasia against people's will. In other words, legalizing euthanasia or PAS will launch us on a slippery slope toward genocide. This argument is sometimes supported by attention to the social inequities that are part of the larger context in which life-and-death decisions are made. Some critics of euthanasia note "the harsh facts of deprivation and inequalities of power" that shape both individual decisions and policies about euthanasia. As Michael Banner notes, euthanasia involves "formal or informal metrics of worth and value," which often favor the privileged and may create pressure on people who are poor, disabled, or chronically ill but not necessarily eager to die.[22] This echoes Roman Catholic and Mennonite arguments for supporting sick, depressed, and dying patients, so that they do not see early death as the best option.[23]

Practices and People

One way to think through some of the issues raised by euthanasia and PAS is to look at the experiences, attitudes, and actions of the people involved in and affected by the issues. Those most obviously involved are the patients and the medical professionals treating them, but many others may be affected, including friends and relatives of the patient, religious advisers, hospital administrators, and other patients whose fate may be shaped by previous decisions. Although this empirical evidence rarely enters into philosophical discussions, a number of studies, from different countries, document the attitudes of medical professionals about euthanasia and assisted suicide. Many find that nurses favor the legalization of euthanasia much more strongly than physicians do. French research found a striking difference in opinions, noting much greater support by nurses. The authors explain the gap by noting that despite the generally greater attention given to physicians' attitudes and practices, "in most cultural contexts, nurses are the cornerstone of end-of-life care, as they play a key role in using a patient-centred approach to understand the wishes of patients and their families and to act on this understanding as advocates for patients and families in the decision-making process." Nurses are thus more aware of the feelings of patients and families and "are frequently the first care givers to receive a patient's request for euthanasia."[24] The authors also cite research showing that nurses may assist with patient-requested euthanasia more frequently than physicians, for example, by not interfering with the patient's plan to hasten death.

The French findings are echoed by research conducted in other regions. A US study found, for example, that "By comparison with physicians, nurses showed more desire for changes in social customs to allow euthanasia."[25] The usual explanation is that because nurses are more involved in day-to-day care, they know the patient's wishes more fully and are witnesses to the suffering of both patients and their loved ones and to physicians' failure, in some cases, to abide by patients' wishes.[26] Similar themes arose in research on the attitudes of Belgian nurses, one of whom explained:

> We are on quite intimate terms with patients, both physically and psychologically. Often, it is during physical care that intimate issues come up; thus, we get to know a lot of minute details about our patients. We are with them much longer [than other healthcare givers], so that these little things come to our attention. Our view is different from that of the physicians. We see problems differently. Difficulty arises sometimes because we are too involved; we can't distance ourselves [from our patients]. The benefit is that we are able to express how difficult it really is for the patient with a [euthanasia] request. Sometimes the physician isn't in touch enough [with the patient] to really express the patient's problem.[27]

This is an implicitly moral reflection, even though nurses often feel they cannot "put into words their ethical thinking."[28] When pressed, the nurses in the study cited principles such as respect for autonomy and quality of life as reasons they supported euthanasia. However, they also found these principles too abstract and not "true guides to the individual character of each patient's complex situation." Research that tries to label nurses' attitudes in such situations may be "imposing static, oversimplified ethical frameworks that may not have a correlation to nurses' actual clinical experiences."[29] This suggests that abstract approaches omit the factors that matter in real cases—personal history, social context, religious and cultural values—and research that uses the dilemmatic model "may shed only limited light on moral views about the difficult dilemmas faced in actual clinical contexts," in the words of an Iranian study of attitudes toward euthanasia.[30]

While the everyday experiences of medical professionals rarely enter into theoretical approaches to these decisions, at least their attitudes have received some scholarly attention. There is much less research on attitudes of those most affected: chronically or terminally ill patients and those close to them. One such study, conducted in the United Kingdom, concluded that many seriously ill people would prefer that the law be changed to allow assisted suicide or voluntary euthanasia. In particular, patients who had seen others die were more likely to favor the legalization of euthanasia or PAS. They believed that these options would reduce both actual pain and anticipated pain, as well as patients' fears of loss of control, cognitive impairment, and burdening others. Some of the patients considered suicide, but they expressed preference for medical help so their deaths could be painless, certain, and socially supported.[31]

This model of death is also easier for the patient's loved ones. Research in the Netherlands shows that the friends and relatives of people who died by euthanasia "coped better with respect to grief symptoms and post-traumatic stress reactions than the bereaved of comparable cancer patients who died a natural death."[32] Euthanasia and PAS, in other words, appear to be significantly easier on relatives, because of the ability to "say goodbye" and also the generally high degree of communication and clarity in the dying process. Their findings, the authors write, "should not be interpreted as a plea for euthanasia, but as a plea for the same level of care and openness in all patients who are terminally ill."[33] The medical and social setting of euthanasia, in other words, entails practices that make the experience of death less traumatic for all concerned. The study authors point to the possibility that many of these practices can be used in other types of death in order to increase communication, address pain effectively, and provide emotional and logistical support for both patients and their loved ones. The practice of medical euthanasia, in this sense, can lead to wider changes in attitudes about death and ultimately to the practical treatment of death in other medical settings.

Nonhuman Euthanasia

When we turn to the euthanasia of nonhuman animals, in one sense the definition remains the same: a painless death, caused by another, for the sake of the dying individual. However, ethical discussions of euthanasia for other animals, and specifically companion species such as cats and dogs, take a very different form from those regarding humans. This is in part because the categories that dominate discussions regarding humans—voluntary and involuntary, active and passive—are not relevant, at least not in the same way. There are two very different categories of euthanasia for companion animals: the mercy killings of gravely ill and dying pets, on the one hand, and the pragmatic killings of healthy animals in shelters, on the other. The former parallels human euthanasia in important ways. The other category of animal euthanasia, however, describes killings that bear no resemblance to human euthanasia. For animals, euthanasia has become a blanket term, "synonymous with any death effected by a veterinarian," in any setting and for any reason, rather than the narrowly defined "good death" of human euthanasia.[34]

This disjuncture stems from the significance of species and how it shapes the value of life and the circumstances under which we think it can be justifiably ended. It is uncommon, and difficult, to bring together conversations about the morality of killing people and those about nonhuman euthanasia (or any kind of animal death). The discussions usually proceed separately, with only implicit and fleeting comparisons. I want to probe more deeply, however, to ask what happens when we make the comparison explicit. This can illuminate different ways to think not just about species and the value of human life but also about relationships, practices of killing, and the connections between individual choices and material structures.

The kind of nonhuman euthanasia that parallels human euthanasia and PAS is the mercy killing of pets that are gravely ill and have no good chance of recovery. This sort of euthanasia is widely accepted and often seen as morally necessary by pet owners and veterinarians. An interesting tension provides the context for these decisions. On the one hand, most people consider animal lives disposable in a way that human lives are not, which means that decisions to kill animals are not morally problematic in the same way. It is taken for granted that we can decide what to do with their lives, including when to end them. On the other hand, some animals' relationships with people turn them into honorary persons, endowing their lives and deaths with great value for those who love them.[35] The close relationship between people and pets transforms the decision about ending life from the utilitarian model that guides most animal killings into a case where the best interests of the patient are foremost.

As I mentioned earlier, in pet euthanasia, the difference between killing and letting die has a different moral resonance from that in human euthanasia. "No one buys this distinction when deciding the fate of non-human animals," Hugh LaFollette points out. "We think it is not just permissible to euthanize an animal in pain; we think it would be grossly inhumane to allow an animal to die slowly and painfully, to let nature take its course." LaFollette uses this example to criticize the use of the distinction between doing and allowing as an argument against PAS. This argument would be valid, he claims, "only if it applies merely to humans. That would be very odd. Most people believe that we should treat humans *better* than we treat non-human animals. Yet here, it seems, we are morally permitted to treat dying animals, but not dying humans, humanely."[36] This is true, ironically, because we value nonhuman lives less than human ones, a moral hierarchy that usually works to the disadvantage of animals. In the case of mercy killing, however, this hierarchy frees decisions about when to end a nonhuman life from the torturous debates that characterize discussions of human euthanasia and often lead to lingering processes of "letting die" that are painful for both patients and their loved ones.

Discussions about euthanasia for pets center not on whether euthanasia is acceptable but rather on the timing. This raises many of the same factors that arise in regard to humans: Are they suffering physical pain that cannot be reliably controlled? Do they have little or no chance of recovery? Is their quality of life such that the bad days clearly outweigh the good? If the answers to these questions are affirmative, then most veterinarians, pet guardians (owners), and animal advocates accept painless killing as the right thing to do. People do not want to lose their pets prematurely, but they also fear waiting too long and causing unnecessary suffering. Decisions often rest on communication from the animal that life is no longer pleasurable, as evidenced by loss of appetite, inability to enjoy favorite activities, and so forth. There is a broad consensus that it is more compassionate not to keep an animal alive in such conditions. It is common, in fact, for people to assert that it would be selfish to do so—they would be doing it for themselves, against the best interests of the animal.

The flip side of this is the possibility of choosing euthanasia too easily, at the first sign of serious illness or age-related debility. As Anne Fawcett points out, many nonhuman animals, like people, "may be willing to persevere with less than perfect fulfilment of their interests in some conditions."[37] Life itself, in other words, may be a value to many animals for some time after a decline begins but before pain is severe and unmanageable. It is possible to view euthanasia as compassionate and in the animal's best interests in some situations while also urging caution about a rush to euthanize any elderly or frail animal. The utilitarian view of animal life becomes a danger if it means that little or no reflection is required before the decision to kill. There is a risk, in other words, that euthanasia may reflect not how much we love our pets but rather, as Pierce writes, "how little we value the lives of animals."[38]

The lower value of animal life is on full display in the world of public shelters. Shelter euthanasia is the most common cause of death of young, healthy companion animals in the United States, killing around three to five million cats and dogs a year in the United States alone. They die not because they are ill or in pain but because they do not have loving guardians able to care for them. Because most public shelters have very limited space and resources, they cannot keep animals indefinitely, and those that are not adopted quickly are usually killed within a few weeks. The number of animals killed in shelters has dropped significantly over the past few decades, primarily as a result of efforts to promote spaying/neutering and increase adoptions of shelter animals. However, the numbers are still enormous, especially in the southern United States and many rural areas.

Even as shelter euthanasia has declined, the debates about its morality have intensified. One position, associated with the "welfarist" camp in animal advocacy, seeks pragmatic and utilitarian reforms to improve the lives of animals, without radically changing human-animal relationships. Welfarists see shelter killings as a sad necessity, which will last as long as there are not enough adopters who seek out shelter animals. Shelter euthanasia is kind, they argue, because homeless animals face fates worse than death, such as abuse, neglect, or a life of hunger and disease on the street. Welfarists insist that they value nonhuman lives and regret the killings but see no feasible alternatives until the population of homeless animals has been significantly reduced. This echoes just war arguments that killing in war is regrettable but unavoidable, the only "realistic" option in an imperfect world.

On the other side, some animal advocates contend that overpopulation is not as extreme as the welfarists suggest and that killing shelter animals is neither necessary nor morally acceptable. On these grounds, they argue that to use the term *euthanasia* "obscures the reality of what's really happening," as Pierce puts it.[39] Animal ethicist Tom Regan elaborates this argument. For a death to be considered true euthanasia, he writes, three conditions must be met: the individual must be killed in the least painful way possible, the one who kills must believe that the death is in the interests of the one killed, and the one who kills must be motivated out of concern for the other's good.[40] If we follow this definition, most killings of nonhuman animals that are described as euthanasia do not in fact count as such. Most animals in shelters are killed, not euthanized, he concludes, and "to persist in calling such practices 'euthanizing animals' is to wrap plain killing in a false verbal cover."[41]

Arguments against shelter euthanasia insist that it can only be justified if it is in the patient's best interest, as in cases of painful, untreatable illness or injury. This is the underlying philosophy of the No Kill movement, according to which "killing healthy or treatable animals is immoral."[42] This argument involves two distinct but related claims: shelter killing is both unnecessary and unethical. The first point rests on a conviction that shelter killings stem not from a surplus of dogs and cats but rather from the failure of shelter staff to implement effective programs to reduce population and increase adoptions.[43] The second point assumes that nonhuman lives have intrinsic value just as human lives do. Animals should receive the same considera-tion as humans, who may not be killed even when their deaths would relieve problems such as overcrowding, resource scarcity, and so forth. Thus, No Kill advocate Nathan Winograd calls on shelters to take killing "off the table" as a solution to practical problems. Because it is acceptable to kill nonhuman animals when they are inconvenient, he asserts, we are less likely to seek solutions that do not involve killing them. Winograd believes that if killing were no longer an option, then "human ingenuity and human compassion would find a way to make it work."[44]

This parallels pacifist arguments about ways to end political conflicts without recourse to war. Both No Kill activists and pacifists assert that when lethal violence is not just available but framed as the realistic, inevitable option, people are much less likely to pursue alternative resolutions to the problem.

Euthanasia, Ethical Theory, and Practice

Attention to practice can shed light on arguments about the morality of euthanasia in a cross-species perspective. Euthanasia is a practice, one that combines the extraordinary decision to end a life with the mundane setting of a shelter, hospital, or home. An ethical analysis focused on practice would examine the actual practices involved in killing, as well as the practices that have created the historical and social context for that killing and shaped the values and beliefs of the people involved. To unpack some of these issues, we can look again at my five organizing themes.

1. Ideas and moral reasoning are not free-floating but always come embedded in concrete circumstances. Ethical reflection about euthanasia involves emotions, relationships, and social structures, even though appeals to autonomy and quality of life suggest abstract principles that can be accessed via "pure reason." Personal and social contexts shape people's attitudes and intentions and also the way other people interpret and respond to them. Perhaps a seriously ill person wants to die because he fears his family cannot afford his care. Or perhaps the person has untreated mental illness or lacks access to effective painkillers. These and many other factors can affect the meaning of a patient's request for PAS or a physician's decision to withdraw care. The practices of euthanasia or suicide, then, make sense only in light of a larger web of actions and structures that determine the value that a life has and the moral significance of killing and dying. In other words, ethicists need to ask not just whether patients consider their lives worth living but also what practices and structures condition the answers to that question. Practices and structures also condition the value of nonhuman lives. Relationships with people give value to pets that place their deaths in a totally different category from shelter animals of the same species. There is no abstract "value of life" at stake but rather the values of particular lives, measured by webs of relationships, available resources, and structural contexts.

2. Related to this, in thinking about euthanasia, form and content cannot be divided. Two of the most important principles in ethical reflections about

euthanasia—quality of life and autonomy—are experienced in different ways by different people in different settings. Understanding them as "thin" values or procedures for decision-making impoverishes discussions about euthanasia. This becomes clear in the cross-species comparison, in which so much hinges on the content-full category of species. We cannot begin to answer some of our moral questions without asking, as Singer puts it, "What, in the end, is so special about the fact that a life is human?"[45]

Singer poses this question in regard to abortion, which, like euthanasia, raises momentous questions about what we value in human life and the practical consequences of that valuation. Very often, and as Singer notes, the moral debates in both cases begin with the specialness of human life as an assumption and not a matter for inquiry. To use Raymond Williams's phrase, humans' unique value is often treated as a "term of analysis," rather than a "term of substance."[46] It is taken as an unquestioned foundation for abstract theorizing rather than as a substantive moral claim that requires support, explanation, and critique. Cross-species comparisons bring humanness to the surface as a variable, if only because we cannot simply transfer ethical arguments from humans to other animals in any thin or formal way. Moral arguments about nonhuman animals require thick details, about their capacities and senses, about their relationships with humans and with ecosystems, and about the material structures that shape their lives. Throughout these themes run practices, through which humans and other creatures exercise capacities, use their senses, and build both structures and relationships.

More specifically, practices help us make sense of principles, such as autonomy and quality of life, that have very different meaning and significance in conversations about human and nonhuman euthanasia. With companion animals, in particular, it is impossible to assert autonomy in a vacuum. Despite the many forms of agency exercised by nonhuman animals, they cannot independently take their own lives in a painless way at a chosen time. The abstract principle of autonomy is not helpful in reflecting on the morality of this kind of killing. Only a thick, detailed understanding of specific circumstances and relationships can bring the proper issues to the fore and answer the question of when, if ever, killing is justified. This kind of thick, nuanced reflection does not take place for most shelter killings; instead, momentous decisions are made on the basis of cost-benefit analysis.

Quality of life similarly takes on texture and differentiation in light of a cross-species comparison. With beloved pets, neither veterinarians nor owners will accept a lingering, increasingly uncomfortable end; active killing is not only permitted but morally required. With humans, however, "letting die" is often considered more acceptable than active euthanasia, in part because it is framed as a non-action. However, if we understand passive euthanasia as a set of practices embedded in relationships, structures, and situations created by other practices, then the distinction between activity and passivity becomes strained. Rather than beginning with these abstract categories and defining particular practices as moral or immoral on that basis, we can begin with the practices and understand the value of the lives at stake on that basis.

3. Euthanasia also underlines the inevitably social nature of moral decisions. Euthanasia is often framed as an individual decision, particularly in light of the emphasis on autonomy. However, euthanasia always involves other people, most immediately the loved ones and caretakers of the patient but also the larger communities in which they are all embedded. Both individual decisions about euthanasia and policymaking are important in large part because of their social impacts. If the issues were purely individual, no one would worry about the "slippery slope" upon which we might launch ourselves by legalizing PAS, for example. It is only because individual life-and-death decisions take place within social contexts that moral debates about euthanasia matter. These social contexts often include nonhuman animals, because people have important relationships not only with humans but also with other creatures. Cross-species relationships define a particular dog or cat either as a beloved pet—an individual who matters—or an anonymous shelter animal whose fate will be decided by cost-benefit analyses.

4. Moral reasoning about euthanasia cannot be separated from other kinds of thinking. It is related to questions about taking life, including war and capital punishment. Euthanasia is a decision that makes sense—or not—only in relation to the whole of a person's life, including social relationships, structures, and larger communities. Autonomy and quality of life are not abstract moral qualities but social relationships determined by economic, political, and cultural factors. Another way to put this is to say that how we think about death is continuous with how we think about life. Further, how we think about the deaths of animals is related to the ways we think about the value of those animals in other contexts. Relationships and structures matter for both humans and other animals. This becomes especially clear in the distinction between shelter and pet euthanasia, where the fate of individual animals depends not on their intrinsic qualities but on their place within particular institutions and webs of relationships.

5. Euthanasia offers a valuable context for thinking about the relations between intentions, actions, and consequences, and in particular about the connection between means and ends. In euthanasia, as in war, what justifies a normally prohibited action—killing another person—is the intention of the person who performs the euthanasia and, in human cases, of the patient or those who care about her. This suggests that euthanasia and PAS are among the situations in which intentions do make a world of difference. In regard to humans, it matters a great deal whether a physician hastens death to honor the patient's request for a quick and painless end to a life of unrelenting suffering, for example, or to collect an expected bequest. And it matters whether the patient makes an informed, rational decision or a hasty choice amid intense but temporary pain. It matters, also, what the patient's loved ones intend, especially in regard to people who cannot make fully informed, rational choices or who cannot express their intentions clearly, such as infants or people with severe developmental delays or advanced dementia. In such cases, moral judgment rests on the extent to which the family's intentions are to advance the patient's best interests. In all these cases, the thought really does count in determining whether a death is morally justified, at least for people who consider euthanasia justifiable in at least some circumstances.

However, the thought is not the only thing that counts, and sometimes it is not the most important. Cross-species comparison shows some of the limitations to ethical theories that prioritize intentions. Sometimes intention makes a decisive moral difference for animals, for example, when a loving pet owner decides, on the basis of veterinary advice and direct experience, that the animal cannot enjoy normal activities, that pain cannot be reliably controlled, and that there is no realistic hope for improvement. This clearly qualifies as euthanasia and may be justified on similar grounds to those for human euthanasia—that is, people who are open to the possibility of justifying euthanasia will find these circumstances persuasive.

When we turn to shelter killings, intentions play a very different role in moral argument. Shelter killings are called euthanasia to justify them by association with the widely accepted practice of pet euthanasia. However, the intentions are not the same. The people doing the killing often believe that they are acting on good intentions, but it is important to distinguish different kinds of intentions, and the motivations behind shelter killing do not parallel those driving pet or human euthanasia. This does not mean that shelter killing is never justified, but when we use "good intentions" to justify a harmful act, we need greater clarity about what is happening and what is at stake, and also about other options. As in just war theory, we might ask who the victims are, what structures provide the contexts in which they live and die, and what relationships determine their social value, as well as the intentions of the people authorizing and carrying out the killing.

Accurate descriptions of the practices of killing and the experiences of those living with illness or pain can help us dig beneath the appeal to intentions as an automatic justification for causing harm. Good intentions only sometimes change the moral character of an act. Saying "I meant well" does not always absolve someone who causes great harm. Euthanasia provides an opportunity to examine these issues in regard to deliberate killings of individuals. The variable of species helps clarify the reasons that not all good intentions are morally equivalent and also the reasons that we need to think about how, when, and why intentions can counter or outweigh harmful actions.

Here the relationship between means and ends is central. Winograd raises this theme explicitly when he asserts that "It is an inherent contradiction to use 'killing' as a means to 'not killing,'" that is, killing a few to save many.[47] This echoes the pacifist criticism of the just war claim that the targeted violence of war will, in the long run, kill fewer people and result in less destruction than the alternatives. Such arguments ground moral justification in claims about necessity, created by resource scarcity (for shelter pets) or military conditions (in war). These claims rest on the priority of intentions over practices: the intention to achieve a greater good justifies committing smaller wrongs, so something normally permitted becomes morally acceptable, even necessary. This calculus is possible because of a hierarchy of value. In shelter killing, the lives of homeless pets are less valuable, first, because of their species identity and, second, because they are not loved by, or at least in the care of, particular humans. This parallels the way the rules of war define certain people as "killable," in Donna Haraway's term.[48] There is a circular logic involved in these arguments: certain animals (or people) are categorized as killable because of their lower value in the eyes of those with power, but at the same time, the fact that they are, in practice, killed means that those in power must characterize them as inferior. The practice of killing, in other words, is not just a result of a prior evaluation but also a factor shaping evaluation.

Conclusions

Discussions about the morality of euthanasia shed new light on some of the themes that have been important throughout this book. One of these is the question of whether it is, after all, the thought that counts. Intentions are central to decisions about euthanasia, and often they are what makes the difference between a justified act of mercy killing and an unjustifiable act of premeditated murder. However, intentions do not matter by themselves, in this situation or any other. The intentions of both patients and physicians are meaningful, and in fact can only emerge, in relation to particular structures, practices, and relationships.

Debates about euthanasia also highlight the central role of relationships in determining value. This becomes especially clear when we consider the valuation of nonhuman life. The comparison between pet euthanasia and shelter killing shows that the worth of an individual's life depends almost entirely on who, if anyone, cares about the individual. The same dogs or cats are killable or not based not on their intrinsic qualities but rather on their position in humanly created structures. As feminist thinkers remind us, practices of care often determine the moral value of particular individuals who are, on the basis of "internal" qualities, indistinguishable. The stark difference that relationships make in the fate of nonhuman animals can help us consider how relationships affect the valuations of particular people's lives as well. This underlines the significance of species, a variable that I have made explicit in this comparison but which plays a role in many other moral and social issues as well. Humanness matters, not in the abstract but in the details, which means in practices.

9

Ideas, Practices, and Climate Change

> The binge the developed world has enjoyed is about over. It's time to
> find our way home and use what little time is left for partial redemp-
> tion of this prodigal generation.
>
> —Wes Jackson[1]

Introduction

Reflections on climate change, the most pressing environmental problem of
our time, can deepen and expand our understanding of practice's role in ethical theory. Human practices are the cause of climate change, and practices
are the only way to address it. We do not necessarily know, however, what it
would mean to address climate change. It is "a structurally 'wicked problem,'"
as Willis Jenkins notes, because "what would count as a solution is ecologically and culturally indeterminate."[2] Solutions are also morally indeterminate, in many cases, in no small part because while we know in general what
causes climate change, we cannot identify specific individuals who are responsible for any given problem, nor can we identify predictable relations
between actions and consequences. Thus, climate change underlines the
need for better ways of thinking about practices, intentions, consequences,
responsibilities, and the relations among them.

The complexity of these issues makes climate change a difficult and also
fruitful site for reflecting on practice's place in ethical theory. In this chapter,
I focus on several themes that build on and expand the discussions in earlier
chapters. I begin with a brief discussion of some of the scientific, economic,
and political dimensions of climate change. I do not go into detail, because
there are countless good studies, including both general overviews and detailed investigations of specific issues.[3] After that overview, I turn to several
themes related to the place of practice in ethics. One is the gap between ideas
and actions, or more precisely the fact that even when people care about a
problem and know what needs to be done, they rarely act in ways consistent

Works Righteousness. Anna L. Peterson, Oxford University Press (2021). © Oxford University Press.
DOI: 10.1093/oso/9780197532232.001.0001.

with their values. I then consider the role of social structures in shaping moral attitudes and practices, focusing on economics and technology. This leads to reflections on the problem of moral responsibility and consequences and, once again, the inadequacy of linear models of moral behavior.

Climate Change: Science, Ethics, and Politics

We can only understand climate change in light of humans' continual, inevitable transformation of the natural world around them. People always change nature, and there is no prehistorical time in which people did not affect their environment. Climate change and many other contemporary environmental problems are different in scale, but they are not unique instances of human intervention. Further, transformation of the environment is not a uniquely human activity. From ants to beavers to elephants, all creatures alter their surroundings in countless ways. Human practices help construct nature, as Steven Vogel explains: "the environment" is not "something we passively *confront* or *experience* or *perceive* or *know*; rather, it is the *object of our practices*."[4] The fact that our influences on natural environments are ubiquitous does not mean that they are necessarily positive, for humans or for ecosystems and other creatures. They are often negative and have been for many centuries. Problems such as air and water pollution, deforestation, erosion, and species eradication or extinction are not unique to our time. Nineteenth-century London, for example, had dangerously poor air quality, and there is evidence of serious deforestation in premodern China and India.[5] Today there is an overwhelming scientific consensus that human activities, mainly fossil-fuel consumption but also deforestation and the release of methane gases by domesticated herbivores, are driving massive ecological change.

Although this is not the first time human practices have caused serious damage to places and ecosystems, the effects of climate change are uniquely dangerous and vast. "The fundamental problem," as Stephen Gardiner explains, "is that it is now possible for humans to alter the underlying dynamics of the planet's climate and so the basic life-support system both for themselves and all other forms of life on Earth."[6] Some of the well-documented effects of climate change include warming land and ocean temperatures, sea-level rise as a result of thermal expansion of the warming oceans along with other factors, habitat range shifts for animals and plants, and a host of other problems, including intensified tropical storm activity, ocean acidification, and desertification. These changes are not distributed evenly across the globe but affect certain regions and communities much more than others. In terms of the human costs, low-lying coastal and island areas will suffer more from flooding, sea-level rise, and extreme weather events. Poorer communities are already being hit harder, because they tend to live in more vulnerable areas and have fewer resources to respond effectively to the challenges. Attention to the nonhuman cost has focused on polar regions affected by melting glaciers and declining ice levels, but climate change affects ecosystems, plants, and animals around the globe.

Given the consensus that climate change is real and that it is caused by human actions, the challenge for scientists now is no longer simply to describe its features and effects but rather to address mitigation and adaptation. The same issues preoccupy ethical and political arguments, which focus mainly on two broad issues: how to slow the rate and extent of change and how to adapt to changes in order to minimize harm to human communities and ecosystems. Some environmental analysts argue that climate change is not "a problem that can be solved . . . a feature of our world that we might end," but rather "it is something to be better managed. The real challenge of climate change is not to produce a world without it, but to sustain ourselves despite it."[7] The emphasis on adapting to climate change does not mean that we should abandon efforts to slow its progress. Part of adaptation must include slowing the rate of change, to reduce as much as possible the costs and challenges of adapting, because there are limits to how far and how fast adaptation can go, especially for nonhuman species. "Adaptation measures will clearly need to be part of any sensible climate policy," as Gardiner writes, "because we are already committed to some warming due to past emissions, and almost all of the proposed abatement strategies envisage that overall global emissions will continue to rise for at least the next few decades, committing us to even more."[8] A combination of strategies, including mitigation and adaptation, is thus necessary.

The climate crisis raises important moral and philosophical questions, which have been explored by environmental ethicists in relation to human attitudes toward and treatment of nature. They have explored a variety of problems, from perspectives focused on a range of religious and secular theories. Here I focus on a few specific issues to explore what we can gain from a focus on practice: the gap between values and actions, the roles of technology and economics in shaping environmental behavior, and the problem of responsibility.

The Values-Practices Gap

Philosophers and theologians have long reflected on the disjuncture between the values people hold and the ways they act. Classical Greek philosophers called this *akrasia*, "a trait of character exhibited in uncompelled, intentional behavior that goes against the agent's best or better judgment."[9] Its opposite is *enkrateia*, defined as continence, self-control, or strength of will, which is also a character trait "exhibited in behavior that conforms with one's best or better judgment in the face of temptation to act to the contrary."[10] The historical evidence for akrasia is overwhelming. As Amelie Rorty puts it, "we have had several centuries of practice producing examples to show the absurdity of [Plato's] claim that 'To know the good is to do the good.'"[11] Plato was sure that people act badly only because they do not know the good and fail to perceive the longer-term benefits of morally correct action. He believed that education and moral development could lead people to desire the good and thus to improve their behavior. This is a linear understanding of intentions and actions: if we can fix the intentions, then proper actions and consequences will follow.

While Plato attributed akrasia to a lack of knowledge, many religious traditions explain the gap between ideals and actions as the result of human sinfulness and weakness of the will. Paul, for example, attributes the failure to do good to the war between body and soul: "For the flesh desires what is contrary to the Spirit, and the Spirit what is contrary to the flesh. They are in conflict with each other, so that you are not to do whatever you want" (Galatians 5:17). This assumes that people are internally divided and that the individual spirit or will alone is not strong enough to conquer the weakness of the flesh. Thus, Paul lamented, "For I do not do the good I want to do, but the evil I do not want to do—this I keep doing" (Romans 7:19). The only way to close this gap, in his view, is with divine assistance. Humans cannot solve their moral problems alone.

Akrasia provides a helpful lens for thinking about environmental problems, and climate change in particular, because there is strong evidence that most people both care about environmental problems and fail to act in ways that would address them.[12] Empirical research about environmental attitudes and behavior consistently shows this contradiction. A 2016 Pew Research Center survey came up with findings typical of other studies over the past few decades: "Three-quarters of Americans are concerned about the environment, but . . . only one-in-five Americans say they make an effort to live in ways that help protect the environment 'all the time.'"[13] This echoes studies published throughout the 1990s and 2000s, in which around 80 percent of Americans express strong environmental concern, but only around 20 percent regularly participate in actions such as recycling, reducing consumption, activism, or voting based on environmental issues.[14] This research suggests a kind of collective akrasia regarding the environment, reflected in the gulf between the large number of people who say they value nature, on the one hand, and the small minority who act in concrete ways to protect it, on the other.

The usual explanation for this discrepancy is a failure of individuals to apply values in real life. This is a contemporary version of Plato's conviction that better knowledge will inevitably lead to better behavior. Scholarship on conservation behavior has called this approach the "knowledge-attitude-behavior" method[15] or, more memorably, "ABC" (attitude-behavior-choice). This model assumes that social change depends "upon values and attitudes (the A), which are believed to drive the kinds of behaviour (the B) that individuals choose (the C) to adopt," as Elizabeth Shove explains. She critiques the assumption that there is, as Anja Kollmus and Julian Agyeman put it, "a linear progression of environmental knowledge leading to environmental awareness and concern (environmental attitudes), which in turn was thought to lead to pro-environmental behaviour."[16] This view of the relationship between knowledge, ideas, and action is based in theories of planned behavior and rational choice, which highlight deliberate individual desires to act in accord with pre-established ideas.[17]

The notion of a gap between values and practices rests on the problematic assumption that people deliberately adopt a certain moral stance and then act on it. This reproduces "precisely that understanding of social change which has generated the problem in the first place," as Shove explains, since "the gap is only mystifying if we suppose that values do (or should) translate into action."[18] In other words, the idea that there is a gap to be closed presupposes both that there is a linear relationship between ideas and actions and that the only factors involved in moral practice are individual attitudes, behavior, and choices. In reality, the relationship is not linear, and of the many things that shape moral practice, relatively few are within the control of a particular individual. Models such as ABC thus do not explain the reasons for complex environmental and social problems, and they are of even less use in efforts to address these issues. A more accurate and holistic approach to behavior change requires understanding social practices not just as the consequence of applied decisions or sites where something happens but rather as "dynamic entities in their own right."[19]

This view challenges the idealist notion that ideas and actions are related in a simple, predictable, and linear way. It also calls into question the individualist assumptions of most approaches to akrasia, which locate both the problem itself and its possible solution in individual mental states. They see the problem as wrong desire, inadequate knowledge, or a weak will; the solution then is to strengthen and correct these individual failings, by self-discipline or with the help of God. Versions of this model still dominate contemporary moral philosophy and theology, much of which finds the answer to immoral actions in individual mental qualities and acts of will. They pay little attention to social factors, even though research shows that these strongly influence moral behavior.[20] It is not enough simply for an individual to acquire more knowledge or different attitudes, because people are embedded in social, economic, cultural, political, and technological contexts that help determine not just what we can do but what we want to do and think it is correct to do.

All of this means it is extremely difficult to change human behavior in meaningful, lasting ways. The evidence is all around us, as Kollmus and Agyeman point out: "Anyone who has ever tried to change a habit, even in a very minor way, will have discovered how difficult it is, even if the new behavior has distinct advantages over the old one."[21] Everyday examples are easy to find: people frequently drink too much, smoke, eat junk food, and fail to exercise, along with many other activities that they know are harmful. If it is hard to change behavior even when our health is at stake, it is not surprising that changing practices for more altruistic reasons is even more challenging.

Economics and Technology

Both what motivates behavior changes and the obstacles to them are complex. Behavior is conditioned by psychological, emotional, and cultural factors and also by structural ones. Among the most significant influences on conservation behavior are economic forces and technologies, both of which shape what people believe they ought to do, as well as creating material possibilities and limitations that condition what people can do.

Economics

Philosophers and theologians rarely address economic structures, even though they shape every aspect of people's lives, including moral ideas and practices; relations with other people, institutions, and nature; and the ability to fulfill personal aspirations and contribute to larger communities. When ethicists do consider economics in relation to environmental problems, and climate change in particular, their topic is usually the individual consumption of natural resources. Criticisms of the destructive consequences of overconsumption and calls for change, especially in relation to food and transportation, are common. However, this focus on consumption habits is problematic, because it identifies the problem as personal decisions and the solution as altered habits, usually seen as the result of better information or moral discipline. This approach is mistaken, first, because it overestimates the impact of individual consumer choices and, second, because it misunderstands the ways individual and collective behavior changes.

A better understanding of consumption is "not just as an individual's choice among goods but as a stream of choices and decisions winding its way through the various stages of extraction, manufacture, and final use, embedded at every step in social relations of power and authority."[22] This holistic approach makes it possible to pose important questions that do not arise within dominant models, such as the reasons people consume and what and how they consume, the social construction of consumption patterns, and the moral, social, and environmental consequences of consumption.[23] When we cease to think about consumption practices as simply a matter of personal choice, we can view our actions in the context of larger social, economic, cultural, and political patterns that have causes and effects far beyond our own households.

Analyses and critiques of consumption, while important, do not provide the bigger picture necessary in order to understand the economic influences on practices related to climate change. More information comes from exploring environmental injustices among individuals, groups, or nations on the basis of ethnic, economic, racial, and gender hierarchies. Environmental injustices are manifested when some groups face disproportionate environmental risks, such as pollution or toxins, or have unequal access to environmental goods, such as clean air and water. Familiar examples include the siting of toxic dumps and harmful industries in low-income neighborhoods, land-use decisions that benefit the privileged, and the prioritization of more affluent regions for environmental services.

The roots of these inequities lie in political and economic structures that give some people and groups less opportunity to participate in decisions about environmental policy.[24] In other words, environmental injustice results from particular practices that organize and distribute material goods. Because of these practices, the people who suffer most from climate change are those who have the least political and economic power. Their greater susceptibility to harms is often due to structural injustices or other human-caused harms that place them in especially vulnerable regions and livelihoods.[25] These are also the people who have, in general, benefited the least from the economic and technological developments made possible by intensive use of fossil fuels. In sum, as environmental ethicist Chris J. Cuomo writes, climate change "was manufactured in a crucible of inequality."[26] Climate change thus requires not merely technological or scientific solutions but rather integrated environmental, economic, and political efforts. Achieving environmental justice requires rethinking economic relationships as well as ecological and social ones and seeing the necessary links among them. Pope Francis I highlights this in his 2015 encyclical *Laudato si'*, writing that climate change underlines the need to "integrate questions of justice in debates on the environment, so as to hear *both the cry of the earth and the cry of the poor.*"[27]

Conventional economic reasoning fails to see these links or capture the value of ecological processes, natural places, species, or individual organisms. Ecological economists challenge the assumptions that monetary measurements can capture all kinds of value and that unrestricted economic growth is always an indication of increased welfare. Drawing on this work, some have pointed out the destructive logic at the core of modern industrial capitalism—the assumption, as Michael Northcott writes, that "constant growth in the transformation of ecological resources into industrially-produced goods and services, and thence into waste to be buried in the ground or emitted into the oceans and atmospheres, promotes human welfare."[28] This model assumes that "money is always substitutable for non-monetary goods and that the money economy exists within a material frame where all goods, even life itself, are theoretically exchangeable for other goods."[29] Marx would say that this understands goods in terms of, and reduces them to, exchange value, extracting them from their material role in people's lives and in nature. The logic of exchange does not capture the value of human relationships, communities, or many other intangible goods, and it certainly does not capture the value of nonhuman nature.[30]

Northcott's critique of the worship of growth and the casual acceptance of waste in modern industrial economies represents one of the infrequent occasions when environmental philosophers mention capitalism. However, he still shies away from directly addressing material structures, concentrating instead on attitudes and ideas about economics. Like most Western critics of unsustainable consumption, in other words, he remains within the hegemonic idealism of theological, philosophical, and moral thought. Another example of this pattern is Lisa Kretz's analysis of the ways "capitalistic narratives dominate the North American imaginary" because of marketing that persuades people to buy and consume ever more. Kretz's answer to this pattern is not structural change as much as more marketing and behavioral psychology, focused on individual behaviors.[31] Her analysis suggests that the problem is narratives about the structures, rather than the structures themselves.

This recalls Marx's critique of the young Hegelians, who assert that they are fighting "phrases." The problem, Marx points out, is that they forget "that to these phrases they themselves are only opposing other phrases, and that they are in no way combating the real existing world when they are merely combating the phrases of this world."[32] For Marx, the main issue is not the ways capitalistic narratives shape our imaginations but rather the way capitalism itself conditions our material practices. Identity issues, the psychological effects of capitalism, and the marketing of consumerism are all important, but they are not the root of the problem. If we only consider phrases and ideas, we will be unable to develop an effective, holistic program to address climate change and other environmental and social challenges. Wes Jackson makes this point, writing that when we confront the interconnected problems of "war and racism, poverty, sexism, the growing gap between the rich and the poor," we hit a brick wall, and "it turns out that brick wall is capitalism. We're going to have to face that." It is so overwhelming to face the structural problems caused by capitalism, however, that "people want to believe it is possible to design around capitalism," rather than changing underlying conditions.[33]

A materialist account of the economic dimensions of climate change would acknowledge the fundamental incompatibility, pinpointed by Jackson, between capitalism and ecologically necessary limits to growth. Effective policies to address climate change require radical reductions in global "extraction, production, and consumption of natural resources," as Jonathan Park notes. However, "the capitalist system as it currently stands is neither designed for nor capable of consciously inhibiting its own propensity for unsustainable growth. The basic assumptions under which neoliberal capitalism operates render it incapable of correcting climate change."[34] The conversion of all value into monetary terms—exchange value—makes capitalism "incapable of accurately assessing and conveying the true value of natural resources." If nature is appreciated only for its instrumental role, Park contends, then "it is irrational and undesirable not to extract and consume the total global supply of fossil fuels."[35] While Park sees the logic of capitalism as opposed to the restraint required to address climate change, others propose a "green" capitalism that uses market mechanisms to address environmental problems, in part by linking sustainability to self-interest, economic and other. Both approaches share an assumption that economic structures help determine what people want, what they consider moral, and how they act in relation to moral issues.

Economic structures shape not only attitudes and values but also practices, including what and how we consume, how we transport ourselves, how we produce food, and so forth. The current model of industrial capitalism encourages, even requires, unsustainable consumption of fossil fuels. Other kinds of economic arrangements—a greener capitalism or socialist alternatives—would encourage and require different kinds of consumption. Beyond the ways practices are shaped by these economic arrangements, it is important to highlight and analyze the ways practices create them. Present economic institutions did not develop spontaneously, any more than alternatives to them will emerge without human efforts. Practices are thus both cause and effect of economic structures, but this causality is never simple, predictable, or deterministic. Practices mediate between structures and individual agency, shaping the ways they are connected and influence each other. A clear example of this mediation can be seen in the interactions between practices and technologies.

Technology and the Built Environment

Like the economy, technology influences how people think and act in multiple ways. Technology receives somewhat more philosophical attention than economics, but the discussions often take place within the constraints of applied ethics, usually in relation to fairly narrow questions about the uses of particular technologies in different situations. I am interested in a broader exploration of the ways technology and the built environment instantiate values or, as Peter-Paul Verbeek puts it, the ways ethics is "materialized" in human products. "When technologies coshape human actions, they give material answers to the ethical question of how to act," he writes. "This implies that engineers are doing 'ethics by other means': they materialize morality."[36] The notion of "materializing morality" offers a helpful perspective on the place of practice in ethical theory. It suggests that material structures, including but not limited to new technologies, influence actions in ethically significant ways, even in the absence of conscious intentions on the part of either designers or users.

Verbeek uses a phrase with pragmatist sensibility, "technologies-in-use," to describe the interactions between technologies and users. This points to the facts that technologies alone are not powerful and also that people do not fully determine the impact of the technologies they use. The interactions are what have power. Just as people shape the meaning and impact of technology, Verbeek writes, technologies "inevitably play a role in the actions of their users," including the ethical dimensions of their behavior.[37] Technologies "mediate people's actions and the way they live their lives." We not only act on our material environments but are shaped and acted on by them.[38] Just as people constitute and are constituted by both social relationships and the natural environment, the same process holds for the built environment and technology. In all cases, as Vogel writes, "The world is not something we *find* ourselves in; it is something we have helped to *make*. But at the same time it is something that helps to make *us*: we are who we are because of the environment that we inhabit. The environment is socially constructed; society is environmentally constructed."[39]

Technology is a crucial part of the socially constructed environment in which humans live and with which we are continually interacting, in mutually transformative ways. The layout of contemporary suburban and rural societies, for example, demands cars, which in turn profoundly affects not only resource consumption but also the ways we use time, the kinds of people to whom we relate, the social relationships we have, and the ways we spend our time at work and at leisure, among many other aspects of our lives.[40] This is dramatically evident in the far-reaching consequences of the Amish decisions to prohibit private ownership of automobiles and telephones. The aim was less to reject technology for its own sake than to keep communities small and tightly knit and reduce dependence on outsiders. The ban on car ownership, along with numerous other decisions about technology, have made it possible for Amish communities to retain the qualities prioritized by their religious faith.[41]

The Amish decision reflects a prophetic awareness of the impact of technology on community life and moral practice. However, many consumers and even designers fail to recognize the materialization of morality in technology and structures and understand the design process as morally neutral. As Verbeek writes, many technologies "possess a 'script' in the sense that they can prescribe the actions of the actors involved."[42] They encourage certain actions and discourage others. A few simple examples illustrate this point: "a speed bump can invite drivers to drive slowly because of its ability to damage a car's shock absorbers, a car can demand from a driver that he or she wear the safety belt by refusing to start if the belt is not used, and a plastic coffee cup has the script 'throw me away after use,' whereas a porcelain cup 'asks' to be cleaned and used again."[43] When we practice these actions—driving slowly, wearing a seat belt, rewashing a cup—we come to take them for granted and to consider them normative. They become habits, as Aristotle and other virtue theorists would note. Habituation makes it seem right to do the things we usually do and wrong to do otherwise. It shapes not just actions but will, as pragmatists emphasize.

Along with pragmatists, Marxists and virtue theorists also recognize the ways social and natural environments teach people to desire particular things. Economic structures, technologies, and experiences in the natural world shape what we want and what we think we can have. The results of our practices, in other words, influence future practices, as well as our values and wishes. These wishes can be for things that are destructive, or we can be educated, as French philosopher Miguel Abensour writes, "to desire better, to desire more, and above all to desire in a different way."[44] This echoes the virtue and pragmatist attention to the power of habit as not just rote activity but an active process of creating and inculcating moral attitudes.

However, we cannot engage in this active process unless we recognize the human origins of our environments and institutions. Here the Marxist criticism of alienation is helpful, insofar as it explains how people "fail to recognize themselves in the world that surrounds them," as Vogel writes. In this situation, "the objects they produce through their labor, instead of appearing as the 'exoteric revelation' of their 'essential powers' or as expressions of their self-realization, become powers over and against them."[45] Alienation obscures both the *produced* and the *social* nature of the objects that our practices produce, including "the environment" itself.[46] It also obscures the produced nature of structures, values, and our practices themselves.

To address environmental problems such as climate change, we must pay attention not only to the practices that generate harm but also to those that shape all aspects of our relationship to nature and the built environment. Technology is, of course, a central part of this environment and of our actions in it. The social roles of technology can illuminate the relations between ideas and practices. In the common view, people start with attitudes and ideas and then apply those in real life—leading to particular technology designs or particular conceptions of moral behavior. This linear model is evident in the planning and marketing of "green" products and practices, which assume that environmental values come first and create demands that then "lead to the production of sustainable technologies that induce environmental benefits."[47] This approach to conservation behavior reflects theories of rational choice and planned behavior, according to which people decide how to act on the basis of preexisting ideas and predetermined goals. This view does not account for the ways people actually use technologies, however. In particular, it fails to understand that practices, such as uses of technology, are never unidirectional; they always involve social interactions between users and technologies that together determine their environmental consequences.[48]

A good example of these complex and often unexpected interactions is the Toyota Prius, introduced in 1997 as one of the first hybrid gasoline-electric vehicles and still the most popular. There are two common ways of conceiving of the relationship between the Prius and environmental values, both of them linear. The first sees the car's creation as an effort to meet already existing demand among environmentally conscious consumers who wanted to reduce their use of fossil fuels. The other assumes that creating a supply of more efficient technologies will change people's attitudes, because their purchase will "magically transform existent behavior into sustainable practices and effects."[49] Whether we start with ideas (demand) or with technology (supply), both approaches assume that causes and effects are easily identified and that the relationship between them is simple and predictable.

As I have been arguing, however, this relationship is neither simple nor predictable. Technologies like the Prius help us understand why. Because many external factors intervene in the use of any product, presumed environmental or social benefits are not intrinsic to the technology itself. Instead, they depend on both the human practices involved in creating the technology and the ongoing practices of users—technologies in use. Technologies shape practices of use but always in interaction with other factors, including the environment in which people and products interact.[50] Neither drivers nor Priuses are solely responsible for the car's environmental effects; rather, they produce these effects together, in their practical interactions.[51] Like streets and stock markets, cars are the products of human practices, and these practices mediate the relationship between values and products from beginning to end.

Economic institutions also materialize values and educate desire, leading people to act in value-laden ways in activities like work, shopping, and tax-paying. These influences are crucial to understanding the ethics of climate change. The human impact on the climate is the result of countless practices, individual and collective, that are made possible and often necessary by the structures in which we live and the kinds of technologies we use. The difference between the Prius and less efficient vehicles is an obvious example of the ways technologies shape practices and values, but many more are hidden in our daily activities: the energy that powers our homes, schools, and workplaces, the food we eat, the transportation choices available in our communities, and much more. In all these cases, structures we did not create have led us to damage the environment in ways that we may not have chosen, were we completely free, rational, and autonomous moral actors. These structures and technologies, the products of human practices, in turn help to create particular kinds of communities which then make possible other practices.

This leads to a more general theme, which is central to ethical theory: the nature and extent of moral responsibility. It is common, in both academic philosophy and everyday life, to link responsibility to intentional actions. Only moral agents can be responsible, in this view, and agency requires intentionality, meaning the ability to act on one's desires and awareness of the likely consequences of one's actions. However, I have been arguing that agency and thus responsibility are mediated by structures that are outside the control of any given individual. The influence of economic, technological, and environmental factors thus muddies the issue of moral responsibility. In relation to climate change, in which both our actions and their consequences are largely outside our control, the question of what we are responsible for and what we should do about it becomes almost impossibly complex.

Moral Responsibility and Consequences

We know that burning fossil fuels releases climate-changing gases into the atmosphere, but we have no way of knowing which specific practice led to any given effect. There are so many different actors and actions involved, all over the globe, that the cause is everyone and no one. Climate change is the consequence of individual, collective, and institutional actions, carried out over many decades, mostly before people knew what was happening. It is a case in which "many independent and uncoordinated actions, all done without malicious intent, can collectively produce a great deal of harm."[52] This harm is the unintended, rarely foreseen cumulative consequence of the actions of almost everyone on earth. We cannot know which of the billions of gallons of fossil fuels consumed caused a particular iceberg to detach, and, as Andrew Kernohan writes, "We will never be able to say who the real perpetrator is, or to say what share of the causal responsibility someone really bears. Accumulative consequences are not reducible to individual consequences."[53] They generate not direct responsibility but a kind of "mediated responsibility," in Derek Parfit's phrase. In this situation, Parfit explains, "Even if an act harms no one, this act may be wrong because it is one of a *set* of acts that *together* harm people".[54] Applying this concept to climate change in particular, Ian Smith argues that if an act is wrong because of its effects, the relevant effects are not limited to those of one particular act.[55]

The notions of cumulative consequences and mediated responsibilities challenge theoretical models that depend on assigning individual responsibility, often based on intention, and identifying the results of particular actions. We are all responsible, and yet no one is responsible. This makes it difficult to account for the moral responsibility of past or present actors, individual or collective. Since each individual action makes a tiny, imperceptible contribution to the cumulative problem, it is tempting to say that no one has the responsibility to fix it.

This contradicts the deeply embedded assumptions of both folk and academic ethical theories, which require us to identify moral actors and determine their responsibility, positive or negative. According to this "moral mathematics," each individual acts in isolation and is only responsible for the consequences of his or her deliberate actions.[56] This approach presupposes the common philosophical emphasis on attitudes and intentions, which make it possible to locate moral culpability or praise "within" a particular individual. This model also presumes the same simple and linear view of cause and effect that I have been criticizing. A better model underlines the ways our actions interact with those of others, who are also acting in the same ways as we are and contributing, together, to a cumulative consequence in which we all have a share of responsibility. We can only address these social, cumulative consequences if we stop trying to break them down so they can be assigned separately to different individuals. Instead, as Kernohan proposes, our solutions must account for "our inability to know who did what to whom."[57]

Cumulative harms, particularly on the scale of global climate change, thus challenge the core assumptions of conventional ethical theory: they drive us to look not at the attitudes of individuals but at the practices of many. This does not mean that we cannot, or should not, distinguish between the contributions of different people and groups. In regard to climate change, for example, wealthier nations have contributed most to the burning of fossil fuels, have benefited the most from that consumption, are best able to pay for the necessary changes, and have the ability to adapt without as much sacrifice as poorer countries.[58]

In understanding the causes and addressing the consequences of climate change, we cannot separate individual and collective actions. Our choices are directed and limited by the material structures into which we are born; as Marx wrote in *The Eighteenth Brumaire*, people always make their own history, "but they do not make it just as they please; they do not make it under circumstances chosen by themselves."[59] We might add that people always make their own environments, although they do not do so in circumstances they have chosen. Both histories and environments are made by practices and constrained by circumstances. So are attitudes about nature and valuations of it in different societies, from indigenous hunter-gatherers to the postindustrial West. Views of nature emerge from human activities, particular ways of living in particular times and places.

Because people's practices shape environments and environmental attitudes, they create environmental problems. They do not, however, create them intentionally and knowingly, at least not always. From local problems such as topsoil erosion to the global crisis of climate change, ecological damage results from the actions of people who are embedded in structures that sometimes leave little room for individual influence— even though people created the structures in the first place. Energy use is a good way to understand this dynamic. As Cuomo writes, "most middle-class consumers of centralized fossil-fuel energy have spent our lives flicking on switches, adjusting thermostats, and paying electric and gas bills without much thought about where the energy originates. It doesn't seem true that we choose coal, although again, we are not devoid of responsibility either."[60] Our choices have been determined, in both deliberate and accidental ways, by the choices of powerful people in industry and government.

The ways those in power have chosen to use fossil fuels are the cause of our present crisis, and that includes creating an economy that benefits them and a government that enables them to pursue their self-interest, even at the cost of great social and ecological harm. Cuomo suggests that economic and political elites can address the crisis by developing and using alternative forms of energy production. If a utility company decided to cease coal operations and focus on providing renewable energy, then "all consumers served by that company would immediately and inadvertently reduce emissions, regardless of their intentions or personal ethics."[61] This is the flip side of our current dilemma, in which it is often impossible for consumers to make a sustainable decision, regardless of their individual commitments or aspirations. Here again, our practices take place inside structures that we did not choose.

Of course, higher-level actors such as governments and corporations often fail to act in sustainable and otherwise socially responsible ways. When this happens, practical responsibility seems to fall on the ordinary people who care enough to change their individual actions. The failure of most corporate actors to take decisive action, and the difficulty of impelling them to do so, is probably a reason so many moral philosophers place "an unfair and possibly unmanageable degree of practical responsibility . . . on citizens and consumers."[62] This creates a double bind for ecologically conscientious citizens. On the one hand, individuals are neither chiefly responsible for the harms nor powerful enough to alleviate them. On the other hand, it often appears that individuals and small communities are the only ones motivated to take action. While such action is necessary, it will never be sufficient, and it is vital that individual actions do not diminish work for change at larger levels.[63] This raises the question of what would lead to the necessary type and scale of changes in individual and collective action. To answer this, we must confront the political nature of our social and environmental arrangements, and especially the way practices both reflect and create power.

Climate Change, Ethics, and Practice

Climate change is perhaps the most complex of the case studies I have examined, because it takes place on a global scale; involves a vast array of natural, political, and economic systems; and involves actions and consequences that are temporally separated from each other. While this complexity muddies the water of ethical analysis, attention to practice can illuminate some of the moral issues raised by climate change. In turn, attention to climate change can clarify some of the contributions of a practice-based theoretical approach. These contributions are especially evident when we think about models of action and the relations between ideas, practices, and consequences.

1. Ideas about nature, just like all moral attitudes, are embedded in larger contexts. People's experiences in both social and natural systems shape their ideas about those systems. Variations in attitudes about nature, therefore, are never merely conflicts of ideas but rather the result of different practices and the structures and environments that they have helped create. "The different 'views' of nature found in hunter-gatherer or agricultural or ancient urban or feudal or industrial or postindustrial societies are not simply 'conceptual schemes' that fell from the sky or just happened to arise at certain historical moments," as Vogel writes. "Rather, they are expressions of the fact that hunter-gatherers and agriculturalists and ancient city-dwellers and inhabitants of feudal or industrial or postindustrial societies *engage in different kinds of practices*, and so live in different (built) environments."[64]

There is no neutral way of thinking about nature, only situated ways of knowing and valuing, rooted in specific situations. This is evident in the ways economic structures and technologies shape not just practices but also attitudes toward nonhuman nature. The dialectical interaction between practices and environments helps give rise to particular ideas about what nature is, what value it has, and how people should treat it.

2. Climate change underlines the unity of form and content, as we see in the relationship between scientific data and moral thinking. We cannot practice a content-free environmental ethic; universal rules and abstract norms will not help us address the novel challenges we face. To reflect on the ethical issues raised by climate change, we need reliable, detailed knowledge about the scientific processes involved in climate change. This content, including knowledge about nonhuman nature and human practices, will in turn change the formal character of ethics. This echoes the ways cross-species comparisons shift discussions about the morality of euthanasia. In both cases, injecting a radically new content powerfully shapes the forms we can use to talk about ethics.

3. Climate change also underlines the social nature of environmental ethics. Ideas about nature are intertwined with ideas about and experiences in human society; as Raymond Williams notes, "What is often being argued . . . in the idea of nature is the idea of man; and this not only generally, or in ultimate ways, but the idea of man in society, indeed the ideas of kinds of societies."[65] Arguments about climate change, similarly, are not just about our relationship to nonhuman nature, as important as that is, but also about the kind of society we wish to live in and to build. Environmental harms are caused by humans collectively, and they affect people as social, not individual, beings. Environmental injustice shows how social conditions and inequities intersect with environmental harms. We must address these harms not as merely scientific problems but also as cultural, political, and economic problems.

Climate change is social in other ways as well. Just as environmental problems have social roots, our social nature is the key to any solutions we might develop. This was affirmed by a major study of environmental values in American culture, which found that information and knowledge about nature shaped ideas and behavior less than affective ties, especially in regard to children and future generations. Environmental values are deeply intertwined with commitment to family and parental responsibility, which give "environmental values a concrete and emotional grounding stronger than that of abstract principles."[66] This echoes research by the Merck Family Fund showing that family and children are central to people's desire to protect the environment.[67] Worry about the effects of environmental problems on the lives of people we love, in short, is one of the most powerful influences on values and actions.

4. Ethical reflection on climate change is tied to virtually all aspects of our lives. It is a truism of ecological science that nothing is separate from the whole, and this is also true of ethical thinking about ecological problems. Nowhere is this more obvious than in regard to climate change, which affects every part of our lives and societies. Consumption offers a helpful lens for thinking about this interconnectedness. We influence the environment and drive climate change through consumption of natural resources, but consumption cannot be isolated; it is everything we do. All our consumption affects other people and nature, including workers, farmers, and producers

and also landscapes, animals, water, and plants. Even when we are not consciously enacting moral stances about nature, we are affecting nature in ways
that are morally significant. There are moral consequences of all our actions,
and there is no separate sphere to which we can relegate thinking about climate change, at least not if we hope to understand it accurately and address it
effectively.

5. Climate change makes clear the inadequacy of linear models of action, such as the ABC approach. We cannot understand moral attitudes
and practices relating to climate change by reference to the Platonic and
Enlightenment notions that knowledge and reason are sufficient to effect
behavioral changes. "Simply put, one cannot assume that increased knowledge about nature leads to a favorable attitude toward nature which in turn
motivates action on behalf of nature," as Kretz writes.[68] Rather than increased
knowledge or abstract principles, behavioral change is motivated by
emotions, relationships, and meaningful narratives, including religious ones.
This means that for environmental philosophers who hope to help close the
gap between values and actions, "it is essential to have theories and practices
that reflect how emotion functions in tandem with critical thinking."[69]

The interconnections between intentions, actions, and consequences in
sorting out the causality of climate change suggests that an equally complex approach will be required to address it. Here the links between means
and ends can be important. Dewey's notion of ends-in-view might be especially helpful, as it shifts us from thinking about once-and-for-all solutions to
thinking about manageable, provisional ones. We can ask, for example, about
the ends-in-view that we might pursue in regard to climate change and how
they might in turn become means to future ends.

Conclusions

This last case study highlights both the complex mutual shaping of structures
and practices and the inadequacies of linear models of moral action. Both of
these themes have important implications for understanding moral responsibility, especially for questions about our capacity to address climate change and
other problems effectively in the public sphere. Worry about this problem has
led some environmental ethicists to lament the failure of their ideas to change
the world. This is particularly true of pragmatists, who believe that the task of

environmental ethics should be, as Bryan Norton writes, "to achieve within democratic societies more reasonable policies that square with human interests, policies that protect nature and natural processes according to our best scientific knowledge and reduce uncertainty and improve our knowledge for future management problems and decisions."[70] Measured by its contributions to this goal, Norton concludes, the evaluation of environmental ethics must be "bleak."[71] Even though concern for the environment is widespread and even mainstream in the United States and many other societies, environmental destruction continues at a frighteningly rapid pace, exemplified most dramatically in climate change.

There are many reasons for the lack of practical progress on a par with the spread of pro-environmental attitudes, and few of them can be laid at the feet of environmental philosophers. Still, there is a difficulty in the way many philosophers conceive of the relationship between moral theory and concrete social change, and it again reminds us of Marx's warning against mistaking "phrases" for the world.[72] We cannot combat anti-environmental attitudes with pro-environmental ones, because both types are shaped by human activities and will only change in concert with altered practices. "We construct the world through our practices, not through our ideas," as Vogel makes clear. "Practices are not 'ideal' but rather are entirely *real*. Engaging in them takes work, meets (indeed, requires) resistance, and frequently leads to failure."[73] Changing practices is often harder than changing ideas, but to change the world, we must change both, together and at the same time.

At the same time, we cannot easily replace unsustainable structures with sustainable ones. This is Marx's point in his critique of Feuerbach: "The materialist doctrine that men are products of circumstances and upbringing, and that, therefore, changed men are products of other circumstances and changed upbringing, forgets that it is men who change circumstances, and that it is essential to educate the educator himself."[74] Neither practices nor ideas can change in a vacuum, any more than individuals and structures can change independently of each other. They are always mutually constituting each other. The inextricable connections between practices and ideas, individuals and structures, underlines the impossibility of separating means and ends. We cannot just think changed structures into being, or even conceive of them in our minds in advance of acting, because, as Anthony Weston writes, "world and thought co-evolve."[75]

Conventional ways of thinking about the ethics of climate change do not help us develop more effective ways of addressing them. One of the strengths of practice-based ethics is its ability to do better in this regard. It directly challenges linear views of causal relationships, not just between ideas and actions but also between individual actions and larger structural change. While the former are important for various reasons, they do not automatically lead to changes in the latter. The person who bicycles or walks to work reduces her personal carbon footprint, for example, but does not necessarily enable other people to make similar changes. For that to happen, we need collective action and communities. Individual practices cannot solve the problem of climate change, but, as Vogel puts it, they can help "to *build the sort of community* capable of averting further climate change."[76] Public policies condition individual moral choices, just as individual actions make possible different policies. Practices can and must create changed structures, not just in technology, agriculture, and land use but also in governance and decision-making. The possibility of social change requires understanding the relations between these different scales and figuring out effective ways to connect them.

This connection between scales does not happen automatically. It requires concerted effort and often direct confrontation with power. Michael Maniates uses the example of the nineteenth-century labor campaign for an eight-hour workday, a struggle that succeeded not because of the personal habits of workers "but because they organized around a set of coherent demands and made their collective presence felt."[77] Addressing climate change will require similar organizations, attentive to the role of economic processes and political structures and willing to confront power. Although personal or local empowerment does not always lead to political power, small-scale successes and personal convictions can contribute to larger change, if they are deliberately and effectively connected to large economic and political structures.[78] Making these connections strong and lasting is a challenge not just for climate change activists but for all movements seeking structural change. The goal, as Raymond Williams noted in relation to British working class organizations, is "to connect particular struggles to a general struggle in one quite special way. . . . to make real what is at first sight the extraordinary claim that the defence and advancement of certain particular interests, properly brought together, are in fact the general interest."[79] Making these connections strong and lasting is the challenge facing all activists, including those focused on climate change. Success in this task requires attending to the actions and ideas of individuals, while always remembering that these individuals are embedded in material structures that profoundly influence all aspects of their lives. Understanding of the practical roots of moral ideas and actions is an important resource in this effort.

10

Conclusion

Thinking in and through Practice

[John Brown] did not use an argument, he was himself an argument.

—W. E. B. Du Bois[1]

Introduction

A practice-based approach to ethics opens up new ways of thinking about the moral dimensions of real-life problems such as war, euthanasia, hate speech, and climate change. However, its contributions are not limited to practical problems. Attention to practice also makes possible alternative approaches to the organization of ethical theory and the relation of ethics to other kinds of thinking and acting. Practice is not a silver bullet that solves all our ethical problems; it is not even, by itself, an ethical theory. However, it is an integral aspect of all our ways of thinking and feeling and thus of all parts of our moral life. Ethical theory should reflect this.

In this concluding chapter, I begin to sketch out what it means for ethical theory to take practice seriously. Drawing on arguments and themes from previous chapters, my goal is to lay out some of the key characteristics and strengths of a practice-based approach to ethical theory—not just of a particular practice-based theory but more broadly of a way of thinking about morality that puts practice front and center. I begin this task with attention to the ways practical experiences change moral attitudes, before reflecting one last time on the overarching themes I have highlighted throughout this book.

Practices Change Us

When we view ethical theory through a practice-centered lens, we see that human activities do not just "enact" values but generate them. What this

Works Righteousness. Anna L. Peterson, Oxford University Press (2021). © Oxford University Press.
DOI: 10.1093/oso/9780197532232.001.0001.

means, first, is that our sensuous activities create relationships, structures, technologies, and societies that in turn make possible and encourage certain ways of acting while discouraging or making impossible others. Thus, practices generate values collectively by mediating between people and their material circumstances. In addition, practices can generate values on a smaller scale. The particular activities of individuals can lead them to value certain things and disregard others. In a simple example, positive interactions with particular people or pets can make those individuals worthy of concern, while negative interactions may diminish the value of other individuals. A more complex example is habit or habituation, as both Aristotle and John Dewey highlight. Habituation results from repeated actions; when these actions embody and inculcate particular values, they create inclinations to continue acting in the same way. These inclinations are virtues if they are directed toward the good. Habitual practices come before, during, and after what we think of as ethical decisions; they are not a one-time "application" of values.

More concisely, when we act as though something is valuable, it changes how we think about it. Composer Philip Glass explains this in relation to his decision to stop eating meat, as part of his commitment to Buddhism:

> By not eating these other sentient-being life forms, we hope gradually to view them in a wholly different light—not as potential meals, snacks, and delicious flavors for our own appetites and pleasures, but as beings worthy of consideration equal to ourselves. This is a slow process: after being a vegetarian for thirty-five years, I still occasionally catch myself regarding fish as a food. But my own view has changed enough so that now I truly believe it is possible to transform our habitual mental patterns through this practice and to arrive at a perception of fellow sentient beings that is in complete accord with a Mahayana Buddhist point of view.[2]

Glass's experience shows the powerful effect that chosen practices can have on values. Applying an ethic, in the sense of living it out, does not require starting with full understanding and acceptance of the moral ideas involved. As Glass's experience shows, it is possible to choose certain practices that will shape attitudes. Glass learned which practices to enact from membership in a religious community that models and teaches certain activities. In aspiring to be a good Buddhist, he took up practices that help define Buddhist identity. This underlines the role of social support and examples, which are necessary for ethical living in any circumstances. A practice-based approach makes these factors clearer and helps us understand their roles in encouraging not just moral actions but also attitudes.

Practices need not be voluntary or deliberate, however, to have a moral impact. An example of this comes from Arun Agrawal's study of forest workers in Kumaon, India. Agrawal began with a question about why some, but not all, residents changed their belief about the need for forest protection, asking what distinguished these "environmental subjects," as he calls them, "from those who continue not to care about or act in relation to the environment."[3] Agrawal initially theorized that variables such as gender or caste would be the most significant predictors of people's attitudes about environmental protection. However, his research showed that the most important factor was participation in environmental projects. The people who were involved in their forest councils or worked in environmental enforcement became much more likely "to agree with the need to protect forests, to say that forests need to be protected for environmental rather than economic reasons, and to accept some reduction in their own use so as to ensure forest protection."[4] Practices of forest protection, in short, gave the forest greater moral value.

There are many other mundane examples of how ideas are shaped by practical experiences, chosen or not. For example, I may start bicycling to work in order to improve my cardiovascular fitness or reduce my use of fossil fuels, but the ride itself becomes pleasant and desirable. A more complex though equally commonplace example is becoming a parent. Although parenthood is not always deliberately chosen, it involves the same moral shift as the adoption of other new practices. Parents do not just rearrange the priority of different values but encounter new ones, created by the activities required in caring for children. For many people, a value that did not exist prior to parenthood—their children's welfare—becomes an overwhelming concern. This transformation of ethical perspective and priorities happens not in some automatic or magical way but in and through the practices of raising children.

According to most Western philosophies, actions done without full awareness are morally lacking; they are shallow, perhaps even dishonest. This judgment is reflected in familiar phrases such as "empty ritualism," "going through the motions," "playacting," and Luther's condemnation of "works righteousness." Even the less dismissive phrase "fake it till you make it" reflects an instrumental view of practice, as a means to achieving the desired attitude that for some reason was not attainable earlier. The example of Glass's vegetarianism, however, suggests that faking it can express not a lack of sincerity or depth but an effort to learn through practice both what is morally good and how best to pursue it and also to inculcate the embodied habits that enable one to continue practicing. By doing good, we learn not only what is good but also that we are capable of enacting it.

It is important to keep in mind the social nature of the changes wrought by practice. As I have argued throughout this book, practices are always social—even when we act alone, we act as social beings indelibly shaped by our histories and relations with other people. And many transformative experiences are explicitly social, involving, for example, participation in religious communities, labor unions, musical performances, military combat, or caring for loved ones. Practices with nonhuman animals and in natural places are also inherently social relationships, even when no other human actors are involved.

The ways experiences transform values are evident in the changes wrought by interactions with people who are different. A good example can be found in one of the most dramatic contemporary social changes, the well-documented and politically momentous shift in attitudes toward lesbian and gay people in the United States in the past few decades.[5] While there are many reasons for this change, a significant factor is practical experience, particularly interactions with ordinary people who are out of the closet. In a 2013 study, 37 percent of respondents cited lesbian or gay friends, family, or acquaintances as the reason for their increasing approval of same-sex marriage, and 32 percent mentioned "knowing someone who is gay."[6] In the past, many Americans believed they did not know anyone who was gay or lesbian, not because there were fewer gay people but because legal and cultural pressures kept them closeted. As decades of activism have diminished these cultural pressures and ensured greater legal protection, more Americans have everyday interactions with people they know to be gay or lesbian. Positive experiences with these people, in their roles as neighbors, coworkers, students, teachers, relatives, customers, religious leaders, and even politicians, diminish fear and increase empathy and respect. This is not a fast or easy process, and personal interactions alone are not adequate to change social structures and laws. However, altered practices, even as simple as everyday interactions with a well-liked colleague or neighbor who you learn is gay, can support changes in moral attitudes, which in turn can contribute to political and legal changes.

More broadly, research demonstrates that isolation from people who are different reduces empathy and tolerance for diversity and that the opposite is also true. One study showed that white college students who lived with African American roommates developed more favorable attitudes about affirmative action and also sought personal contacts with members of other ethnic groups, even after their year of living with a black roommate had ended. Overall, the researchers conclude, "mixing with members of other groups tends to make individuals more empathetic to these groups."[7] Other studies have confirmed that people who have close personal interactions with members of different groups gain greater understanding of and empathy for them.

On the other hand, "whites become less supportive of redistributive policies when they are assigned roommates from wealthy families."[8] Wealth in general is negatively correlated with generosity, honesty, compassion, and rule-following. A series of recent empirical studies shows repeatedly that "upper class individuals are worse at recognizing the emotions of others and less likely to pay attention to people they are interacting with."[9] Correlation, of course, is not causation, and it is not always clear whether a lack of compassion or honesty is a root cause of wealth or a consequence of it. The authors of the research mentioned here hypothesize both that "The less we have to rely on others, the less we may care about their feelings" and that wealthier people may have more positive attitudes toward greed. The relations between material conditions and moral attitudes, including experiences of privilege and attitudes toward those who have less, are always complex and multicausal. It is clear, however, that practical experiences can challenge or strengthen inherited values about race and class; they can make people more compassionate and open-minded, or they can reinforce entitlement and intolerance.

Empirical research, as well as anecdotal accounts such as Glass's story, contradicts "the common presumption that actions follow from beliefs," as Agrawal writes.[10] Changes in practice may be prompted by different factors, including economic imperatives, self-interest, and legal compulsion, but in any of these cases, they can help generate changes in values. In describing these processes, it is important to avoid suggesting a simple cause-effect determinism. In other words, there is a risk of simply inverting the idealist logic, so that instead of ideas causing actions, actions now cause ideas, in a kind of crude materialism that mirrors the crude idealism of linear models. No simplistic or unilateral explanation can capture the complexity of what actually happens when we think and act morally. When we pay attention to practices, however, we are better able to understand the origins and the nature of moral attitudes, as well as their consequences.

Toward a Practice-Centered Approach to Ethical Theory

My overarching goal in this book is to begin the task of building a practice-based ethical theory. Toward this goal, I have explored a variety of different theoretical models, which show a wide range of ways practice can enter ethical theory and of interpretations of this relationships. These various perspectives can prevent some of the weaknesses of idealist models and also illuminate specific ways attention to practice addresses these weaknesses. Without revisiting all my earlier discussions, I want to highlight some of my critiques and contributions, organized in relation to the five themes I have highlighted throughout the book.

1. In every alternative model I have examined, ideas are embedded in practices and in the cultures and structures that practices create. There are no autonomous ideas, no disembodied mind, will, or faith. Cognition, rather, is embodied—"essentially bound up with the agent's bodily capacities."[11] Moral thought and action engage all human faculties, including physical and emotional ones. Further, moral decisions are rarely made in the reasoned, careful way that philosophers describe. Rather, as Greg Miller puts it, "explicit conscious reasoning is not where the action is."[12] Emotion and habit are crucial to moral decision-making, and both emotion and habit are conditioned by social institutions and collective experiences.

Critiques of the identification of ethics with disembodied reason have been made familiar in recent decades by feminists, cognitive scientists, and a variety of other scholars. Rather than rehash their arguments, I want to highlight how this complex, holistic view of ethics is enriched by attention to practice. The central themes of contemporary critiques of rationalist ethics—the emphases on emotion, embodiment, and habituation—all hinge on practices, because practices are the way in which we are embodied and interact with the world beyond ourselves. Thus, a practice-focused approach to ethical theory both reinforces and expands other efforts to challenge the Enlightenment worship of universal laws and abstract, disembodied reason.

2. A practice-based approach also shows the impossibility of dividing form and content. Any ethic that is lived out must be thick and substantive. In thick moral theories, the content shapes the form, and vice versa. This is related to practices in at least two ways. First, because they are substantive and detailed, thick theories are full of practices, which are by definition always rooted in particular times and places, enacted in the lives and histories of concrete people, places, and cultures. Life is composed of practices, as Marx would remind us, and we cannot describe any important part of our lives, including morality, without attention to specific activities.

In addition, there can be no thin or formalist account of practice itself. An ethical theory focused on practices cannot be empty of content. This may suggest that when we inject practice, ethical theory necessarily becomes partial, narrow, and limited in its capacity to make claims on, or even speak to, people outside a locally shared set of practices. Thickness appears to prevent a critical stance that can assess and judge different ideas, practices, and events.[13] Thus, thick accounts of morality seem relevant only to particular situations and places, for example, in arguments about the details of a policy or position.

This account of thickness and thinness suggests that we must choose between substantive detail and the ability to connect across differences. However, as John O'Neill argues, we do not need a minimalist, cosmopolitan language to talk about values across cultures. "Greater depth need not be associated with a shift away from claims that make wider contributions to global conversations about value," he writes.[14] Many shared goods are expressed in different ways across cultures, locally rooted but not limited to local meanings. They can be, as O'Neill puts it, local cultural specifications of a good, rather than goods that are unique to a single culture. Examples include appreciation for family relationships, nonhuman nature, or character traits such as loyalty or generosity. Although each takes distinctive local forms, they are easily recognizable across geographic, linguistic, religious, and cultural boundaries. We can be rooted in these details and still find common ground with other people on things that matter.

Building ethical conversations around thick meanings requires us to look at what people really do and how their values and priorities are evident in and shaped by these practices. It is possible to value equity and justice without ignoring the substantive details that give meaning to both lives and moral problems. It is even possible, and perhaps necessary, to root ethical claims about equity and justice, among other values, in these details. This recalls

Cornel West's critique of liberal philosophy's attempt to remove itself from "the flux of history." Rather than seeking distance from everyday life, West argues, ethical theory can find its grounds in "consciously identifying with—and digesting *critically* the values of—a particular community or tradition."[15] These particularities provide both socially grounded values and thicker descriptions of moral problems, which in turn enable people to clarify and communicate their values and engage in conversations that can lead to substantive agreements and constructive practical programs.[16] Understanding local and personal perspectives is necessary for such conversations, not a hindrance to them. In shared practices, we build local meanings and also connect with others, even those whose locales differ.

3. Practice-based approaches to ethics share an assumption that ethics is social. This is true, first, because humans are social animals whose values are the product of past and present interactions with others. It is in our nature to be social, and we cannot think, speak, or practice outside of social relationships. Ethics is also social because they address social relationships and structures; their content, as well as their actors, are social—embedded in economic and political institutions as well as cultures, neighborhoods, and families. Ethics is social, further, because a good life in common with others is the end toward which moral thought and action aim: "No one lives enisled in a sea of alien humanity," as the early-twentieth-century philosopher W. F. Lofthouse wrote. "That would not be life. It would be death. We are persons, in constant and inevitable touch with other persons, invading them, so to speak, and invaded by them in turn. So far as we are ourselves, we transcend ourselves. We can be called real only so far as we are approaching a community not yet realized."[17] This communal life, further, is not just the end we seek but also the means to attaining this end. Relationships, between two people or an entire community, "can never be complete. At the very moment of attainment, we are conscious of something else to be reached."[18] Our social life, in this sense, is a kind of pragmatist end-in-view; it is always at once a good in itself and the only way we have to pursue other goods. For all these reasons, ethics is inevitably social.

Our moral thinking is not just necessarily social but better for being social. Two heads are better than one, and multiple voices will present alternative questions and solutions that may prove crucial to finding a better solution and one that reflects multiple interests, as pragmatists would point out. To put it another way, only a sociopath would try to make a life-or-death decision for others all by himself. No single actor has—or should have—enough power to solve big problems alone.[19]

4. Practice-based ethics shows the impossibility of separating morality from other spheres of life or drawing sharp lines between ethical reasoning and action and other kinds of human practice. This means, first, that ethics is practiced by everyone. This echoes Antonio Gramsci's insistence that every person is a philosopher, because philosophy is not separate from the rest of life. As he elaborated, "Each man, finally, outside his professional activity, carries on some form of intellectual activity, that is, he is a 'philosopher,' an artist, a man of taste, he participates in a particular conception of the world, has a conscious line of moral conduct, and therefore contributes to sustain a conception of the world or to modify it, that is, to bring into being new modes of thought."[20] I want to make a similar argument about the relationship of ethics to other areas of life and forms of thought. Ethics is not a separate compartment of life or something that only a few skilled professionals engage in but rather a practice in which virtually all people participate. It is proper to humans as such.

The fact that ethics is integrated into every aspect of life can, paradoxically, make it harder to change how we think about ethics. Our ways of thinking about ethics are constructed by and embedded in everyday practices, language, cultural forms, and material structures, all of which reinforce the idealism of dominant academic models. This idealism is evident not only in philosophical arguments about ethical theory but also in the everyday notion that it is the thought that counts. Such assumptions are hegemonic, in the academy and in everyday life. We cannot alter these powerful ways of thinking ethically, or about ethical theory, simply by an act of will. Thus, we must turn to the complex, unpredictable, and far from linear ways practices shape not only what we value but what we think about the process of valuing.

This task encompasses every aspect of our lives, for moral understandings are as varied as our activities. We act ethically and learn about ethics in caring for others, riding a bicycle, working in an office, planting trees, volunteering at an animal shelter, defending a military base, or playing in an orchestra. Of course, most of these are not only, or even primarily, moral undertakings. This is a strength of practice-based ethics, because it shows how practices connect different areas of our lives and also the various communities and institutions in which we participate.

Because they mediate between varied spheres and communities, practices reveal the shortcomings in theories that limit ethics to a specific kind of thinking or subject matter. This criticism finds support from thinkers who insist that ethics cannot be separated from other forms of thought, notably perennial gadflies Dewey and Marx. Both assert, for example, that ethics is tied up with not only epistemology but also history, science, economics, and politics. They reject in particular the separation between morals and experience, carried to its logical conclusion by Kant, who excluded from principles "all connection with empirical details," as Dewey writes, and "all reference of any kind to consequences." Because of this exclusion, Dewey asserts, Kant's concept of "reason becomes entirely empty; nothing is left except the universality of the universal."[21] While Kant pushed this model to the extreme, his insistence that ethics must be a distinctive kind of thought, unaffected by and separate from ordinary activities, shapes other major theories as well.

Compartmentalizing different kinds of ideas further denies the historical and material roots of all thinking. Thus, Marx would assert, and Dewey would likely agree, that Kant's effort to present his ideas as universal is a way to separate the ruling ideas from the people whose interests they serve.[22] The notion that ideas can have a life of their own—a "semblance of independence," as Marx puts it—rests on a denial of the way ideas are created by real people who, "developing their material production and their material intercourse, alter, along with this, their real existence, their thinking and the products of their thinking."[23] Idealism, in other words, depends on a denial of practice. When we bring practice into the heart of ethics, we necessarily consider the material structures that are created and shaped by human activity, including economic forces, technologies, political institutions, workplaces, cultural and religious communities, and more. Ethics is not just the product of practices, further, but is itself a practice that shapes other practices, people, and structures, wherever we perceive, experience, and construct value. Understood in this way, ethics has its place in almost every aspect of human life. To paraphrase Gramsci, we are all ethicists; every person, regardless of professional activity, carries on some form of moral activity, that is, she is an ethicist, a valuer, a person with duties and priorities; she participates in a particular conception of value, has a conscious line of moral conduct, and therefore contributes to sustain a valuation of the world or to modify it, that is, to bring into being new modes of moral thought.

5. A practice-focused approach to ethical theory views the relationship between ideas, actions, and consequences as complex, fluid, mutual, and unpredictable. Because of this, means and ends cannot be separated. They are convertible terms, as Gandhi put it. As a result, we cannot describe practices

as merely the result of prior decisions or the causes of desired effects. Sometimes a practice we adopt as a means to a goal becomes an end in itself, sometimes an objective we pursued becomes a means to a different goal, and quite often, the same practice is both means and end at the same time. Throughout all these permutations, our experiences and practices alter what we value.

Making practices central reveals that the relations between ideas, actions, and consequences are fluid, unpredictable, multidirectional, and socially embedded. This makes ethics an inherently risky activity.[24] We never have complete certainty about the results of our acts or even our own intentions in acting. To do justice to this complexity, we need an ethical vocabulary and an ethical theory that are concrete, flexible, multidirectional, and even improvisational. This theory, based on a more accurate account of ethical action, can ground a conception of intentions, actions, and consequences as related not in terms of cause and effect but rather in terms of means and ends, as reflected in Dewey's notion of ends-in-view and Gandhi's description of means as ends in the process of becoming. Practices are the key to these models, because they link means and ends in dynamic, fluid interactions.

Conclusions

I want to return to this chapter's epigraph and the question of what it means to say that John Brown "was himself an argument." I read this as a claim similar to John Howard Yoder's assertion that the kingdom of God is a social ethic. This means, Yoder explains, that "The alternative community discharges a modeling mission. The church is called to be now what the world is called to be ultimately."[25] In both cases, a concrete, living, material reality constitutes a moral claim, or a set of related claims. Brown not only articulated, defended, and preached his beliefs, but he lived them. They were his moral critique of society, his vision of how society should change, and his conviction about the good life for human beings. His practices embodied these values, and at the same time, they contributed toward the creation of a society in which people could live as they should. This echoes the conviction, held by Anabaptists, Gandhi, and King, that particular forms of community are central to the social changes that they pursued. In each case, a concrete form of life embodies a moral argument, by showing how people should live and at the same time helping them live that way.

The heart of this vision of ethics is the unity of ends and means. The ends that are desired—a free society or a Christian community—can be pursued only by living as free or truly Christian persons. In practicing those values, we make them real. This echoes Glass's account of how his vegetarianism transformed his valuation of other animals. The question, of course, is how we know what practices to undertake, if we can only know what is valuable in and through practices. The moral practices of Glass, like those of Gandhi, King, and Yoder, are rooted in religious traditions and communities of memory that provide both ideas and institutions that guide participants. W. E. B. Du Bois would note that Brown's approach to moral life was also shaped by a community, the radical abolitionist movement. In all cases, values came embedded in institutions, stories, and practices, providing models for behavior and a supportive setting within which individuals engage in their own practices. In this process, they do not merely mimic or follow instructions but experiment, change, challenge, and expand the traditions. Practice, in this perspective, "is no longer some application of ethical knowledge," as Jim Cheney and Anthony Weston write. "Practice is now *constitutive of ethics itself*, our very mode of access to the world's possibilities."[26] In doing, we learn not just what has value but also what it is possible to do.

The communities and movements that can ground a practice-based ethic have thickly normative identities as well as material expressions that enable members to witness the process and consequences of acting in one or another way and try out different ways of acting. This suggests that the way to change destructive attitudes or misplaced values is to act differently. This is what Glass's Buddhism proposes: in order to stop thinking of animals as food, stop treating them as such. We can add other examples. In order to believe that people of different races or cultures are fully human, treat them as such. In order to think of nonhuman nature as valuable in its own right, work to protect it. Weston expresses this in his reflection on the possibility of a non-human-centered ethic. Such an ethic, he argues, requires as its precondition a non-human-centered practice: "We need to deanthropocentrize the world rather than, first and foremost, to develop and systematize non-anthropocentrism—for world and thought co-evolve. We can only create an appropriate non-anthropocentrism as we begin to build a progressively less anthropocentric world."[27] Brown might have added that we can only create an appropriate antiracism as we begin to build a progressively less racist world.

This is a challenging task. It begins with finding compelling visions of moral practice. Particular communities can model and support moral practices, providing the context for the development of what Alasdair MacIntyre calls a narrative self, for which "the story of my life is always embedded in the story of those communities from which I derive my identity."[28] Thus, Glass can become vegetarian because he can draw on a long history of Buddhist practice and ideas, as well as the support of contemporary Buddhist communities. For people who are not committed to a specific moral community, however, there is a poignant uncertainty to MacIntyre's assertion that "I can only answer the question 'What am I to do?' if I can answer the prior question 'Of what story or stories do I find myself a part?' "[29] We are not always sure which stories include us, and how those stories might anchor our efforts to live good lives.

In addition, communities, traditions, and narratives are not the exclusive possessions of the virtuous. Many communities, and the stories they tell, can be parochial and intolerant or even cruel to outsiders. The German doctors who collaborated with the Nazis were rooted in particular values and acted as part of a story, no less than the communists who resisted the Nazis. Chilean Catholics who enabled the Augusto Pinochet regime to come to power acted within a narrative, as did the laypeople and Church leaders who aided the victims of the dictatorship. It can be difficult for people inside a community to critique it and its foundational stories. This brings us again to MacIntyre's question—we are all part of stories, but some people are part of stories that they reject or that reject them.

Thus, we face a paradox: practice-based ethics requires stories and structures that support moral action and inquiry, but there is no guarantee that we have the right ones. We need to ask, then, how to change the narratives in which we are embedded. The answer, again, lies in practice, but here again, we have to ask what can guide practice, in this situation. This seems circular, but pragmatist insights can help us clarify the moral logic at work here. One source of guidance comes from the open-ended task of inquiry that is so central to pragmatism. Dewey's social ethics was grounded in a view of democracy not as "a perfected end-state to be attained" but rather as "the development of critical intelligence and a method of living with regard to the past, present, and future."[30] For Dewey and other pragmatists, empirical evidence and constant testing are the key to knowing what is good. This is the substance of his normative claim that growth itself is the only moral end. Democracy, he wrote, "is the faith that the process of experience is more important than any special result attained, so that special results achieved are of ultimate value only as they are used to enrich and order the ongoing process."[31] These results are ends-in-view: one goal leads to another, as our practices lead to knowledge that generates new goals, just as scientific research leads to new questions as often as, or more than, it leads to definitive answers. This is an infinite process, without any final end, only ends-in-view.

This model seems to offer no firm guiding principles, apart from the open-ended advice to pursue knowledge and continually experiment, test, and revise our conclusions in community with other people. Inquiry may show that experience with people of different races and backgrounds leads to greater compassion and tolerance, but the path of inquiry does not tell us why we would value compassion and tolerance in the first place. If we are all ethicists, and our ethics are rooted in and shaped by our practices, there seems to be little ground for judging among different values. Since this problem is posed in part by pragmatism, it is fitting to offer a pragmatist answer. In 1891, William James gave an address in which he declared:

> The philosopher, then, qua philosopher, is no better able to determine the best universe in the concrete emergency than other men. He sees, indeed, somewhat better than most men what the question always is—not a question of this good or that good simply taken, but of the two total universes with which these goods respectively belong. He knows that he must vote always for the richer universe, for the good which seems most organizable, most fit to enter into complex combinations, most apt to be a member of a more inclusive whole. But which particular universe this is he cannot know for certain in advance; he only knows that if he makes a bad mistake the cries of the wounded will soon inform him of the fact.[32]

While there are no magic solutions, putting practice at the center of our ethical thinking can make our universe richer, help us organize the good in our lives and our societies, and open us to the cries of the wounded.

Notes

Chapter 1

1. Bertolt Brecht, "On Form and Subject Matter," in *Brecht on Theatre: The Development of an Aesthetic*, edited by John Willett (New York: Hill and Wang, 1964), 29.
2. Ali Altaf Mian, "Intention as Moral Attentiveness in Islamic Ethics," In *Hadith and Ethics: Concepts, Approaches and Theoretical Foundations*, ed. Mutaz al-Khatib (Leiden: Brill, forthcoming).
3. Margaret Urban Walker, *Moral Understandings: A Feminist Study in Ethics*, 2nd ed. (New York: Oxford University Press, 2007), 67.
4. I have not been able to find an original source for the phrase "add women and stir." I first heard it in the late 1980s in a graduate class with feminist theologian Anne Carr, who also quotes it in her book *Transforming Grace: Christian Tradition and Women's Experience* (New York: Harper & Row, 1990), 74. It is used frequently in feminist scholarship, e.g., Nel Noddings, "The Care Tradition: Beyond 'Add Women and Stir,'" *Theory into Practice* 40, no. 1 (Winter 2001): 29–34.
5. Martha C. Nussbaum, *Frontiers of Justice: Disability, Nationality, Species Membership* (Cambridge, MA: Harvard University Press, 2006), 2.
6. Gary Dorrien, *Social Ethics in the Making: Interpreting an American Tradition* (Malden, MA: Wiley-Blackwell, 2011), 3.
7. Anna L. Peterson, *Being Human: Ethics, Environment, and Our Place in the World* (Berkeley: University of California Press, 2001).
8. Alasdair MacIntyre, "Marxism: An Interpretation," in *Alasdair MacIntyre's Engagement with Marxism: Selected Writings 1953–1974*, edited by Paul Blackledge and Neil Davidson (Chicago: Haymarket Books, 2009), 15.
9. Alfred R. Mele, "Introduction," in *The Philosophy of Action*, edited by Alfred R. Mele (Oxford: Oxford University Press, 1997), 16.
10. John Dewey, *Reconstruction in Philosophy* (Boston: Beacon, 1957), 181.
11. Karl Marx, "Theses on Feuerbach," in *The Marx-Engels Reader*, edited by Robert C. Tucker (New York: W. W. Norton, 1978), 143.
12. Antonio Damasio, *Descartes' Error: Emotion, Reason, and the Human Brain* (New York: Avon, 1994), is a good introduction to these discussions.
13. Clifford Geertz, "Thick Description," in *The Interpretation of Cultures* (New York: Basic Books, 1973), 18.
14. Walker, *Moral Understandings*, ix.

Chapter 2

1. Immanuel Kant, *Fundamental Principles of the Metaphysics of Morals*, in *Ethics: History, Theory, and Contemporary Issues*, edited by Steven M. Cahn and Peter Markie (New York: Oxford University Press, 1998), 279.

2. Charlene Haddock Seigfried, *Pragmatism and Feminism: Reweaving the Social Fabric* (Chicago: University of Chicago Press, 1996), 241.

3. Walker, *Moral Understandings*, 8.

4. Walker, *Moral Understandings*, 7–8.

5. Walker, *Moral Understandings*, 9.

6. Antonio Gramsci, "Critical Notes on an Attempt at a Popular Presentation of Marxism by Bukharin," in *The Modern Prince & Other Writings* (New York: International Publishers, 1957), 108.

7. Walker, *Moral Understandings*, 19.

8. Walker, *Moral Understandings*, 19.

9. Robert Holmes, *Pacifism: A Philosophy of Nonviolence* (London: Bloomsbury, 2017), 75.

10. Augustine, *Homilies on the First Epistle of John 7.7*, http://www.newadvent.org/fathers/170207.htm. Quoted in Holmes, *Pacifism*, 75.

11. Augustine, *The City of God*, Book XIV, Ch.6. https://www.newadvent.org/fathers/1201.htm.

12. Holmes, *Pacifism*, 75. See also Lisa Sowle Cahill, *Love Your Enemies: Discipleship, Pacifism, and Just War Theory* (Minneapolis: Fortress Press, 1994), 70.

13. Augustine, *The Enchiridion*, ch. IX, para. 30, http://www.tertullian.org/fathers/augustine_enchiridion_02_trans.htm.

14. James Bissett Pratt, "The Ethics of St. Augustine," *International Journal of Ethics* 13, no. 2 (January 1903): 224.

15. James Turner Johnson, "Can a Pacifist Have a Conversation with Augustine? A Response to Alain Epp Weaver." *Journal of Religious Ethics* 29, no. 1 (Spring 2001): 90.

16. Martin Luther, "On Secular Authority: To What Extent It Should Be Obeyed," in *Martin Luther: Selections from His Writings*, edited by John Dillenberger (Garden City, NY: Anchor, 1961), 370.

17. Martin Luther, "On the Freedom of a Christian," in *Martin Luther: Selections from His Writings*, edited by John Dillenberger (Garden City, NY: Anchor, 1961), 53.

18. Luther, "On the Freedom," 53.

19. Luther, "On the Freedom," 64.

20. Luther, "On the Freedom," 55.

21. Luther, "Commentary on St. Paul's Epistle to the Galatians," in *Martin Luther: Selections from His Writings*, edited by John Dillenberger (Garden City, NY: Anchor, 1961), 105.

22. Martin Luther, "Commentary," 120.

23. Luther, "On the Freedom," 75.

24. Luther, "On the Freedom," 75.

25. Luther, "Commentary," 139.

26. Luther, "Commentary," 139; see also 144 and "On the Freedom," 67.

27. Luther, "On the Freedom," 75.

28. Luther, "On the Freedom," 70.

29. Daniel N. Robinson and Rom Harré, "The Demography of the Kingdom of Ends," *Philosophy* 69, no. 267 (January 1994): 10.

30. Kant, *Fundamental Principles*, 277.

31. Kant, *Fundamental Principles*, 277.

32. Kant, *Fundamental Principles*, 277.

33. Kant, *Fundamental Principles*, 277.

34. Immanuel Kant, "On a Supposed Right to Lie from Benevolent Motives," 1792, archived at https://philpapers.org/rec/KANOAS-2.

35. Immanuel Kant, *Perpetual Peace, Appendix I: On the Opposition between Morality and Politics with Respect to Perpetual Peace* (1795), https://www.mtholyoke.edu/acad/intrel/kant/append1.htm.

36. Christine M. Korsgaard, "The Right to Lie: Kant on Dealing with Evil." *Philosophy & Public Affairs* 15, no. 4 (Autumn 1986): 345.

37. Kant, *Fundamental Principles*, 284.

38. Immanuel Kant, *Foundation for the Metaphysic of Morals*, in *Ethical Theory: Classic and Contemporary Readings*, edited by Louis P. Pojman (Belmont, CA: Wadsworth, 2001), 274.

39. It is acceptable, presumably, to treat a person sometimes as partially a means to an end, such as a waiter who serves a meal or an employee who helps complete certain tasks. However, moral agents must not ever forget or deny that such persons have intrinsic value and are, therefore, also ends in themselves.

40. Judith Jarvis Thomson, "Afterword," in *Rights, Restitution, and Risk: Essays in Moral Theory* (Cambridge, MA: Harvard University Press, 1986), 252. James uses the phrase "cash value" in "What Pragmatism Means," in *Pragmatism: The Classic Writings*, edited by H. S. Thayer (Indianapolis: Hackett, 1982), 213.

41. Philippa Foot, "Abortion and the Doctrine of Double Effect," in *Virtues and Vices* (Oxford: Oxford University Press, 2002), 23.

42. Foot, "Abortion," 23.

43. Foot, "Abortion," 29.

44. Judith Jarvis Thomson, "The Trolley Problem," in *Rights, Restitution, and Risk: Essays in Moral Theory* (Cambridge, MA: Harvard University Press, 1986), 94–116.

45. Judith Jarvis Thomson, "A Defense of Abortion," in *Rights, Restitution, and Risk: Essays in Moral Theory* (Cambridge, MA: Harvard University Press, 1986), 10.

46. Bernard Williams, "A Critique of Utilitarianism," in *Utilitarianism: For and Against*, by J. J. C. Smart and Bernard Williams (Cambridge: Cambridge University Press, 1973), 99.

47. Foot, "Abortion," 29.

48. There are countless versions of this dilemma. Kohlberg discussed his in Lawrence Kohlberg, *Essays on Moral Development*, Vol. 1: *The Philosophy of Moral Development* (San Francisco: Harper & Row, 1981).

49. Carol Gilligan, *In a Different Voice: Psychological Theory and Women's Development* (Cambridge, MA: Harvard University Press, 1982).

50. Thomson, "Afterword," 257.

51. Thomson, "Afterword," 257.

52. Kwame Anthony Appiah, *Experiments in Ethics* (Cambridge, MA: Harvard University Press, 2008), 84.

53. Thomson, "Afterword," 257.

54. Tom Regan, *The Case for Animal Rights* (Berkeley: University of California Press, 2004), xvii.

55. Regan, *The Case*, 285.

56. Regan, *The Case*, 324.

57. Anthony Weston, *A Practical Companion to Ethics* (New York: Oxford University Press, 1997), 35.

58. Williams, "A Critique," 97.

59. Weston, *A Practical Companion*, 50.

60. For a discussion of this issue in relation to bioethics, see J. Liaschenko, N. Y. Oguz, and D. Brunnquell, "Critique of the 'Tragic Case' Method in Ethics Education," *Journal of Medical Ethics* 32, no. 11 (November 2006): 672–677.

61. Judith Jarvis Thomson, "Killing, Letting Die, and the Trolley Problem," in *Rights, Restitution, and Risk: Essays in Moral Theory* (Cambridge, MA: Harvard University Press, 1986), 86.

62. In real life, we need to know about them, but hypothetical dilemmas minimize details in order to present a stark choice between theoretical options.

63. Ruth Barcan Marcus, "Moral Dilemmas and Consistency," *Journal of Philosophy* 77, no. 3 (March 1980): 121.

64. Weston, *A Practical Companion*, 34–35.

65. Sara Ruddick, *Maternal Thinking: Toward a Politics of Peace* (Boston: Beacon, 1995), 95.

66. Ruddick, *Maternal Thinking*, 95.

67. Damasio, *Descartes' Error*, xvi–xvii.

68. Steven Fesmire, *John Dewey and Moral Imagination: Pragmatism in Ethics* (Bloomington: Indiana University Press, 2003), 83.

69. Mark Johnson, "Mind Incarnate: From Dewey to Damasio." *Daedalus* 135, on. 3 (Summer 2006): 48.

70. Johnson, "Mind Incarnate," 46.

71. Mark Johnson, *Moral Imagination: Implications of Cognitive Science for Ethics* (Chicago: University of Chicago Press, 1993), 163; quoting John Dewey, *Theory of the Moral Life* (New York: Holt, Rinehart, and Winston, 1960), 150–151.

72. William James, quoted in Johnson, "Mind Incarnate," 48.

73. Michael Banner, *The Ethics of Everyday Life: Moral Theology, Social Anthropology, and the Imagination of the Human* (Oxford: Oxford University Press, 2014), 7.

74. Geertz, "Thick Description," 18.

75. Michael Walzer, *Thick and Thin: Moral Argument at Home and Abroad* (Notre Dame, IN: University of Notre Dame Press, 1994).

76. Robert Bellah et al., *Habits of the Heart: Individualism and Commitment in American Life* (Berkeley: University of California Press, 1984), 80.

Chapter 3

1. Second Vatican Council, *Gaudium et spes*, http://www.vatican.va/archive/hist_councils/ii_vatican_council/documents/vat-ii_cons_19651207_gaudium-et-spes_en.html.
2. Aristotle, *Nichomachean Ethics* (New York: Penguin, 2004), 1103a14–18.
3. Aristotle, *Nichomachean Ethics*, 1103b17–26.
4. Aristotle, *Nichomachean Ethics*, 1103b8–17.
5. Aristotle, *Nichomachean Ethics*, 1106a5–8.
6. Aristotle, *Nichomachean Ethics*, 1104a1–5.
7. Aristotle, *Nichomachean Ethics*, 1105b10–18.
8. Julia Annas, "Being Virtuous and Doing the Right Thing," *Proceedings and Addresses of the American Philosophical Association* 78, no. 2 (November 2004): 70.
9. Annas, "Being Virtuous," 68.
10. Annas, "Being Virtuous," 68.
11. Alasdair MacIntyre, *After Virtue: A Study in Moral Theory* (Notre Dame, IN: University of Notre Dame Press, 1981), 201.
12. MacIntyre, *After Virtue*, 179.
13. MacIntyre, *After Virtue*, 58.
14. Pontifical Council for Justice and Peace, "Compendium of the Social Doctrine of the Church" (2004), no. 189, http://www.vatican.va/roman_curia/pontifical_councils/justpeace/documents/rc_pc_justpeace_doc_20060526_compendio-dott-soc_en.html.
15. Second Vatican Council, *Gaudium et spes*, no. 33; see also Pontifical Council for Justice and Peace, "Compendium," no. 287.
16. Second Vatican Council, *Gaudium et spes*, no. 33.
17. John Paul II, *Laborem Exercens: On Human Work*, no. 9, http://w2.vatican.va/content/john-paul-ii/en/encyclicals/documents/hf_jp-ii_enc_14091981_laborem-exercens.html
18. John Paul II, *Laborem Exercens*, no. 25.
19. John Paul II, *Laborem Exercens*, no. 25.
20. Pontifical Council for Justice and Peace, "Compendium," no. 58.
21. Luther, "On the Freedom," 56.
22. See Lilian Calles Barger, *The World Come of Age: An Intellectual History of Liberation Theology* (New York: Oxford University Press, 2018), for an expansive history which includes many Protestant and North American thinkers under the rubric of "liberation theology."
23. Gustavo Gutiérrez, *A Theology of Liberation* (Maryknoll, NY: Orbis Books, 1973), 11.
24. Justin Sands, "Introducing Cardinal Cardijn's See–Judge–Act as an Interdisciplinary Method to Move Theory into Practice," *Religions* 9 (2018): 4.

25. CELAM (Conference of Latin America Bishops), *The Church in the Present-Day Transformation of Latin America in the Light of the Council: Medellín Conclusions* (Washington, DC: National Conference of Catholic Bishops, 1979), 26.

26. Gutiérrez, *A Theology of Liberation*, 15.

27. Juan Luis Segundo, *The Liberation of Theology* (Maryknoll, NY: Orbis Books, 1976), 9.

28. Gutiérrez, *A Theology of Liberation*, 6.

29. Gustavo Gutiérrez, "Notes for a Theology of Liberation," *Theological Studies* 31, no. 2 (1970): 244; see also Gutiérrez, *A Theology of Liberation*, 56.

30. Jon Sobrino, *The True Church and the Poor* (Maryknoll, NY: Orbis Books, 2004), 24.

31. Segundo, *The Liberation of Theology*, 40.

32. Segundo, *The Liberation of Theology*, 8.

33. Gutiérrez, "Notes," 255; see also Gutiérrez, *A Theology of Liberation*, 11, 153.

34. Enrique Dussel, *History and the Theology of Liberation* (Maryknoll, NY: Orbis Books, 1976), 157.

35. Gutiérrez, *A Theology of Liberation*, 150.

36. Gutiérrez, *A Theology of Liberation*, 194.

37. Gutiérrez, "Notes," 257.

38. Gustavo Gutiérrez, *The Power of the Poor in History* (Maryknoll, NY: Orbis Books, 2004), 101.

39. Marilyn Friedman, "Beyond Caring: The De-moralization of Gender," in *Justice and Care: Essential Readings in Feminist Ethics*, edited by Virginia Held (Boulder: Westview, 1995), 63.

40. Gilligan, *In a Different Voice*, 19.

41. Gilligan, *In a Different Voice*, 28.

42. Friedman, "Beyond Caring," 62.

43. Nel Noddings, *Caring: A Feminine Approach to Ethics and Moral Education* (Berkeley: University of California Press, 1984), 3.

44. Ruddick, "Maternal Thinking," 359.

45. Virginia Held, "Feminist Moral Inquiry and the Feminist Future," in *Justice and Care: Essential Readings in Feminist Ethics*, edited by Virginia Held (Boulder: Westview, 1995), 154.

46. Ruddick, *Maternal Thinking*, xi.

47. Geertz, "Thick Description," 28.

48. Walker, *Moral Understandings*, 67.

49. Walker, *Moral Understandings*, 10.

Chapter 4

1. John Dewey, *Reconstruction in Philosophy* (Boston: Beacon Press, 1948), 167.

2. William James, quoted in Louis Menand, "Introduction," in *Pragmatism: A Reader*, edited by Louis Menand (New York: Vintage Books, 1997), xxv.

3. Menand, "Introduction," xxvi.

4. John Dewey, "Moral Theory and Practice," *International Journal of Ethics* 1, no. 2 (January 1891), 203.

5. Dewey, "Moral Theory and Practice," 188.

6. Charles Sanders Peirce, "What Pragmatism Is," in *Charles S. Peirce: Selected Writings (Values in a Universe of Chance)*, edited by Philip P. Wiener (New York: Dover, 1958), 183.

7. Charles Sanders Peirce, "How to Make Our Ideas Clear," in *Charles S. Peirce: Selected Writings (Values in a Universe of Chance)*, edited by Philip P. Wiener (New York: Dover, 1958), 124; see also Peirce, "What Pragmatism Is," 192.

8. Dewey, *Reconstruction in Philosophy*, 156.

9. William James, "What Pragmatism Means," in *Pragmatism: The Classic Writings*, edited by H. S. Thayer (Indianapolis and Cambridge: Hackett, 1982), 210.

10. James, "What Pragmatism Means," 213.

11. Dewey, *Reconstruction in Philosophy*, 156.

12. James, "What Pragmatism Means," 213. See also William James, *The Varieties of Religious Experience: A Study in Human Nature* (New York: Penguin, 1982).

13. Andrew Altman, "Pragmatism and Applied Ethics," *American Philosophical Quarterly* 20, no. 2 (April 1983): 233.

14. Anthony Weston, "Beyond Intrinsic Value: Progress in Environmental Ethics." *Environmental Ethics* 7, no. 4 (1985): 334–335.

15. John Dewey, "Means and Ends," in *Their Morals and Ours: Marxist versus Liberal Views on Morality*, edited by Leon Trotsky, John Dewey, and George Novack (New York: Merit, 1969), 53.

16. Dewey, "Moral Theory and Practice," 201.

17. Erin McKenna, *The Task of Utopia: A Pragmatist and Feminist Perspective* (Lanham, MD: Rowman & Littlefield, 2001), 99. McKenna provides a helpful list of five pragmatist criteria for good ends-in-view and good societies. I draw on her list but have modified it for this discussion.

18. McKenna, *The Task of Utopia*, 108.

19. McKenna, *The Task of Utopia*, 108.

20. McKenna, *The Task of Utopia*, 108.

21. McKenna, *The Task of Utopia*, 98.

22. Seigfried, *Pragmatism and Feminism*, 6.

23. James, "What Pragmatism Means," 213. See also James, *The Varieties of Religious Experience*.

24. Fesmire, *John Dewey*, 73, 70.

25. Joseph Margolis, "Peirce's Fallibilism," *Transactions of the Charles S. Peirce Society* 34, no. 3 (Summer 1998): 537.

26. John Dewey, quoted in Richard J. Bernstein, "Pragmatism, Pluralism, and the Healing of Wounds," in *Pragmatism: A Reader*, edited by Louis Menand (New York: Vintage Books, 1997), 388.

27. John Dewey, *Human Nature and Conduct* (New York: Henry Holt, 1922), 42, http://www.gutenberg.org/files/41386/41386-h/41386-h.htm.

28. Michael Eldridge, "Ethics," in *The Bloomsbury Companion to Pragmatism*, edited by Sami Pihlström (London: Bloomsbury, 2015), 143.

29. Peirce, "How to Make Our Ideas Clear," 121.

30. Dewey, *Human Nature and Conduct*, 20–21.

31. Dewey, *Human Nature and Conduct*, 20.

32. Dewey, *Human Nature and Conduct*, 29.

33. Elena Cuffari, "Habits of Transformation," *Hypatia* 26, no. 3 (Summer 2011): 537.

34. Fesmire, *John Dewey*, 10.

35. Dewey, *Human Nature and Conduct*, 16.

36. Dewey, *Human Nature and Conduct*, 21.

37. Dewey, *Human Nature and Conduct*, 21.

38. Dewey, *Human Nature and Conduct*, 21.

39. Dewey, *Human Nature and Conduct*, 24.

40. Steven Knapp and Walter Benn Michaels, "Against Theory," in *Against Theory: Literary Studies and the New Pragmatism*, edited by W. J. T. Mitchell (Chicago: University of Chicago Press, 1985), 380.

41. Theodore R. Schatzki, "Introduction: Practice Theory," in *The Practice Turn in Contemporary Theory*, edited by Theodore R. Schatzki, Karin Knorr Cetina, and Eike von Savigny (London: Routledge, 2001), 11.

42. Schatzki, "Introduction," 12.

43. Despite many areas of agreement with Marxism, pragmatists shy away from a fully materialist approach to social analysis or normative claims; see Cornel West, *The American Evasion of Philosophy: A Genealogy of Pragmatism* (Madison: University of Wisconsin Press, 1989).

44. Albert Weinberg, "A Critique of Pragmatist Ethics," *Journal of Philosophy* 20, no. 21 (October 11, 1923), 566.

45. Dewey, *Reconstruction in Philosophy*, 177.

46. Dewey, *Human Nature and Conduct*, 113.

47. William James, "The Moral Philosopher and the Moral Life," *International Journal of Ethics* 1, no. 3 (April; 1891): 330; quoted in Eldridge, "Ethics," 139.

48. Dewey, *Human Nature and Conduct*, 73.

49. Dewey, *Theory of the Moral Life*, 172; quoted in Marvin E. Kanne, "John Dewey's Conception of Moral Good," *Journal of Economic Issues* 22, no. 4 (December 1988): 1213.

50. Dewey, *Human Nature and Conduct*, 11.

51. Peirce, "How to Make Our Ideas Clear," 121.

52. Dewey, *Human Nature and Conduct*, 8.

53. Joshua August Skorburg, "Beyond Embodiment: John Dewey and the Integrated Mind," *The Pluralist* 8, no. 3 (Fall 2013): 67.

54. Dewey, quoted in Fesmire, *John Dewey*, 11.

55. Seigfried, *Pragmatism and Feminism*, 224.

56. Eldridge, "Ethics," 142.

57. Dewey, "Moral Theory and Practice," 188.

58. Sami Pihlström, "Research Methods and Problems," in *The Bloomsbury Companion to Pragmatism*, edited by Sami Pihlström (London: Bloomsbury, 2015), 56.

59. Pihlström, "Research Methods and Problems," 57.

60. Dewey, *Human Nature and Conduct*, 78.

61. Kanne, "John Dewey's Conception," 1220.

62. Altman, "Pragmatism and Applied Ethics," 233.

63. Dewey, *Reconstruction in Philosophy*, xviii; see also 170–171.

64. Dewey, *Human Nature and Conduct*, 18.

65. Dewey, *Human Nature and Conduct*, 17.

66. Charles L. Stevenson, "Reflections on John Dewey's Ethics," *Proceedings of the Aristotelian Society* 62 (1961–1962): 88.

67. Kanne, "John Dewey's Conception," 1217.

68. McKenna, *The Task of Utopia*, 86.

69. Sterling P. Lamprecht, "Ends and Means in Ethical Theory," *Journal of Philosophy, Psychology, and Scientific Methods* 17, no. 19 (September 9, 1920): 508.

70. Dewey, *Human Nature and Conduct*, 17.

71. Dewey, *Human Nature and Conduct*, 18.

Chapter 5

1. Karl Marx, "The German Ideology," in *The Marx-Engels Reader*, edited by Robert Tucker (New York: W. W. Norton, 1978), 149.

2. Antonio Gramsci, *Selections from the Prison Notebooks*, edited and translated by Quintin Hoare and Geoffrey Nowell-Smith (New York: International Publishers, 1971), 330–331.

3. Gramsci, *Selections*, 330–331.

4. Nancy Bancroft, "Does Marx Have an Ethical Theory?" *Soundings* 63, no. 2 (Summer 1980): 214.

5. Marx, "Theses on Feuerbach," 143.

6. Richard J. Bernstein, *Praxis and Action: Contemporary Philosophies of Human Activity* (Philadelphia: University of Pennsylvania Press, 1971), 13.

7. Bernstein, *Praxis and Action*, 76.

8. Bernstein, *Praxis and Action*, 43.

9. Marx, "Theses on Feuerbach," 144.

10. Marx, "The German Ideology," 165.

11. Marx, "The German Ideology," 149.

12. Bernstein, *Praxis and Action*, 43.

13. Karl Marx, quoted in Ernst Fischer, *The Necessity of Art: A Marxist Approach*, translated by Anna Bostock (New York: Penguin Books, 1981), 15.

14. Marx, "The German Ideology," 154.

15. Karl Marx, "Economic and Philosophic Manuscripts of 1844," in *The Marx-Engels Reader*, edited by Robert Tucker (New York: W. W. Norton, 1978), 113–114.

16. Marx, "The German Ideology," 154–155.

17. Karl Marx, "Contribution to the Critique of Hegel's *Philosophy of Right*," in *The Marx-Engels Reader*, edited by Robert Tucker (New York: W. W. Norton, 1978), 53–54.

18. Marx, "The German Ideology," 154.

19. Marx, "The German Ideology," 172; this echoes the claim made in the *Communist Manifesto* that the ruling ideas are the ideal expression of dominant material relations. See Karl Marx and Friedrich Engels, *The Manifesto of the Communist Party*, in *The Marx-Engels Reader*, edited by Robert Tucker (New York: W. W. Norton, 1978), 489.

20. Marx, "The German Ideology," 174–175.

21. Karl Marx, *The Eighteenth Brumaire of Louis Bonaparte*, in *The Marx-Engels Reader*, edited by Robert Tucker (New York: W. W. Norton, 1978), 595.

22. Bertell Ollman, *Alienation: Marx's Concept of Man in Capitalist Society* (Cambridge: Cambridge University Press, 1971), 131.

23. Paul Tillich, *Love, Power, and Justice: Ontological Analyses and Ethical Applications* (New York: Oxford University Press, 1960), 25.

24. Marx, "Contribution to the Critique," 53.

25. Marx, "Contribution to the Critique," 53–54.

26. Marx, "Contribution to the Critique," 54.

27. Marx, "Contribution to the Critique," 53–54.

28. Bernstein, *Praxis and Action*, 44.

29. Bernstein, *Praxis and Action*, 44–45.

30. Marx, "Economic and Philosophic Manuscripts," 77.

31. Marx, "Contribution to the Critique," 54.

32. Bernstein, *Praxis and Action*, 47.

33. Ollman, *Alienation*, 27.

34. Ollman, *Alienation*, 71.

35. Ollman, *Alienation*, 27–28.

36. E. P. Thompson, *The Making of the English Working Class* (New York: Vintage Books, 1966), 9.

37. Thompson, *The Making of the English Working Class*, 11.

38. Steven Lukes, *Marxism and Morality* (Oxford: Oxford University Press, 1987), 3.

39. Lukes, *Marxism and Morality*, 29.

40. Lukes, *Marxism and Morality*, 145.

41. Lukes, *Marxism and Morality*, 122.

42. Lukes, *Marxism and Morality*, 146.

43. Michel Foucault, *Power/Knowledge: Selected Interviews and Other Writings, 1972–1977*, edited by Colin Gordon (New York: Pantheon Books, 1980), 135.

44. Lukes, *Marxism and Morality*, iii.

45. Lukes, *Marxism and Morality*, 146–147.

46. Lukes, *Marxism and Morality*, 149.

47. Cornel West, *The Ethical Dimensions of Marxist Thought* (New York: Monthly Review, 1991), 91–92.

48. West, *The Ethical Dimensions*, 3.

49. West, *The Ethical Dimensions*, 65.

50. West, *The Ethical Dimensions*, xxi.

51. West, *The Ethical Dimensions*, xxiv.

52. Raymond Williams, "Literature and Sociology," in *Problems in Materialism and Culture: Selected Essays* (London: Verso, 1980), 22.

53. Paul Blackledge, *Marxism and Ethics: Freedom, Desire, and Revolution* (Albany: State University of New York Press, 2012), 3.

54. Blackledge, *Marxism and Ethics*, 3.

55. Blackledge, *Marxism and Ethics*, 4.

56. Blackledge, *Marxism and Ethics*, 207.

57. Marx, "Contribution to the Critique," 53.

58. Marx, "The German Ideology," 172; see also Marx and Engels, *The Manifesto*, 489.

59. Marx, "Theses on Feuerbach," 144.

60. Ollman, *Alienation*, 49.

61. Ollman, *Alienation*, 49.

62. Ollman, *Alienation*, 49.

63. Alasdair MacIntyre, "Notes from the Moral Wilderness," in *Alasdair MacIntyre's Engagement with Marxism: Selected Writings 1953–1974* (Chicago: Haymarket, 2009), 65.

64. Marx, "The German Ideology," 160.

65. MacIntyre, "Notes," 67.

66. Agnes Heller, *Everyday Life* (London: Routledge Kegan Paul, 1984), 87.

67. Heller, *Everyday Life*, 82.

68. Lukes, *Marxism and Morality*, 27; quoting Karl Marx, "On the Jewish Question," in *The Marx-Engels Reader*, edited by Robert Tucker (New York: W. W. Norton, 1978), 42, 43.

69. Raymond Williams, "Alignment and Commitment," in *Marxism and Literature* (Oxford: Oxford University Press, 1977), 200.

70. MacIntyre, "Notes," 55.

71. MacIntyre, "Notes," 55.

72. Raymond Williams, "Base and Superstructure in Marxist Cultural Theory," in *Problems in Materialism and Culture: Selected Essays* (London: Verso, 1980), 34.

73. Marx, "Theses on Feuerbach," 145.

Chapter 6

1. Mohandas K. Gandhi, *The Essential Gandhi*, edited by Louis Fischer (New York: Vintage Books, 1962), 173–174.

2. A. A. Milne, "The Pacifist Spirit," in *Nonviolence in Theory and Practice*, edited by Robert L. Holmes (Long Grove, IL: Waveland, 1990), 117.

3. J. Denny Weaver, *Anabaptist Theology in Face of Postmodernity: A Proposal for the Third Millennium* (Telford, PA: Pandora, 2000), 44.

4. James Childress, "Moral Discourse about War in the Early Church," *Journal of Religious Ethics* 12, no. 1 (Spring 1984): 2.

5. Robert L. Holmes, *On War and Morality* (Princeton, NJ: Princeton University Press, 1989), 181.

6. Robert L. Holmes, "Can War Be Morally Justified? The Just War Theory," in *Just War Theory*, edited by Jean Bethke Elshtain (New York: New York University Press, 1992), 200. See also Childress, "Moral Discourse," 6.

7. Michael Walzer, *Just and Unjust Wars: A Moral Argument with Historical Illustrations*, 3rd ed. (New York: Basic Books, 2000), 151.

8. Holmes, *On War and Morality*, 176.

9. Alex J. Bellamy, "Supreme Emergencies and the Protection of Non-Combatants in War," *International Affairs* 80, no. 5 (October 2004): 829.

10. Holmes, "Can War Be Morally Justified?" 223–224.

11. Laurie Calhoun, "The Metaethical Paradox of Just War Theory," *Ethical Theory and Moral Practice* 4, no. 2 (March 2001): 51.

12. Holmes, *On War and Morality*, 179.

13. John Howard Yoder, *The War of the Lamb: The Ethics of Nonviolence and Peacemaking*, edited by Glen Stassen, Mark Thiessen Nation, and Matt Hamsher (Grand Rapids, MI: Brazos, 2009), 36.

14. Helmut David Baer and Joseph E. Capizzi, "Just War Theories Reconsidered: Problems with Prima Facie Duties and the Need for a Political Ethic," *Journal of Religious Ethics* 33, no. 1 (March 2005): 125.

15. John Howard Yoder, *The Politics of Jesus* (Grand Rapids, MI: Eerdmans, 1994), 52.

16. Tertullian, "Apology," in *Christian Social Teachings: A Reader in Christian Social Ethics from the Bible to the Present*, edited by George Forell and James Childs (Philadelphia: Fortress, 2012), 27.

17. Luther, "On Secular Authority," 381.

18. The Schleitheim Confession of Faith, 1527, https://courses.washington.edu/hist112/ SCHLEITHEIM%20CONFESSION%20OF%20FAITH.htm.

19. The Schleitheim Confession.

20. The Schleitheim Confession.

21. The Schleitheim Confession.

22. David Kline, "God's Spirit and a Theology for Living," in *Creation and the Environment: An Anabaptist Perspective on a Sustainable World*, edited by Calvin Redekop (Baltimore: Johns Hopkins University Press, 2000).

23. David Weaver-Zercher, *The Amish in the American Imagination* (Baltimore: Johns Hopkins University Press, 2001), 153; John A. Hostetler, *Amish Society*, 4th ed. (Baltimore: Johns Hopkins University Press, 1993), 306.

24. *Confession of Faith in a Mennonite Perspective* (Scottdale, PA: Herald, 1995), 65–66.

25. *Confession of Faith*, 65–66.

26. James Cone, *Malcolm & Martin & America: A Dream or a Nightmare* (Maryknoll, NY: Orbis Books, 1991), 64.

27. Martin Luther King Jr., "Letter from a Birmingham Jail," April 14, 1963, 5, https:// www.africa.upenn.edu/Articles_Gen/Letter_Birmingham.html.

28. King, "Letter," 6.

29. Martin Luther King Jr., "Declaration of Independence from the War in Vietnam," speech at Riverside Church, New York, April 4, 1967, https://www.commondreams.org/views04/0115-13.htm.
30. King, "Declaration."
31. Mohandas K. Gandhi, *Non-Violent Resistance (Satyagraha)* (Minneola, NY: Dover, 2001), 3.
32. Mark Juergensmeyer, *Fighting with Gandhi: A Step-by-Step Strategy for Resolving Everyday Conflicts* (San Francisco: Harper & Row, 1984), 18.
33. Juergensmeyer, *Fighting with Gandhi*, 17.
34. Juergensmeyer, *Fighting with Gandhi*, 14.
35. Gandhi, *Non-Violent Resistance*, 6. See also Gandhi, *The Essential Gandhi*, 173.
36. This phrase is widely attributed to Gandhi and frequently quoted, but I have been unable to document its origin in his published writings.
37. Juergensmeyer, *Fighting with Gandhi*, 38.
38. Juergensmeyer, *Fighting with Gandhi*, 39.
39. Gandhi, *Non-Violent Resistance*, 13.
40. Gandhi, *The Essential Gandhi*, 166.
41. Gandhi, *The Essential Gandhi*, 132.
42. A. Whitney Sanford, "Being the Change: Gandhi, Intentional Communities, and the Process of Social Change," *Social Sciences Directory* 2, no. 3 (August 2013): 99.
43. Karuna Mantena, "Gandhi and the Means-Ends Question in Politics," Institute for Advanced Study School of Social Science Occasional Papers, no. 46 (June 2012), 14.
44. Yoder, John Howard, "The Kingdom as Social Ethic," in *The Priestly Kingdom: Social Ethics as Gospel* (Notre Dame, IN: University of Notre Dame Press, 1984), 80–101.
45. James F. Childress, "Just-War Criteria," in *War or Peace? The Search for New Answers*, edited by Thomas A. Shannon (Maryknoll, NY: Orbis Books, 1982), 52.
46. Childress, "Just-War Criteria," 52.
47. Yoder, *The War of the Lamb*, 36.
48. Yoder, *The War of the Lamb*, 36.
49. Gandhi, *The Essential Gandhi*, 266.
50. Martin Luther King Jr., quoted in Adam Fairclough, "Was Martin Luther King a Marxist?" *History Workshop Journal* 15, no. 1 (Spring 1983): 122.
51. Weaver, *Anabaptist Theology*, 114.
52. *Confession of Faith*, 86.
53. *Confession*, 89–90.
54. Yoder, *The War of the Lamb*, 83.
55. Yoder, *The War of the Lamb*, 83.
56. Yoder, *The War of the Lamb*, 84.
57. Holmes, *On War and Morality*, 178–179.
58. Yoder, *The War of the Lamb*, 61–62.
59. Martin Luther King Jr., "A Christmas Sermon on Peace," December 24, 1967, https://www.beaconbroadside.com/broadside/2017/12/martin-luther-king-jrs-christmas-sermon-peace-still-prophetic-50-years-later.html.
60. Yoder, *The Politics of Jesus*, 232.

61. John Howard Yoder, *For the Nations: Essays Public and Evangelical* (Grand Rapids, MI: Eerdmans, 1997), 41.
62. Cahill, *Love Your Enemies*, 2.
63. Sanford, "Being the Change," 32.
64. A. Whitney Sanford, "Being the Change: Food, Nonviolence, and Self-Sufficiency in Contemporary Intentional Communities," *Communal Societies* 34, no. 1 (2014): 49.
65. Walter Klaasen, "Pacifism, Nonviolence, and the Peaceful Reign of God," in *Creation and the Environment: An Anabaptist Perspective on a Sustainable World*, edited by Calvin Redekop (Baltimore: Johns Hopkins University Press, 2000), 140.
66. Klaasen, "Pacifism," 148.
67. Klaasen, "Pacifism," 149.

Chapter 7

1. *Cohen v. California*, 403 US 15 (1971), https://supreme.justia.com/cases/federal/us/403/15/.
2. Richard Delgado and Jean Stefancic, "Hateful Speech, Loving Communities: Why Our Notion of 'A Just Balance' Changes So Slowly," *California Law Review* 82, no. 4 (July 1994): 856.
3. Richard Spencer, "Facing the Future as a Minority," speech at American Renaissance Conference, 2013; reprinted on the Occidental Observer, a white nationalist website, http://www.theoccidentalobserver.net/2013/05/14/facing-the-future-as-a-minority/.
4. Southern Poverty Law Center, "Richard Bertrand Spencer," n.d., https://www.splcenter.org/fighting-hate/extremist-files/individual/richard-bertrand-spencer-0.
5. Daniel Lombroso and Yoni Applebaum, "White Nationalists Salute the President-Elect," November 21, 2016, https://www.theatlantic.com/politics/archive/2016/11/richard-spencer-speech-npi/508379/.
6. National Policy Institute, "Who Are We?" https://nationalpolicy.institute/whoarewe.
7. James Doubek, "Richard Spencer Leads Group Protesting Sale of Confederate Statue," NPR, May 14, 2017, http://www.npr.org/sections/thetwo-way/2017/05/14/528363829/richard-spencer-leads-group-protesting-sale-of-confederate-statue.
8. Fields pleaded guilty to federal hate crimes in March 2019. See https://www.washingtonpost.com/local/public-safety/neo-nazi-sympathizer-pleads-guilty-to-federal-hate-crimes-for-plowing-car-into-crowd-of-protesters-at-unite-the-right-rally-in-charlottesville/2019/03/27/2b947c32-50ab-11e9-8d28-f5149e5a2fda_story.html?utm_term=.cdffd4f1fffe.
9. Susan Svrluga, "'We Will Keep Coming Back': Richard Spencer Leads Another Torchlight March in Charlottesville," *Washington Post*, October 9, 2017, https://www.washingtonpost.com/news/grade-point/wp/2017/10/07/richard-spencer-leads-another-torchlight-march-in-charlottesville/?utm_term=.b981e7c73a2c.
10. US Supreme Court. *National Socialist Party of America v. Village of Skokie*," 432 U.S. 43 (1977), https://supreme.justia.com/cases/federal/us/432/43/case.html.
11. Ruth McGaffey, "The Heckler's Veto," *Marquette Law Review* 57, no. 1 (1973): 39–64.

12. Andrew Caplan, "Latest Tab for Richard Spencer Visit: $793,000," *Gainesville Sun*, January 25, 2018, http://www.gainesville.com/news/20180125/latest-tab-for-richard-spencer-visit-793000.

13. The site, freespeech.ufl.edu, has been deactivated since the event.

14. Comments posted on https://www.facebook.com/events/118168255546347/.

15. Chris Quintana, "An Anti-Hate Group Has This Advice for When the Alt-Right Comes to Campus," *Chronicle of Higher Education*, August 10, 2017, http://www.chronicle.com/article/An-Anti-Hate-Group-Has-This/240901. See also "SPLC: Don't Protest Spencer, That's What He Wants," *Auburn Plainsman*, April 10, 2017, http://www.theplainsman.com/article/2017/04/splc-dont-protest-spencer-thats-what-he-wants.

16. Bob Moser, "Richard Spencer Wins," *New Republic*, October 20, 2017, https://newrepublic.com/article/145402/richard-spencer-wins.

17. For example, see comments on https://www.facebook.com/NoWhiteSupremacyAtUF/.

18. https://www.facebook.com/events/118168255546347/.

19. Andrea Diaz and Nicole Chavez, "College's Bell Tower Trolled White Supremacist with Black National Anthem," CNN, October 20, 2017, http://www.cnn.com/2017/10/20/us/university-florida-bell-tower-trnd/index.html.

20. One of the Spencer supporters involved in the attempted shooting was sentenced to fifteen years. See https://www.gainesville.com/news/20190227/richard-spencer-supporter-tenbrink-gets-15-year-term.

21. K. A. Gross and D. R. Kinder, "A Collision of Principles? Free Expression, Racial Equality and the Prohibition of Racist Speech," *British Journal of Political Science* 28, no. 3 (1998): 449.

22. Richard Delgado, "Words That Wound: A Tort Action for Racial Insults, Epithets, and Name-Calling," *Harvard Civil Rights–Civil Liberties Law Review* 17 (1982): 135–136.

23. Delgado, "Words That Wound," 140.

24. Carl Cohen, "Free Speech Extremism: How Nasty Are We Free to Be?" *Law and Philosophy* 7, no. 3 (1988–1989): 263–279.

25. Lydialyle Gibson, "Growing Numbers," *University of Chicago Magazine*, September–October 2013), https://mag.uchicago.edu/law-policy-society/growing-numbers. See also Tom Smith, Benjamin Schapiro, and Jaesok Son, *General Social Survey Final Report: Trends in Public Attitudes about Civil Liberties, 1972–2014* (Chicago: NORC, 2015), 5.

26. Scott Clement, "Americans' Growing Support for Free Speech Doesn't Include Racist Speech," *Washington Post*, March 16, 2015, https://www.washingtonpost.com/news/wonk/wp/2015/03/16/americans-growing-support-for-free-speech-doesnt-include-racist-speech/?utm_term=.3aa907736731.

27. Gibson, "Growing Numbers."

28. Erica Goldberg, "Free Speech Consequentialism," *Columbia Law Review* 116, no. 3 (2016): 687–756.

29. Karen L. Bird, "Racist Speech or Free Speech? A Comparison of the Law in France and the United States," *Comparative Politics* 32, no. 4 (2000): 399–418.

30. Jeremy Waldron, "Dignity and Defamation: The Visibility of Hate," *Harvard Law Review* 123, no. 7 (2010): 1600.

31. Mari Matsuda, "Public Response to Racist Speech: Considering the Victim's Story," *Michigan Law Review* 87, no. 8 (1989): 2357.

32. Waldron, "Dignity and Defamation," 1656.

33. Sami Pihlström, "New Directions," in *The Bloomsbury Companion to Pragmatism*, edited by Sami Pihlström (London: Bloomsbury, 2015), 250.

34. Alison Kadlec, "Reconstructing Dewey: The Philosophy of Critical Pragmatism," *Polity* 38, no. 4 (2006): 254.

35. The quote was attributed to Voltaire in *The Friends of Voltaire*, written by Beatrice Evelyn Hall under the pseudonym S. G. Tallentyre and published in 1906; see https://www.themarysue.com/voltaire-beatrice-evelyn-hall/.

36. Kant, *Fundamental Principles*, 293.

37. Raymond Williams, "Structures of Feeling," in *Marxism and Literature* (Oxford: Oxford University Press, 1977), 129.

38. Marx, *The German Ideology*, 172.

39. Marx, *The German Ideology*, 174–175.

40. Anatole France, *The Red Lily* (1894), ch. 7, https://www.gutenberg.org/files/3922/3922-h/3922-h.htm.

41. Leonard Boasberg, "How the Poor Are Made Equal with the Rich," *New York Times*, July 13, 1988, https://www.nytimes.com/1988/07/13/opinion/l-how-the-poor-are-made-equal-with-the-rich-095688.html.

42. Ted Yoho, statement on Richard Spencer, October 16, 2017, https://www.facebook.com/plugins/post.php?href=https%3A%2F%2Fwww.facebook.com%2FCongressmanTedYoho%2Fposts%2F2185231301502836.

43. Meagan Flynn, "Calling Racism a 'Leftist Lie,' White Vandals Target California Black Lives Matter Slogan," *Washington Post* (July 6, 2020). https://www.washingtonpost.com/nation/2020/07/06/california-blm-mural-vandalized/

44. John Haltiwanger, "People Are Using Houston to Criticize 'All Lives Matter,'" *Newsweek*, August 29, 2017. http://www.newsweek.com/people-are-using-houston-talk-about-why-all-lives-matter-dumb-perspective-and-656442.

45. Marx, "On the Jewish Question," 42.

46. Max Cohen, "Trump: Black Lives Matter Is a 'Symbol of Hate,'" *Politico* (July 1, 2020). https://www.politico.com/news/2020/07/01/trump-black-lives-matter-347051

47. Erik Nielsen, "If We Silence Hate Speech, Will We Silence Resistance?" *New York Times*, August 9, 2018, https://www.nytimes.com/2018/08/09/opinion/if-we-silence-hate-speech-will-we-silence-resistance.html.

48. For a thoughtful analysis of another sense in which "blue lives matter," linked to the identity and relationships among police officers which sometimes override considerations of justice, see Matthew Guariglia, "'Blue Lives' Do Matter—That's the Problem," *Washington Post*, November 30, 2017, https://www.washingtonpost.com/news/made-by-history/wp/2017/11/30/why-blue-lives-matter/?utm_term=.bc2e5bd3ace9.

49. Joseph Mello, "Free Speech from Left to Right: Exploring How Liberals and Conservatives Conceptualize Speech Rights through the Works of Lenny Bruce and Milo Yiannopoulos," *Law, Culture and the Humanities* (Jan. 2018): 4.

50. Bellah et al., *Habits of the Heart*, 153.

51. John O'Neill, "Environmental Values through Thick and Thin," *Conservation and Society* 3, no. 2 (July–December 2005): 480.

52. O'Neill, "Environmental Values," 480.

53. O'Neill, "Environmental Values," 493.

54. O'Neil, "Environmental Values," 494.

55. MacIntyre, *After Virtue*, 58.

56. Marx, *The German Ideology*, 150.

Chapter 8

1. John Paul II, *The Gospel of Life (Evangelium vitae)* (New York: Times Books, 1995), 26.

2. John M. Crisp, "Physician-Assisted Suicide Needs Discussion," *Gainesville Sun*, June 17, 2015, 7A. The original text says "assure," which I have corrected to "ensure."

3. For a rare exception, see Jessica Pierce, "Human and Animal Euthanasia: Dare to Compare," *Psychology Today*, November 29, 2011 https://www.psychologytoday.com/blog/all-dogs-go-heaven/201111/human-and-animal-euthanasia-dare-compare.

4. Jessica Pierce, *The Last Walk: Reflections on Our Pets at the End of Their Lives* (Chicago: University of Chicago Press, 2012), 2.

5. Brad Hooker, "Rule-Utilitarianism and Euthanasia," in *Ethics in Practice*, 3rd ed., edited by Hugh LaFollette (Malden, MA: Blackwell, 2007), 66–67.

6. Jessica Pierce, "When We Kill Our Pets," *Chronicle of Higher Education*, September 10, 2012, https://www.chronicle.com/article/When-We-Kill-Our-Pets/134142.

7. Philippa Foot, "Euthanasia," in *Virtues and Vices* (Oxford: Oxford University Press, 2002), 33.

8. American Medical Association, "Code of Medical Ethics: Opinion 2.21—Euthanasia www.ama-assn.org/delivering-care/ethics/euthanasia.

9. Peter Singer, *Rethinking Life and Death: The Collapse of Our Traditional Ethics* (New York: St. Martin's, 1994), 151.

10. Helga Kuhse, "Euthanasia," in *A Companion to Ethics*, edited by Peter Singer (Malden, MA: Blackwell, 1993), 296.

11. American Medical Association, "Code of Medical Ethics: Opinion 2.21—Euthanasia."

12. American Medical Association, "Code of Medical Ethics Opinion 2.20—Withholding or Withdrawing Life-Sustaining Medical Treatment," www.ama-assn.org/delivering-care/ethics/withholding-or-withdrawing-life-sustaining-treatment.

13. Aaron Mackler, *Introduction to Jewish and Catholic Bioethics: A Comparative Analysis* (Washington, DC: Georgetown University Press, 2003), 66.

14. The Pew Research Center provides a helpful summary in "Religious Groups' Views on End-of-Life Issues," http://www.pewforum.org/2013/11/21/religious-groups-views-on-end-of-life-issues/.

15. Lois Snyder and Daniel P. Sulmasy, "Physician-Assisted Suicide," *Annals of Internal Medicine* 135, no. 3 (August 7, 2001): 209.

16. Snyder and Sulmasy, "Physician-Assisted Suicide," 209.

17. Tom L. Beauchamp, "Justifying Physician-Assisted Deaths," in *Ethics in Practice*, 3rd ed., edited by Hugh LaFollette (Malden, MA: Blackwell, 2007), 72, 73.

18. James Rachels, "Active and Passive Euthanasia.," in *Ethics: History, Theory, and Contemporary Issues*, edited by Steven M. Cahn and Peter Markie (New York: Oxford University Press, 1998), 779.

19. Foot, "Euthanasia," in *Ethics: History, Theory, and Contemporary Issues*, edited by Steven M. Cahn and Peter Markie (New York: Oxford University Press, 1998), 794.

20. Singer, *Rethinking Life and Death*, 80.

21. John Paul II, *The Gospel of Life*, 115–116.

22. Banner, *The Ethics of Everyday Life*, 117.

23. Banner, *The Ethics of Everyday Life*, 116; see also Mennonite Church Canada, "Life Worth Living: Issues in Euthanasia and Assisted Suicide" (Winnipeg: Mennonite Church Canada Council on Faith and Life, 1995).

24. M-K. Bendiane et al., "French District Nurses' Opinions towards Euthanasia, Involvement in End-of-Life Care and Nurse-Patient Relationship: A National Phone Survey," *Journal of Medical Ethics* 33, no. 12 (December 2007): 708.

25. Norman K. Brown et al., "How Do Nurses Feel about Euthanasia and Abortion?" *American Journal of Nursing* 71, no. 7 (July 1971): 1415.

26. Brown et al., "How Do Nurses Feel?" 1415. For similar research in Japan, see Atsushi Asai et al., "Doctors' and Nurses' Attitudes towards and Experiences of Voluntary Euthanasia: Survey of Members of the Japanese Association of Palliative Medicine." *Journal of Medical Ethics* 27, no. 5 (October 2001): 329.

27. B. Dierckx de Casterlé et al., "Nurses' Views on Their Involvement in Euthanasia: A Qualitative Study in Flanders (Belgium)." *Journal of Medical Ethics* 32, no. 4 (April 2006): 189.

28. Dierckx et al., "Nurses' Views," 189.

29. M. Berghs, B. Dierckx de Casterlé, and C. Gastmans, "The Complexity of Nurses' Attitudes toward Euthanasia: A Review of the Literature." *Journal of Medical Ethics* 31, no. 8 (August 2005): 444.

30. Naser Aghababaei, "Attitudes towards Euthanasia in Iran: The Role of Altruism," *Journal of Medical Ethics* 40, no. 3 (March 2014): 175.

31. A. Chapple et al., "What People Close to Death Say about Euthanasia and Assisted Suicide: A Qualitative Study." *Journal of Medical Ethics* 32, no. 12 (December 2006): 706.

32. Nikkie B. Swarte et al., "Effects of Euthanasia on the Bereaved Family and Friends: A Cross Sectional Study," *British Medical Journal* 327, no. 7408 (July 26, 2003): 189.

33. Swarte et al., "Effects of Euthanasia," 189.

34. Anne Fawcett, "Euthanasia and Morally Justifiable Killing in a Veterinary Clinical Context," in *Animal Death*, edited by Jay Johnston and Fiona Probyn-Rapsey (Sydney: Sydney University Press, 2013), 206.

35. Clinton R. Sanders, "Killing with Kindness: Veterinary Euthanasia and the Social Construction of Personhood," *Sociological Forum* 10, no. 2 (June 1995): 196–197.

36. Hugh LaFollette, *The Practice of Ethics* (Malden, MA: Blackwell, 2007), 127.

37. Fawcett, "Euthanasia," 206.

38. Pierce, *The Last Walk*, 165.
39. Pierce, *The Last Walk*, 184.
40. Regan, *The Case for Animal Rights*, 110.
41. Regan, *The Case for Animal Rights*, 119.
42. Nathan Winograd, *Irreconcilable Differences: The Battle for the Heart and Soul of America's Animal Shelters* (n.p., 2009), 94.
43. Winograd, *Irreconcilable Differences*, xv.
44. Winograd, *Irreconcilable Differences*, xiv.
45. Singer, *Rethinking Life and Death*, 105.
46. Williams, "Structures of Feeling," 129.
47. Winograd, *Irreconcilable Differences*, 19, 20.
48. Donna Haraway, *When Species Meet* (Minneapolis: University of Minnesota Press, 2008), 80.

Chapter 9

1. Wes Jackson, *Becoming Native to This Place* (Lexington: University Press of Kentucky, 1994), 5.
2. Willis Jenkins, *The Future of Ethics: Sustainability, Social Justice, and Religious Creativity* (Washington, DC: Georgetown University Press, 2013), 20.
3. Among the most valuable resources are reports available from the Intergovernmental Panel on Climate Change, https://www.ipcc.ch/reports/. Another good overview is J. T. Houghton, *Global Warming: The Complete Briefing*, 5th ed. (Cambridge: Cambridge University Press, 2015).
4. Steven Vogel, *Thinking Like a Mall: Environmental Philosophy after the End of Nature* (Cambridge, MA: MIT Press, 2015), 56.
5. Carolyn Merchant, *The Death of Nature: Women, Ecology, and the Scientific Revolution* (New York: Harper & Row, 1980), 241.
6. Stephen M. Gardiner, "Ethics and Global Climate Change," *Ethics* 114, no. 3 (April 2004): 559.
7. Thom Brooks, "The Real Challenge of Climate Change," *PS: Political Science & Politics* 46, no. 1 (January 2013): 34.
8. Gardiner, "Ethics and Global Climate Change," 573.
9. Alfred Mele, "Weakness of Will and Akrasia," *Philosophical Studies* 150, no. 3 (September 2010): 392.
10. Mele, "Weakness of Will," 392.
11. Amelie Rorty, "Plato and Aristotle on Belief, Habit, and 'Akrasia,'" *American Philosophical Quarterly* 7, no. 1 (January 1970): 50.
12. Elizabeth Shove, "Beyond the ABC: Climate Change Policy and Theories of Social Change," *Environment and Planning A* 42, no. 6 (2010): 1276.
13. Monica Anderson, "For Earth Day, Here's How Americans View Environmental Issues," Pew Research Center, April 20, 2017, http://www.pewresearch.org/fact-tank/2017/04/20/for-earth-day-heres-how-americans-view-environmental-issues/.

14. Eco-America, "The American Environmental Values Survey: American Views on the Environment in an Era of Polarization and Conflicting Priorities," October 2006, https://ecoamerica.org/wp-content/uploads/2013/02/AEVS_Report.pdf; Willett Kempton, James S. Boster, and Jennifer A. Hartley, *Environmental Values in American Culture* (Cambridge, MA: MIT Press, 1995).

15. Lissy Goralnik and Michael Nelson, "Forming a Philosophy of Environmental Action: Aldo Leopold, John Muir, and the Importance of Community," *Journal of Environmental Education* 42, no. 3 (2011): 183.

16. Kollmus and Agyeman, "Mind the Gap," 241.

17. Shove, "Beyond the ABC," 1274.

18. Shove, "Beyond the ABC," 1276.

19. Shove, "Beyond the ABC," 1277.

20. See, for example, Anja Kollmus and Julian Agyeman, "Mind the Gap: Why Do People Act Environmentally and What Are the barriers to Pro-Environmental Behavior?" *Environmental Education and Research* 8, no. 2 (2002): 239–260; and Thomas Princen, Michael Maniates, and Ken Conca, "Confronting Consumption," in *Confronting Consumption*, edited by T. Princen, M. Maniates, and K. Conca (Cambridge, MA: MIT Press, 2002).

21. Kollmus and Agyeman, "Mind the Gap," 241.

22. Princen, Maniates, and Conca, "Confronting Consumption," 12.

23. Princen, Maniates, and Conca, "Confronting Consumption," 5.

24. Kristin Schrader-Frechette, *Environmental Justice: Creating Equality, Reclaiming Democracy* (Oxford: Oxford University Press, 2002), 3.

25. Chris J. Cuomo, "Climate Change, Vulnerability, and Responsibility," *Hypatia* 26, no. 4 (Fall 2011): 695.

26. Cuomo, "Climate Change," 693.

27. Francis I, "*Laudato si*': On Care for Our Common Home," May 24, 2015, para. 49 http://w2.vatican.va/content/francesco/en/encyclicals/documents/papa-francesco_20150524_enciclica-laudato-si.html; italics in original.

28. Michael S. Northcott, *A Moral Climate: The Ethics of Global Warming* (Maryknoll, NY: Orbis Books, 2007), 143.

29. Northcott, *A Moral Climate*, 148.

30. Jonathan T. Park, "Climate Change and Capitalism," *Consilience* 14, no. 2 (2015): 192.

31. Lisa Kretz, "Climate Change: Bridging the Theory-Action Gap," *Ethics and the Environment* 17, no. 2 (Fall 2012): 18–19.

32. Marx, *The German Ideology*, 149.

33. Robert Jensen, "An Interview with Wes Jackson," *CounterPunch*, July 10, 2003, https://www.counterpunch.org/2003/07/10/an-interview-with-wes-jackson/.

34. Park, "Climate Change and Capitalism," 189.

35. Park, "Climate Change and Capitalism," 202.

36. Peter-Paul Verbeek, "Materializing Morality: Design Ethics and Technological Mediation," *Science, Technology, & Human Values* 31, no. 3 (May 2006): 361.

37. Verbeek, "Materializing Morality," 368–369.

38. Verbeek, "Materializing Morality," 366.

39. Vogel, *Thinking Like a Mall*, 44.

40. Juliet Schor, *The Overspent American: Why We Want What We Don't Need* (New York: Harper & Row, 1999), 102.

41. Marc A. Olshan, "Modernity, the Folk Society, and the Old Order Amish: An Alternative Interpretation," *Rural Sociology* 46, no. 2 (1981): 297–309.

42. Verbeek, "Materializing Morality," 362.

43. Verbeek, "Materializing Morality," 362.

44. Miguel Abensour, "William Morris: The Politics of Romance," in *Revolutionary Romanticism: A Drunken Boat Anthology*, edited by Max Blechman (San Francisco: City Lights, 1999), 146; quoted in E. P. Thompson, *William Morris: Romantic to Revolutionary* (Stanford, CA: Stanford University Press, 1981), 790–791. See also Anna L. Peterson, *Everyday Ethics and Social Change: The Education of Desire* (New York: Columbia University Press, 2009).

45. Vogel, *Thinking Like a Mall*, 74.

46. Vogel, *Thinking Like a Mall*, 74.

47. Ritsuko Ozaki, Isabel Shaw, and Mark Dodgson, "The Coproduction of 'Sustainability': Negotiated Practices and the Prius," *Science, Technology, & Human Values* 38, no. 4 (July 2013): 518–519.

48. Ozaki, Shaw, and Dodgson, "The Coproduction of 'Sustainability,' " 521, 518–519.

49. Ozaki, Shaw, and Dodgson, "The Coproduction of 'Sustainability,' " 519.

50. Ozaki, Shaw, and Dodgson, "The Coproduction of 'Sustainability,' " 520, 524.

51. Ozaki, Shaw, and Dodgson, "The Coproduction of 'Sustainability,' " 524.

52. Andrew Kernohan, "Individual Acts and Accumulative Consequences," *Philosophical Studies* 97, no. 3 (February 2000): 343.

53. Kernohan, "Individual Acts and Accumulative Consequences," 345.

54. Derek Parfit, *Reasons and Persons* (Oxford: Oxford University Press, 1984), 70.

55. Ian Smith, "On Explaining Individual and Corporate Culpability in the Global Climate Change Era." *Journal of Business Ethics* 112, no. 4 (February 2013): 552.

56. Cuomo, "Climate Change," 700–701.

57. Kernohan, "Individual Acts and Accumulative Consequences," 364.

58. Kretz, "Climate Change," 11; see also Mathias Frisch, "Climate Change Justice," *Philosophy & Public Affairs* 40, no. 3 (Summer 2012): 225–253; and Eric Posner and David Weisbach, *Climate Change Justice* (Princeton, NJ: Princeton University Press, 2010).

59. Marx, *The Eighteenth Brumaire*, 595.

60. Cuomo, "Climate Change," 704.

61. Cuomo, "Climate Change," 704.

62. Cuomo, "Climate Change," 708.

63. Cuomo, "Climate Change," 708.

64. Vogel, *Thinking Like a Mall*, 57; italics in original.

65. Raymond Williams, "Ideas of Nature," in *Problems in Materialism and Culture: Selected Essays* (London: Verso, 1980), 70–71.

66. Kempton, Boster, and Hartley, *Environmental Values*; cited in Richard Louv, *Last Child in the Woods: Saving Our Children from Nature-Deficit Disorder* (Chapel Hill, NC: Algonquin Books, 2005), 298.

67. Harwood Group, "Yearning for Balance: Views of Americans on Consumption, Materialism, and the Environment," Merck Family Fund, July 1995. https://enb.iisd.org/consume/harwood.html

68. Kretz, "Climate Change," 15. See also Carol Booth, "A Motivational Turn for Environmental Ethics," *Ethics & the Environment* 14, no. 1 (Spring 2009): 53–78; and Goralnik and Nelson, "Forming a Philosophy."

69. Kretz, "Climate Change," 15, 16.

70. Bryan G. Norton, "Why I Am Not a Nonanthropocentrist: Callicott and the Failure of Monistic Inherentism," *Environmental Ethics* 17 (Winter 1995): 355.

71. Norton, "Why I Am Not a Nonanthropocentrist," 343.

72. Marx, *The German Ideology*, 149.

73. Vogel, *Thinking Like a Mall*, 122.

74. Marx, "Theses on Feuerbach," 144.

75. Anthony Weston, "Non-Anthropocentrism in a Thoroughly Anthropocentrized World," *Trumpeter* 8, no. 3 (1991): 1, http://trumpeter.athabascau.ca/index.php/trumpet/article/download/459/760?inline=1.

76. Vogel, *Thinking Like a Mall*, 214. Italics in original.

77. Michael Maniates, "In Search of Consumptive Resistance: The Voluntary Simplicity Movement," in *Confronting Consumption*, edited by Thomas Princen, Michael Maniates, and Ken Conca (Cambridge, MA: MIT Press, 2002), 227.

78. Daniel Levine, *Popular Voices in Latin American Catholicism* (Princeton, NJ: Princeton University Press, 1992), 317, 318.

79. Raymond Williams, "The Forward March of Labour Halted?" in *Resources of Hope: Culture, Democracy, Socialism* (London: Verso: 1989), 249.

Chapter 10

1. W. E. B. Du Bois, *John Brown* (Philadelphia: George W. Jacobs, 1909), 341.

2. Philip Glass, "Vegetarianism as Practice," in *Dharma Rain: Sources of Buddhist Environmentalism*, edited by Stephanie Kaza and Kenneth Kraft (Boston: Shambhala, 2000), 343.

3. Arun Agrawal, "Environmentality: Community, Intimate Government, and the Making of Environmental Subjects in Kumaon, India," *Current Anthropology* 46, no. 2 (April 2005): 162.

4. Agrawal, "Environmentality," 177.

5. Pew Research Center, "Support for Same-Sex Marriage Grows, Even among Groups That Had Been Skeptical," June 26, 2017), http://www.people-press.org/2017/06/26/support-for-same-sex-marriage-grows-even-among-groups-that-had-been-skeptical/. Also see Pew Research Center, "Changing Attitudes on Gay Marriage," June 26, 2017, at http://www.pewforum.org/fact-sheet/

changing-attitudes-on-gay-marriage/; Hannah Fingerhut, "Support steady for same-sex marriage and acceptance of homosexuality," Pew Research Center FactTank, May 12, 2016 at http://www.pewresearch.org/fact-tank/2016/05/12/support-steady-for-same-sex-marriage-and-acceptance-of-homosexuality/; and David Cox, Juhem Navarro-Rivera, and Robert P. Jones, "A Shifting Landscape: A Decade of Change in American Attitudes about Same-Sex Marriage and LGBT Issues," *PRRI*, February 26, 2014 at https://www.prri.org/research/2014-lgbt-survey/.

6. Pew Research Center, "Changing Minds: Behind the Rise in Support for Gay Marriage," March 21, 2013), http://www.people-press.org/2013/03/21/gay-marriage-changing-opinions/; see also Pew Research Center, "Growing Support for Gay Marriage: Changed Minds and Changing Demographics," March 20, 2013, at http://www.people-press.org/2013/03/20/growing-support-for-gay-marriage-changed-minds-and-changing-demographics/.

7. Johanne Boisjoly et al., "Empathy or Antipathy? The Impact of Diversity," *American Economic Review* 96, no. 5 (December 2006), 1891.

8. Boisjoly et al., "Empathy or Antipathy?" 1902.

9. Daisy Grewal, "How Wealth Reduces Compassion," *Scientific American*, April 10, 2012, https://www.scientificamerican.com/article/how-wealth-reduces-compassion/. The recent university admissions scandal highlights some of the moral consequences of privilege, as explained in David Mayer, "Why Rich Parents Are More Likely to Be Unethical," *The Conversation*, March 15, 2019, https://theconversation.com/why-rich-parents-are-more-likely-to-be-unethical-113605.

10. Agrawal, "Environmentality," 162–163.

11. Komarine Romdenh-Romluc, "Agency and Embodied Cognition," *Proceedings of the Aristotelian Society* n.s. 111 (2011): 93–94. For a pioneering discussion of these issues, see Mark Johnson, *The Body in the Mind: The Bodily Basis of Meaning, Imagination, and Reason* (Chicago: University of Chicago Press, 1987).

12. Greg Miller, "The Roots of Morality," *Science* 320, no. 5877 (May 9, 2008): 734.

13. John O'Neill, "Environmental Values through Thick and Thin," *Conservation and Society* 3, no. 2 (July–December 2005): 482.

14. O'Neill, "Environmental Values," 494.

15. West, *The Ethical Dimensions*, 3.

16. O'Neill, "Environmental Values"; see also Walzer, *Thick and Thin*.

17. W. F. Lofthouse, "The Good as Means and as End," *Philosophy* 16, no. 64 (October 1941): 382.

18. Lofthouse, "The Good," 384.

19. See Sharon Welch, *A Feminist Ethic of Risk* (Minneapolis: Fortress, 1990).

20. Gramsci, *Selections*, 9.

21. Dewey, *Human Nature and Conduct*, 100.

22. Marx, *The German Ideology*, 174–175.

23. Marx, *The German Ideology*, 154–155.

24. Welch, *A Feminist Ethic*.

25. Yoder, "The Kingdom as Social Ethic," 92.

26. Jim Cheney and Anthony Weston, "Environmental Ethics as Environmental Etiquette," *Environmental Ethics* 21, no. 2 (Summer 1999): 125.
27. Weston, "Non-Anthropocentrism," 1.
28. MacIntyre, *After Virtue*, 205.
29. MacIntyre, *After Virtue*, 201.
30. McKenna, *The Task of Utopia*, 83.
31. McKenna, *The Task of Utopia*, 95, quoting John Dewey, "Creative Democracy: The Task before Us," in *John Dewey: The Later Works*, Vol. 1: *1925*, edited by Jo Ann Boydston (Carbondale: Southern Illinois University Press, 1981), 229.
32. James, "The Moral Philosopher," 350.

Bibliography

Adams, Carol. "The War on Compassion." In *The Feminist Care Tradition in Animal Ethics*, ed. Donovan, Josephine and Carol J. Adams. New York: Columbia University Press, 2007.

Aghababaei, Naser. "Attitudes towards Euthanasia in Iran: The Role of Altruism." *Journal of Medical Ethics* 40, no. 3 (March 2014): 173–176.

Agrawal, Arun. "Environmentality: Community, Intimate Government, and the Making of Environmental Subjects in Kumaon, India." *Current Anthropology* 46, no. 2 (April 2005): 161–181.

Altman, Andrew. "Pragmatism and Applied Ethics." *American Philosophical Quarterly* 20, no. 2 (April 1983): 227–235.

American Medical Association. "Code of Medical Ethics: Opinion 2.20—Withholding or Withdrawing Life-Sustaining Medical Treatment." www.ama-assn.org/delivering-care/ethics/withholding-or-withdrawing-life-sustaining-treatment.

American Medical Association. "Code of Medical Ethics: Opinion 2.21—Euthanasia." www.ama-assn.org/delivering-care/ethics/euthanasia.

Anderson, Monica. "For Earth Day, Here's How Americans View Environmental Issues." Pew Research Center, April 20, 2017. http://www.pewresearch.org/fact-tank/2017/04/20/for-earth-day-heres-how-americans-view-environmental-issues/.

Annas, Julia. "Being Virtuous and Doing the Right Thing." *Proceedings and Addresses of the American Philosophical Association* 78, no. 2 (November 2004): 61–75.

Appiah, Kwame Anthony. *Experiments in Ethics*. Cambridge, MA: Harvard University Press, 2008.

Aristotle. *Nichomachean Ethics*. New York: Penguin, 2004.

Asai, Atsushi, Motoki Ohnishi, Shizuko K. Nagata, Noritoshi Tanida, and Yasuji Yamazaki. "Doctors' and Nurses' Attitudes towards and Experiences of Voluntary Euthanasia: Survey of Members of the Japanese Association of Palliative Medicine." *Journal of Medical Ethics* 27, no. 5 (October 2001): 324–330.

Augustine. *The Enchiridion*. http://www.tertullian.org/fathers/augustine_enchiridion_02_trans.htm.

Augustine. *The City of God*. https://www.newadvent.org/fathers/1201.htm

Augustine. *Homilies on the First Epistle of John 7.7*. http://www.newadvent.org/fathers/170207.htm.

Baer, Helmut David, and Joseph E. Capizzi. "Just War Theories Reconsidered: Problems with Prima Facie Duties and the Need for a Political Ethic." *Journal of Religious Ethics* 33, no. 1 (March 2005): 119–137.

Bancroft, Nancy. "Does Marx Have an Ethical Theory?" *Soundings* 63, no. 2 (Summer 1980): 214–229.

Banner, Michael. *The Ethics of Everyday Life: Moral Theology, Social Anthropology, and the Imagination of the Human*. Oxford: Oxford University Press, 2014.

Barger, Lilian Calles. *The World Come of Age: An Intellectual History of Liberation Theology*. New York: Oxford University Press, 2018.

Beauchamp, Tom L. "Justifying Physician-Assisted Deaths." In *Ethics in Practice*, 3rd ed., edited by Hugh LaFollette,72–80. Malden, MA: Blackwell, 2007.

Bellah, Robert N., Richard Madsen, William Sullivan, Ann Swidler, and Steven Tipton. *Habits of the Heart: Individualism and Commitment in American Life.* Berkeley: University of California Press, 1985.

Bellamy, Alex J. "Supreme Emergencies and the Protection of Non-Combatants in War." *International Affairs* 80, no. 5 (October 2004): 829–850.

Bendiane, M-K., A. Galinier, R. Favre, C. Ribiere, J-M. Lapiana, Y. Obadia, and P. Peretti-Watel. "French District Nurses' Opinions towards Euthanasia, Involvement in End-of-Life Care and Nurse-Patient Relationship: A National Phone Survey." *Journal of Medical Ethics* 33, no. 12 (December 2007): 708–711.

Berghs, M., B. Dierckx de Casterlé, and C. Gastmans. "The Complexity of Nurses' Attitudes toward Euthanasia: A Review of the Literature." *Journal of Medical Ethics* 31, no. 8 (August 2005): 441–446.

Bernstein, Richard J. "Pragmatism, Pluralism, and the Healing of Wounds." In *Pragmatism: A Reader*, edited by Louis Menand, 382–401. New York: Vintage Books, 1997.

Bernstein, Richard J. *Praxis and Action: Contemporary Philosophies of Human Activity.* Philadelphia: University of Pennsylvania Press, 1971.

Bird, Karen L. "Racist Speech or Free Speech? A Comparison of the Law in France and the United States." *Comparative Politics* 32, no. 4 (2000): 399–418.

Blackledge, Paul. *Marxism and Ethics: Freedom, Desire, and Revolution*. Albany: State University of New York Press, 2012.

Boasberg, Leonard. "How the Poor Are Made Equal with the Rich." *New York Times*, July 13, 1988. https://www.nytimes.com/1988/07/13/opinion/l-how-the-poor-are-made-equal-with-the-rich-095688.html.

Boisjoly, Johanne, Greg J. Duncan, Michael Kremer, Dan M. Levy, and Jacque Eccles. "Empathy or Antipathy? The Impact of Diversity." *American Economic Review* 96, no. 5 (December 2006): 1890–1905.

Booth, Carol. "A Motivational Turn for Environmental Ethics." *Ethics & the Environment* 14, no. 1 (Spring 2009): 53–78.

Brecht, Bertolt. *Brecht on Theatre: The Development of an Aesthetic*, edited by John Willett. New York: Hill and Wang, 1964.

Brooks, Thom. "The Real Challenge of Climate Change." *PS: Political Science & Politics* 46, no. 1 (January 2013): 34–36.

Brown, Norman K., Donovan J. Thompson, Roger J. Bulger, and E. Harold Laws. "How Do Nurses Feel about Euthanasia and Abortion?" *American Journal of Nursing* 71, no. 7 (July 1971): 1413–1416.

Cahill, Lisa Sowle. *Love Your Enemies: Discipleship, Pacifism, and Just War Theory.* Minneapolis: Fortress, 1994.

Calhoun, Laurie. "The Metaethical Paradox of Just War Theory." *Ethical Theory and Moral Practice* 4, no. 1 (March 2001): 41–58.

Caplan, Andrew. "Latest Tab for Richard Spencer Visit: $793,000." *Gainesville Sun*, January 25, 2018. http://www.gainesville.com/news/20180125/latest-tab-for-richard-spencer-visit-793000.

Carr, Anne. *Transforming Grace: Christian Tradition and Women's Experience.* New York: Harper & Row, 1990.

CELAM (Conference of Latin America Bishops). *The Church in the Present-Day Transformation of Latin America in the Light of the Council: Medellín Conclusions.* Washington, DC: National Conference of Catholic Bishops, 1979.

Chapple, A., S. Ziebland, A. McPherson, and A. Herxheimer. "What People Close to Death Say about Euthanasia and Assisted Suicide: A Qualitative Study." *Journal of Medical Ethics* 32, no. 12 (December 2006): 706–710.

Cheney, Jim, and Anthony Weston. "Environmental Ethics as Environmental Etiquette." *Environmental Ethics* 21, no. 2 (Summer 1999): 115–134.

Childress, James F. "Just-War Criteria." In *War or Peace? The Search for New Answers,* edited by Thomas A. Shannon, 40–58. Maryknoll, NY: Orbis Books, 1982.

Childress, James F. "Moral Discourse about War in the Early Church." *Journal of Religious Ethics* 12, no. 1 (Spring 1984): 2–18.

Clement, Scott. "Americans' Growing Support for Free Speech Doesn't Include Racist Speech." *Washington Post,* March 16, 2015. https://www.washingtonpost.com/news/wonk/wp/2015/03/16/americans-growing-support-for-free-speech-doesnt-include-racist-speech/?utm_term=.3aa907736731.

Cohen, Carl. "Free Speech Extremism: How Nasty Are We Free to Be?" *Law and Philosophy* 7, no. 3 (1988–1989): 263–279.

Cohen, Max. "Trump: Black Lives Matter Is a 'Symbol of Hate.'" *Politico,* July 1, 2020. https://www.politico.com/news/2020/07/01/trump-black-lives-matter-347051

Cone, James. *Martin & Malcolm & America: A Dream or a Nightmare.* Maryknoll, NY: Orbis Books, 1991.

Confession of Faith in a Mennonite Perspective. Scottdale, PA: Herald, 1995.

Cox, David, Juhem Navarro-Rivera, and Robert P. Jones. "A Shifting Landscape: A Decade of Change in American Attitudes about Same-Sex Marriage and LGBT Issues." *PRRI,* February 26, 2014. https://www.prri.org/research/2014-lgbt-survey/.

Crisp, John M. "Physician-Assisted Suicide Needs Discussion." *Gainesville Sun,* June 17, 2015, 7A.

Cuffari, Elena. "Habits of Transformation." *Hypatia* 26, no. 3 (Summer 2011): 535–553.

Cuomo, Chris J. "Climate Change, Vulnerability, and Responsibility." *Hypatia* 26, No. 4, (Fall 2011): 690–714.

Damasio, Antonio R. *Descartes' Error: Emotion, Reason, and the Human Brain.* New York: Avon, 1994.

Delgado, Richard. "Words That Wound: A Tort Action for Racial Insults, Epithets, and Name-Calling." *Harvard Civil Rights–Civil Liberties Law Review* 17 (1982): 133–181.

Delgado, Richard, and Jean Stefancic. "Hateful Speech, Loving Communities: Why Our Notion of 'A Just Balance' Changes So Slowly." *California Law Review* 82, no. 4 (July 1994): 851–869.

Dewey, John. "Creative Democracy: The Task before Us." In *John Dewey: The Later Works,* Vol. 14: *1925–1953,* edited by Jo Ann Boydston, 224–230. Carbondale: Southern Illinois University Press, 1981.

Dewey, John. *Human Nature and Conduct.* New York: Henry Holt, 1922. http://www.gutenberg.org/files/41386/41386-h/41386-h.htm.

Dewey, John. "Means and Ends." In *Their Morals and Ours: Marxist versus Liberal Views on Morality,* edited by Leon Trotsky, John Dewey, and George Novack, 51–56. New York: Merit, 1969.

Dewey, John. "Moral Theory and Practice." *International Journal of Ethics* 1, no. 2 (January 1891): 186–203.

Dewey, John. *Reconstruction in Philosophy*. Boston: Beacon, 1957.

Dewey, John. *Theory of the Moral Life*. New York: Holt, Rinehart, and Winston, 1960.

Diaz, Andrea, and Nicole Chavez. "College's Bell Tower Trolled White Supremacist with Black National Anthem." CNN, October 20, 2017. http://www.cnn.com/2017/10/20/us/university-florida-bell-tower-trnd/index.html.

Dierckx de Casterlé, B., C. Verpoort, N. De Bal, and C. Gastmans. "Nurses' Views on Their Involvement in Euthanasia: A Qualitative Study in Flanders (Belgium)." *Journal of Medical Ethics* 32, no. 4 (April 2006): 187–192.

Dorrien, Gary. *Social Ethics in the Making: Interpreting an American Tradition*. Malden, MA: Wiley-Blackwell, 2011.

Doubek, James. "Richard Spencer Leads Group Protesting Sale of Confederate Statue." NPR, May 14, 2017. http://www.npr.org/sections/thetwo-way/2017/05/14/528363829/richard-spencer-leads-group-protesting-sale-of-confederate-statue.

Du Bois, W. E. B. *John Brown*. Philadelphia: George W. Jacobs, 1909.

Dussel, Enrique. *History and the Theology of Liberation*. Maryknoll, NY: Orbis Books, 1976.

Eco-America. "The American Environmental Values Survey: American Views on the Environment in an Era of Polarization and Conflicting Priorities." October 2006. https://ecoamerica.org/wp-content/uploads/2013/02/AEVS_Report.pdf.

Eldridge, Michael. "Ethics." In *The Bloomsbury Companion to Pragmatism*, edited by Sami Pihlström, 138–153. London: Bloomsbury, 2015.

Fairclough, Adam. "Was Martin Luther King a Marxist?" *History Workshop* 15, no. 1 (Spring,1983): 117–125.

Fawcett, Anne. "Euthanasia and Morally Justifiable Killing in a Veterinary Clinical Context." In *Animal Death*, edited by Jay Johnston and Fiona Probyn-Rapsey, 205–219. Sydney: Sydney University Press, 2013.

Fesmire, Steven. *John Dewey and Moral Imagination: Pragmatism in Ethics*. Bloomington: Indiana University Press, 2003.

Fingerhut, Hannah. "Support steady for same-sex marriage and acceptance of homosexuality." Pew Research Center FactTank, May 12, 2016. http://www.pewresearch.org/fact-tank/2016/05/12/support-steady-for-same-sex-marriage-and-acceptance-of-homosexuality/.

Fischer, Ernst. *The Necessity of Art: A Marxist Approach*, translated by Anna Bostock. New York: Penguin Books, 1981.

Flynn, Meagan. "Calling Racism a 'Leftist Lie,' White Vandals Target California Black Lives Matter Slogan." *Washington Post*, July 6, 2020. https://www.washingtonpost.com/nation/2020/07/06/california-blm-mural-vandalized/.

Foot, Philippa. "Abortion and the Doctrine of the Double Effect." In *Virtues and Vices*, 19–31. Oxford: Oxford University Press, 2002.

Foot, Philippa. "Euthanasia." In *Ethics: History, Theory, and Contemporary Issues*. Edited by Steven M. Cahn and Peter Markie, 783–798. New York: Oxford University Press, 1998.

Foot, Philippa. "Euthanasia." In *Virtues and Vices*, 33–61. Oxford: Oxford University Press, 2002.

Foucault, Michel. *Power/Knowledge: Selected Interviews and Other Writings, 1972–1977*, edited by Colin Gordon. New York: Pantheon Books, 1980.

France, Anatole. *The Red Lily*. 1894. https://www.gutenberg.org/files/3922/3922-h/ 3922-h.htm.

Francis I. "*Laudatosi*': On Care for Our Common Home." May 24, 2015. http://w2.vatican. va/content/francesco/en/encyclicals/documents/papa-francesco_20150524_ enciclica-laudato-si.html.

Friedman, Marilyn. "Beyond Caring: The De-moralization of Gender." In *Justice and Care: Essential Readings in Feminist Ethics*, edited by Virginia Held, XXX–XXX. Boulder: Westview, 1995.

Frisch, Mathias. "Climate Change Justice." *Philosophy & Public Affairs* 40, no. 3 (Summer 2012): 225–253.

Gandhi, Mohandas K. *The Essential Gandhi*, edited by Louis Fischer. New York: Vintage Books, 1962.

Gandhi, Mohandas K. *Non-Violent Resistance (Satyagraha)*. Minneola, NY: Dover, 2001.

Gardiner, Stephen M. "Ethics and Global Climate Change." *Ethics* 114, no. 3 (April 2004): 555–600.

Geertz, Clifford. "Thick Description." In *The Interpretation of Cultures*, 3–33. New York: Basic Books, 1973.

Gibson, Lydialyle. "Growing Numbers." *University of Chicago Magazine*, September–October 2013.https://mag.uchicago.edu/law-policy-society/growing-numbers.

Gilligan, Carol. *In a Different Voice: Psychological Theory and Women's Development*. Cambridge, MA: Harvard University Press, 1982.

Glass, Philip. "Vegetarianism as Practice." In *Dharma Rain: Sources of Buddhist Environmentalism*, edited by Stephanie Kaza and Kenneth Kraft, 342–343. Boston: Shambhala, 2000.

Goldberg, Erica. "Free Speech Consequentialism." *Columbia Law Review* 116, no. 3 (2016): 687–756.

Goralnik, Lissy, and Michael Nelson. "Forming a Philosophy of Environmental Action: Aldo Leopold, John Muir, and the Importance of Community." *Journal of Environmental Education* 42, no. 3 (2011): 181–192.

Gramsci, Antonio. *The Modern Prince & Other Writings*. New York: International Publishers, 1957.

Gramsci, Antonio. *Selections from the Prison Notebooks*, edited and translated by Quintin Hoare and Geoffrey Nowell-Smith. New York: International Publishers, 1971.

Grewal, Daisy. "How Wealth Reduces Compassion." *Scientific American*, April 10, 2012. https://www.scientificamerican.com/article/how-wealth-reduces-compassion/.

Gross, K. A., and D. R. Kinder. "A Collision of Principles? Free Expression, Racial Equality and the Prohibition of Racist Speech." *British Journal of Political Science* 28, no. 3 (1998): 445–471.

Guariglia, Matthew. "'Blue Lives' Do Matter—That's the Problem." *Washington Post*, November 30, 2017. https://www.washingtonpost.com/news/made-by-history/wp/ 2017/11/30/why-blue-lives-matter/?utm_term=.bc2e5bd3ace9.

Gutiérrez, Gustavo. "Notes for a Theology of Liberation." *Theological Studies* 31, no. 2 (1970): 243–261.

Gutiérrez, Gustavo. *The Power of the Poor in History*. Maryknoll, NY: Orbis Books, 2004.

Gutiérrez, Gustavo. *A Theology of Liberation*. Maryknoll, NY: Orbis Books, 1973.

Haltiwanger, John. "People Are Using Houston to Criticize 'All Lives Matter.'" *Newsweek*, August 29, 2017. http://www.newsweek.com/people-are-using-houston-talk-about-why-all-lives-matter-dumb-perspective-and-656442.

Haraway, Donna. *When Species Meet*. Minneapolis: University of Minnesota Press, 2008.

Harwood Group. "Yearning for Balance: Views of Americans on Consumption, Materialism, and the Environment." Merck Family Fund, July 1995. https://enb.iisd.org/consume/harwood.html

Held, Virginia. "Feminist Moral Inquiry and the Feminist Future." In *Justice and Care: Essential Readings in Feminist Ethics*, edited by Virginia Held, 153–177. Boulder: Westview, 1995.

Heller, Agnes. *Everyday Life*. London: Routledge Kegan Paul, 1984.

Holmes, Robert L. "Can War Be Morally Justified? The Just War Theory." In *Just War Theory*, edited by Jean Bethke Elshtain, 197–233. New York: New York University Press, 1992.

Holmes, Robert L. *On War and Morality*. Princeton, NJ: Princeton University Press, 1989.

Holmes, Robert L. *Pacifism: A Philosophy of Nonviolence*. London: Bloomsbury, 2017.

Hooker, Brad. "Rule Utilitarianism and Euthanasia." In *Ethics in Practice*, 3rd ed., edited by Hugh LaFollette, 62–71. Malden, MA: Blackwell, 2007.

Hostetler, John A. *Amish Society*, 4th ed. Baltimore: Johns Hopkins University Press, 1993.

Houghton, J. T. *Global Warming: The Complete Briefing*, 5th ed. Cambridge: Cambridge University Press, 2015.

Jackson, Wes. *Becoming Native to This Place*. Lexington: University Press of Kentucky, 1994.

James, William. "The Moral Philosopher and the Moral Life." *International Journal of Ethics* 1, no. 3 (April 1891): 330–354. James, William. "What Pragmatism Means." In *Pragmatism: The Classic Writings*, edited by H. S. Thayer, 209–226. Indianapolis: Hackett, 1982.

James, William. *The Varieties of Religious Experience: A Study in Human Nature*. New York: Penguin, 1982.

Jenkins, Willis. *The Future of Ethics: Sustainability, Social Justice, and Religious Creativity*. Washington, DC: Georgetown University Press, 2013.

Jensen, Robert. "An Interview with Wes Jackson." *CounterPunch* (July 10, 2003). https://www.counterpunch.org/2003/07/10/an-interview-with-wes-jackson/.

John Paul II. *The Gospel of Life (Evangelium vitae)*. New York: Times Books, 1995.

John Paul II. *Laborem exercens: On Human Work*. 1981. http://w2.vatican.va/content/john-paul-ii/en/encyclicals/documents/hf_jp-ii_enc_14091981_laborem-exercens.html.

Johnson, James Turner. "Can a Pacifist Have a Conversation with Augustine? A Response to Alain Epp Weaver." *Journal of Religious Ethics* 29, no. 1 (Spring 2001): 87–93.

Johnson, Mark. *The Body in the Mind: The Bodily Basis of Meaning, Imagination, and Reason*. Chicago: University of Chicago Press, 1987.

Johnson, Mark. "Mind Incarnate: From Dewey to Damasio." *Daedalus* 135, no. 3 (Summer 2006): 46–54.

Johnson, Mark. *Moral Imagination: Implications of Cognitive Science for Ethics*. Chicago: University of Chicago Press, 1993.

Johnson, Mark. "What Cognitive Science Brings to Ethics." In *Morality, Ethics, and Gifted Minds*, edited by Don Ambrose and Tracy Cross, 147–150. New York: Springer, 2009.

Juergensmeyer, Mark. *Fighting with Gandhi: A Step-by-Step Strategy for Resolving Everyday Conflicts*. San Francisco: Harper & Row, 1984.

Kadlec, Alison. "Reconstructing Dewey: The Philosophy of Critical Pragmatism." *Polity* 38, no. 4 (2006): 519–542.

Kanne, Marvin E. "John Dewey's Conception of Moral Good." *Journal of Economic Issues* 22, no. 4 (December 1988): 1213–1223.

Kant, Immanuel. *Foundation for the Metaphysic of Morals*. In *Ethical Theory: Classic and Contemporary Readings*, edited by Louis P. Pojman, 255–274. Belmont, CA: Wadsworth, 2001.

Kant, Immanuel. *Fundamental Principles of the Metaphysics of Morals*. In *Ethics: History, Theory, and Contemporary Issues*, edited by Steven M. Cahn and Peter Markie, 275–318. New York: Oxford University Press, 1998.

Kant, Immanuel. "On a Supposed Right to Lie from Benevolent Motives," 1792. Archived at https://philpapers.org/rec/KANOAS-2.

Kant, Immanuel. *Perpetual Peace, Appendix I: On the Opposition between Morality and Politics with Respect to Perpetual Peace* (1795). https://www.mtholyoke.edu/acad/intrel/kant/append1.htm.

Kempton, Willett, James S. Boster, and Jennifer A. Hartley. *Environmental Values in American Culture*. Cambridge, MA: MIT Press, 1995.

Kernohan, Andrew. "Individual Acts and Accumulative Consequences." *Philosophical Studies* 97, no. 3 (February 2000): 343–366.

King, Martin Luther, Jr. "A Christmas Sermon on Peace." December 24, 1967. https://www.beaconbroadside.com/broadside/2017/12/martin-luther-king-jrs-christmas-sermon-peace-still-prophetic-50-years-later.html.

King, Martin Luther, Jr. "Declaration of Independence from the War in Vietnam." Speech at Riverside Church, New York, April 4, 1967. https://www.commondreams.org/views04/0115-13.htm.

King, Martin Luther, Jr. "Letter from a Birmingham Jail." April 14, 1963. https://www.africa.upenn.edu/Articles_Gen/Letter_Birmingham.html.

Klaasen, Walter. "Pacifism, Nonviolence, and the Peaceful Reign of God." In *Creation and the Environment: An Anabaptist Perspective on a Sustainable World*, edited by Calvin Redekop, 139–153. Baltimore: Johns Hopkins University Press, 2000.

Kline, David. "God's Spirit and a Theology for Living." In *Creation and the Environment: An Anabaptist Perspective on a Sustainable World*, edited by Calvin Redekop, 61–69. Baltimore: Johns Hopkins University Press, 2000.

Knapp, Steven, and Walter Benn Michaels. "Against Theory." In *Against Theory: Literary Studies and the New Pragmatism*, edited by W. J. T. Mitchell, 11–30. Chicago: University of Chicago Press, 1985.

Kohlberg, Lawrence. *Essays on Moral Development*, Vol. 1: *The Philosophy of Moral Development*. San Francisco: Harper & Row, 1981.

Kollmus, Anja, and Julian Agyeman. "Mind the Gap: Why Do People Act Environmentally and What Are the Barriers to Pro-Environmental Behavior?" *Environmental Education and Research* 8, no. 2 (2002): 239–260.

Korsgaard, Christine M. "The Right to Lie: Kant on Dealing with Evil." *Philosophy & Public Affairs* 15, no. 4 (Autumn 1986): 325–349.

Kretz, Lisa. "Climate Change: Bridging the Theory-Action Gap." *Ethics and the Environment* 17, no. 2 (Fall 2012): 9–27.

Kuhse, Helga. "Euthanasia." In *A Companion to Ethics*, edited by Peter Singer, 294–302. Malden, MA: Blackwell, 1993.

LaFollette, Hugh. *The Practice of Ethics*. Malden, MA: Blackwell, 2007.

Lamprecht, Sterling P. "Ends and Means in Ethical Theory." *Journal of Philosophy, Psychology, and Scientific Methods* 17, no. 19 (September 9, 1920): 505–513.

Leo XIII. *Rerum novarum.* http://w2.vatican.va/content/leo-xiii/en/encyclicals/documents/hf_l-xiii_enc_15051891_rerum-novarum.html.

Levine, Daniel. *Popular Voices in Latin American Catholicism.* Princeton, NJ: Princeton University Press, 1992.

Liaschenko, J., N. Y. Oguz, and D. Brunnquell. "Critique of the 'Tragic Case' Method in Ethics Education." *Journal of Medical Ethics* 32, no. 11 (November 2006): 672–677.

Lofthouse, W. F. "The Good as Means and as End." *Philosophy* 16, no. 64 (October 1941): 372–385.

Lombroso, Daniel, and Yoni Appelbaum. "White Nationalists Salute the President-Elect." *Atlantic*, November 21, 2016. https://www.theatlantic.com/politics/archive/2016/11/richard-spencer-speech-npi/508379/.

Louv, Richard. *Last Child in the Woods: Saving Our Children from Nature-Deficit Disorder.* Chapel Hill, NC: Algonquin Books, 2005.

Lukes, Steven. *Marxism and Morality.* Oxford: Oxford University Press, 1987.

Luther, Martin. "Commentary on St. Paul's Epistle to the Galatians." In *Martin Luther: Selections from His Writings*, edited by John Dillenberger, 99–165. Garden City, NY: Anchor Books, 1961.

Luther, Martin. "On the Freedom of a Christian." In *Martin Luther: Selections from His Writings*, edited by John Dillenberger, 42–85. Garden City, NY: Anchor Books, 1961.

Luther, Martin. "On Secular Authority: To What Extent It Should Be Obeyed." In *Martin Luther: Selections from His Writings*, edited by John Dillenberger, 363–402. Garden City, NY: Anchor Books, 1961.

MacIntyre, Alasdair. *After Virtue: A Study in Moral Theory.* Notre Dame, IN: University of Notre Dame Press, 1981.

MacIntyre, Alasdair. "Marxism: An Interpretation." In *Alasdair MacIntyre's Engagement with Marxism: Selected Writings 1953–1974*, edited by Paul Blackledge and Neil Davidson, 1–23. Chicago: Haymarket, 2009 (originally Leiden: Brill, 2005).

MacIntyre, Alasdair. "Notes from the Moral Wilderness." In *Alasdair MacIntyre's Engagement with Marxism: Selected Writings 1953–1974*, edited by Paul Blackledge and Neil Davidson, 45–68. Chicago: Haymarket, 2009 (originally Leiden: Brill, 2005).

Mackler, Aaron. *Introduction to Jewish and Catholic Bioethics: A Comparative Analysis.* Washington, DC: Georgetown University Press, 2003.

Maniates, Michael. "In Search of Consumptive Resistance: The Voluntary Simplicity Movement." In *Confronting Consumption*, edited by Thomas Princen, Michael Maniates, and Ken Conca, 199–236. Cambridge, Mass.: MIT Press, 2002.

Mantena, Karuna. "Gandhi and the Means-Ends Question in Politics." Institute for Advanced Study School of Social Science Occasional Papers, no. 46 (June 2012).

Marcus, Ruth Barcan. "Moral Dilemmas and Consistency." *Journal of Philosophy* 77, no. 3 (March 1980): 121–136.

Margolis, Joseph. "Peirce's Fallibilism." *Transactions of the Charles S. Peirce Society* 34, no. 3 (Summer 1998): 535–569.

Marx, Karl. "Contribution to the Critique of Hegel's *Philosophy of Right*." In *The Marx-Engels Reader*, edited by Robert Tucker, 16–25. New York: W. W. Norton, 1978.

Marx, Karl. "Economic and Philosophic Manuscripts of 1844." In *The Marx-Engels Reader*, edited by Robert Tucker, 66–125. New York: W. W. Norton, 1978.

Marx, Karl. *The Eighteenth Brumaire of Louis Bonaparte.* In *The Marx-Engels Reader*, edited by Robert Tucker, 594–617. New York: W. W. Norton, 1978.

Marx, Karl. *The German Ideology*. In *The Marx-Engels Reader*, edited by Robert Tucker, 146–200. New York: W. W. Norton, 1978.

Marx, Karl. "On the Jewish Question." In *The Marx-Engels Reader*, edited by Robert Tucker, 26–53. New York: W. W. Norton, 1978.

Marx, Karl. "Theses on Feuerbach." In *The Marx-Engels Reader*, edited by Robert C. Tucker, 143–154. New York: W. W. Norton, 1978.

Marx, Karl, and Friedrich Engels. *The Manifesto of the Communist Party*. In *The Marx-Engels Reader*, edited by Robert Tucker, 469–500. New York: W. W. Norton, 1978.

Matsuda, Mari. "Public Response to Racist Speech: Considering the Victim's Story." *Michigan Law Review* 87, no. 8 (1989): 2320–2381.

Mayer, David. "Why Rich Parents Are More Likely to Be Unethical." *The Conversation*, March 15, 2019. https://theconversation.com/why-rich-parents-are-more-likely-to-be-unethical-113605.

McGaffey Ruth. "The Heckler's Veto." *Marquette Law Review* 57, no. 1 (1973): 39–64.

McKenna, Erin. *The Task of Utopia: A Pragmatist and Feminist Perspective*. Lanham, MD: Rowman & Littlefield, 2001.

Mele, Alfred R. "Introduction." In *The Philosophy of Action*, edited by Alfred R. Mele, 1–26. Oxford: Oxford University Press, 1997.

Mele, Alfred R. "Weakness of Will and Akrasia." *Philosophical Studies* 150, no. 3 (September 2010): 391–404.

Mello, Joseph. "Free Speech from Left to Right: Exploring How Liberals and Conservatives Conceptualize Speech Rights through the Works of Lenny Bruce and Milo Yiannopoulos." *Law, Culture and the Humanities* (January 2018): 1–20.

Menand, Louis. "An Introduction to Pragmatism." In *Pragmatism: A Reader*, edited by Louis Menand, xi–xxxiv. New York: Vintage Books, 1997.

Mennonite Church Canada. "Life Worth Living: Issues in Euthanasia and Assisted Suicide." Winnipeg: Mennonite Church Canada Council on Faith and Life, 1995.

Merchant, Carolyn. *The Death of Nature: Women, Ecology, and the Scientific Revolution*. New York: Harper & Row, 1980.

Mian, Ali Altaf. "Intention as Moral Attentiveness in Islamic Ethics." In *Hadith and Ethics: Concepts, Approaches and Theoretical Foundations*, edited by Mutaz al-Khatib. Leiden: Brill, forthcoming.

Miller, Greg. "The Roots of Morality." *Science* 320, no. 5877 (May 9, 2008): 734–737.

Milne, A. A. "The Pacifist Spirit." In *Nonviolence in Theory and Practice*, edited by Robert L. Holmes, 115–120. Long Grove, IL: Waveland, 1990.

Moser, Bob. "Richard Spencer Wins." *New Republic*, October 20, 2017. https://newrepublic.com/article/145402/richard-spencer-wins.

National Policy Institute. "Who Are We?" https://nationalpolicy.institute/whoarewe.

Nielsen, Erik. "If We Silence Hate Speech, Will We Silence Resistance?" *New York Times*, August 9, 2018. https://www.nytimes.com/2018/08/09/opinion/if-we-silence-hate-speech-will-we-silence-resistance.html.

Noddings, Nel. "The Care Tradition: Beyond 'Add Women and Stir.'" *Theory into Practice* 40, no. 1 (Winter 2001): 29–34.

Noddings, Nel. *Caring: A Feminine Approach to Ethics and Moral Education*. Berkeley: University of California Press, 1984.

Northcott, Michael S. *A Moral Climate: The Ethics of Global Warming*. Maryknoll, NY: Orbis Books, 2007.

Norton, Bryan G. "Why I Am Not a Nonanthropocentrist: Callicott and the Failure of Monistic Inherentism." *Environmental Ethics* 17 (Winter 1995): 341–358.

Nussbaum, Martha C. *Frontiers of Justice: Disability, Nationality, Species Membership.* Cambridge, MA: Harvard University Press, 2006.

Ollman, Bertell. *Alienation: Marx's Conception of Man in Capitalist Society.* Cambridge: Cambridge University Press, 1971.

Olshan, Marc A. "Modernity, the Folk Society, and the Old Order Amish: An Alternative Interpretation." *Rural Sociology* 46, no. 2 (1981): 297–309.

O'Neill, John. "Environmental Values through Thick and Thin." *Conservation and Society* 3, no. 2 (July–December 2005): 479–500.

Ozaki, Ritsuko, Isabel Shaw, and Mark Dodgson. "The Coproduction of 'Sustainability': Negotiated Practices and the Prius." *Science, Technology, & Human Values* 38, no. 4 (July 2013): 518–541.

Parfit, Derek. *Reasons and Persons.* Oxford: Oxford University Press, 1984.

Park, Jonathan T. "Climate Change and Capitalism." *Consilience* 14, no. 2 (2015): 189–206.

Peirce, Charles Sanders. "How to Make Our Ideas Clear." In *Charles S. Peirce: Selected Writings (Values in a Universe of Chance),* edited by Philip P. Wiener, 113–136. New York: Dover, 1958.

Peirce, Charles S. "What Pragmatism Is." In *Charles S. Peirce: Selected Writings (Values in a Universe of Chance),* edited by Philip P. Wiener, 180–202. New York: Dover, 1958.

Peterson, Anna L. *Being Human: Ethics, Environment, and Our Place in the World.* Berkeley: University of California Press, 2001.

Peterson, Anna L. *Everyday Ethics and Social Change: The Education of Desire.* New York: Columbia University Press, 2009.

Pew Research Center. "Attitudes on Same-Sex Marriage." June 26, 2017. http://www.pewforum.org/fact-sheet/changing-attitudes-on-gay-marriage/.

Pew Research Center. "Changing Minds: Behind the Rise in Support for Gay Marriage." March 21, 2013. http://www.people-press.org/2013/03/21/gay-marriage-changing-opinions/.

Pew Research Center. "Growing Support for Gay Marriage: Changed Minds and Changing Demographics." March 20, 2013. http://www.people-press.org/2013/03/20/growing-support-for-gay-marriage-changed-minds-and-changing-demographics/.

Pew Research Center. "Religious Groups' Views on End-of-Life Issues." http://www.pewforum.org/2013/11/21/religious-groups-views-on-end-of-life-issues/.

Pew Research Center. "Support for Same-Sex Marriage Grows, Even among Groups That Had Been Skeptical." June 26, 2017. http://www.people-press.org/2017/06/26/support-for-same-sex-marriage-grows-even-among-groups-that-had-been-skeptical/.

Pierce, Jessica. "Human and Animal Euthanasia: Dare to Compare." *Psychology Today,* November 29, 2011. https://www.psychologytoday.com/blog/all-dogs-go-heaven/201111/human-and-animal-euthanasia-dare-to-compare.

Pierce, Jessica. *The Last Walk: Reflections on Our Pets at the End of Their Lives.* Chicago: University of Chicago Press, 2012.

Pierce, Jessica. "When We Kill Our Pets." *Chronicle of Higher Education,* September 10, 2012. https://www.chronicle.com/article/When-We-Kill-Our-Pets/134142.

Pihlström, Sami. "New Directions." In *The Bloomsbury Companion to Pragmatism,* edited by Sami Pihlström, 238–254. London: Bloomsbury, 2015.

Pihlström, Sami. "Research Methods and Problems." In *The Bloomsbury Companion to Pragmatism,* edited by Sami Pihlström, 37–63. London: Bloomsbury, 2015.

Pontifical Council for Justice and Peace. "Compendium of the Social Doctrine of the Church." 2004.

Posner, Eric, and David Weisbach. *Climate Change Justice*. Princeton, NJ: Princeton University Press, 2010.

Pratt, James Bissett. "The Ethics of St. Augustine." *International Journal of Ethics* 13, no. 2 (January 1903): 222–235.

Princen, Thomas, Michael Maniates, and Ken Conca. "Confronting Consumption." In *Confronting Consumption*, edited by T. Princen, M. Maniates, and K. Conca, 1–20. Cambridge, MA: MIT Press, 2002.

Quintana, Chris. "An Anti-Hate Group Has This Advice for When the Alt-Right Comes to Campus." *Chronicle of Higher Education*, August 10, 2017. http://www.chronicle.com/article/An-Anti-Hate-Group-Has-This/240901.

Rachels, James. "Active and Passive Euthanasia." In *Ethics: History, Theory, and Contemporary Issues*, edited by Steven M. Cahn and Peter Markie, 778–782. New York: Oxford University Press, 1998.

Regan, Tom. *The Case for Animal Rights*. Berkeley: University of California Press, 2004.

Robinson, Daniel N., and Rom Harré. "The Demography of the Kingdom of Ends." *Philosophy* 69, no. 267 (January 1994): 5–19.

Romdenh-Romluc, Komarine. "Agency and Embodied Cognition." *Proceedings of the Aristotelian Society* n.s. 111 (2011): 79–95.

Rorty, Amelie. "Plato and Aristotle on Belief, Habit, and 'Akrasia.'" *American Philosophical Quarterly* 7, no. 1 (January 1970): 50–61.

Ruddick, Sara. "Maternal Thinking." *Feminist Studies* 6, no. 2 (Summer 1980): 342–367.

Ruddick, Sara. *Maternal Thinking: Toward a Politics of Peace*. Boston: Beacon, 1995.

Sanders, Clinton R. "Killing with Kindness: Veterinary Euthanasia and the Social Construction of Personhood." *Sociological Forum* 10, no. 2 (June 1995): 195–214.

Sands, Justin. "Introducing Cardinal Cardijn's See–Judge–Act as an Interdisciplinary Method to Move Theory into Practice." *Religions* 9 (2018): 1–10.

Sanford, A. Whitney. "Being the Change: Food, Nonviolence, and Self-Sufficiency in Contemporary Intentional Communities." *Communal Societies Journal* 34, no. 1 (2014): 28–53.

Sanford, A. Whitney. "Being the Change: Gandhi, Intentional Communities, and the Process of Social Change." *Social Sciences Directory* 2, no. 3 (August 2013): 106–113.

Schatzki, Theodore R. "Introduction: Practice Theory." In *The Practice Turn in Contemporary Theory*, edited by Theodore R. Schatzki, Karin Knorr Cetina, and Eike von Savigny, 1–14. London: Routledge, 2001.

The Schleitheim Confession of Faith. 1527. https://courses.washington.edu/hist112/SCHLEITHEIM%20CONFESSION%20OF%20FAITH.htm.

Schor, Juliet. *The Overspent American: Why We Want What We Don't Need*. New York: Harper & Row, 1999.

Schrader-Frechette, Kristin. *Environmental Justice: Creating Equality, Reclaiming Democracy*. Oxford: Oxford University Press, 2002.

Second Vatican Council. *Gaudium et spes*. http://www.vatican.va/archive/hist_councils/ii_vatican_council/documents/vat-ii_cons_19651207_gaudium-et-spes_en.html.

Segundo, Juan Luis. *The Liberation of Theology*. Maryknoll, NY: Orbis Books, 1976.

Seigfried, Charlene Haddock. *Pragmatism and Feminism: Reweaving the Social Fabric*. Chicago: University of Chicago Press, 1996.

Shove, Elizabeth. "Beyond the ABC: Climate Change Policy and Theories of Social Change." *Environment and Planning A* 42, no. 6 (2010): 1273–1285.

Singer, Peter. *Rethinking Life and Death: The Collapse of Our Traditional Ethics.* New York: St. Martin's, 1994.

Skorburg, Joshua August. "Beyond Embodiment: John Dewey and the Integrated Mind." *The Pluralist* 8, no. 3 (Fall 2013): 66–78.

Smith, Ian. "On Explaining Individual and Corporate Culpability in the Global Climate Change Era." *Journal of Business Ethics* 112, no. 4 (February 2013): 551–558.

Smith, Tom, Benjamin Schapiro, and Jaesok Son. *General Social Survey Final Report: Trends in Public Attitudes about Civil Liberties, 1972–2014.* Chicago: NORC, 2015.

Snyder, Lois, and Daniel P. Sulmasy, "Physician-Assisted Suicide." *Annals of Internal Medicine* 135, no. 3 (August 7, 2001): 209–216.

Sobrino, Jon. *The True Church and the Poor.* Maryknoll, NY: Orbis Books, 2004.

Southern Poverty Law Center. "Richard Bertrand Spencer." N.d. https://www.splcenter. org/fighting-hate/extremist-files/individual/richard-bertrand-spencer-0.

Spencer, Richard. "Facing the Future as a Minority." Speech at American Renaissance Conference, 2013. Reprinted on the Occidental Observer, a white nationalist website, http://www.theoccidentalobserver.net/2013/05/14/facing-the-future-as-a-minority/.

"SPLC: Don't Protest Spencer, That's What He Wants." *Auburn Plainsman.* April 10, 2017.   http://www.theplainsman.com/article/2017/04/splc-don't-protest-spencer-thats-what-he-wants.

Stevenson, Charles L. "Reflections on John Dewey's Ethics." *Proceedings of the Aristotelian Society* 62 (1961–1962): 77–98.

Svrluga, Susan. "'We Will Keep Coming Back': Richard Spencer Leads Another Torchlight March in Charlottesville." *Washington Post*, October 9, 2017. https://www. washingtonpost.com/news/grade-point/wp/2017/10/07/richard-spencer-leads-another-torchlight-march-in-charlottesville/?utm_term=.b981e7c73a2c.

Swarte, Nikkie B., Marije L. van der Lee, Johanna G. van der Bom, Jan van den Boutand, and A. Peter M. Heintz. "Effects of Euthanasia on the Bereaved Family and Friends: A Cross Sectional Study." *British Medical Journal* 327, no. 7408 (July 26, 2003): 189–192.

Tertullian. *Apology.* In *Christian Social Teachings: A Reader in Christian Social Ethics from the Bible to the Present*, edited by George Forell and James Childs, 26–31. Philadelphia: Fortress, 2012.

Thompson, E. P. *The Making of the English Working Class.* New York: Vintage Books, 1966.

Thompson, E. P. *William Morris: Romantic to Revolutionary.* Stanford, CA: Stanford University Press, 1981.

Thomson, Judith Jarvis. "Afterword." In *Rights, Restitution, and Risk: Essays in Moral Theory*, 251–262. Cambridge, MA: Harvard University Press, 1986.

Thomson, Judith Jarvis. "A Defense of Abortion." In *Rights, Restitution, and Risk: Essays in Moral Theory*, 1–19. Cambridge, MA: Harvard University Press, 1986.

Thomson, Judith Jarvis. "Killing, Letting Die, and the Trolley Problem." In *Rights, Restitution, and Risk: Essays in Moral Theory*, 78–93. Cambridge, MA: Harvard University Press, 1986.

Thomson, Judith Jarvis. "The Trolley Problem." In *Rights, Restitution, and Risk: Essays in Moral Theory*, 94–116. Cambridge, MA: Harvard University Press, 1986.

Tillich, Paul. *Love, Power, and Justice: Ontological Analyses and Ethical Applications.* New York: Oxford University Press, 1960.

Trotsky, Leon, John Dewey, and George Novack. *Their Morals and Ours: Marxist versus Liberal Views on Morality*. New York: Merit, 1969.

US Supreme Court. *Cohen v. California*. 403 US 15 (1971). https://supreme.justia.com/cases/federal/us/403/15/.

US Supreme Court. *National Socialist Party of America v. Village of Skokie*. 432 US 43 (1977). https://supreme.justia.com/cases/federal/us/432/43/case.html.

Verbeek, Peter-Paul. "Materializing Morality: Design Ethics and Technological Mediation." *Science, Technology, & Human Values* 31, no. 3 (May 2006): 361–380.

Vogel, Steven. *Thinking Like a Mall: Environmental Philosophy after the End of Nature*. Cambridge, MA: MIT Press, 2015.

Waldron, Jeremy. "Dignity and Defamation: The Visibility of Hate." *Harvard Law Review* 123, no. 7 (2010): 1596–1657.

Walker, Margaret Urban. *Moral Understandings: A Feminist Study in Ethics*, 2nd ed. New York: Oxford University Press, 2007.

Walzer, Michael. *Just and Unjust Wars: A Moral Argument with Historical Illustrations*, 3rd ed. New York: Basic Books, 2000.

Walzer, Michael. *Thick and Thin: Moral Argument at Home and Abroad*. Notre Dame, IN: University of Notre Dame Press, 1994.

Weaver, J. Denny. *Anabaptist Theology in the Face of Postmodernity: A Proposal for the Third Millennium*. Telford, PA: Pandora, 2000, 114.

Weaver-Zercher, David. *The Amish in the American Imagination*. Baltimore: Johns Hopkins University Press, 2001.

Weinberg, Albert. "A Critique of Pragmatist Ethics." *Journal of Philosophy* 20, no. 21 (October 11, 1923): 561–566.

Welch, Sharon. *A Feminist Ethic of Risk*. Minneapolis: Fortress, 1990.

West, Cornel. *The American Evasion of Philosophy: A Genealogy of Pragmatism*. Madison: University of Wisconsin Press, 1989.

West, Cornel. *The Ethical Dimensions of Marxist Thought*. New York: Monthly Review, 1991.

Weston, Anthony. "Beyond Intrinsic Value: Pragmatism in Environmental Ethics." *Environmental Ethics* 7, no. 4 (1985): 321–339.

Weston, Anthony. "Non-Anthropocentrism in a Thoroughly Anthropocentrized World," *Trumpeter* 8, no. 3 (1991): 1–9. http://trumpeter.athabascau.ca/index.php/trumpet/article/download/459/760?inline=1.

Weston, Anthony. *A Practical Companion to Ethics*. New York: Oxford University Press, 1997.

Williams, Bernard. "A Critique of Utilitarianism." In *Utilitarianism: For and Against*, by J. J. C. Smart and Bernard Williams, 77–150. Cambridge: Cambridge University Press, 1973.

Williams, Raymond. "Alignment and Commitment." In *Marxism and Literature*, 199–205. Oxford: Oxford University Press, 1977.

Williams, Raymond. "Base and Superstructure in Marxist Theory." In *Problems in Materialism and Culture: Selected Essays*, 31–49. London: Verso, 1980.

Williams, Raymond. "The Forward March of Labour Halted?" In *Resources of Hope: Culture, Democracy, Socialism*, 247–255. London: Verso, 1989.

Williams, Raymond. "Ideas of Nature." In *Problems in Materialism and Culture: Selected Essays*, 67–85. London: Verso, 1980.

Williams, Raymond. "Literature and Sociology." In *Problems in Materialism and Culture: Selected Essays*, 11–30. London: Verso, 1980.

Williams, Raymond. "Structures of Feeling." In *Marxism and Literature*, 128–125. Oxford: Oxford University Press, 1977.

Winograd, Nathan. *Irreconcilable Differences: The Battle for the Heart and Soul of America's Animal Shelters*. N.p., 2009.

Yoder, John Howard. *For the Nations: Essays Public and Evangelical*. Grand Rapids, MI: Eerdmans, 1997.

Yoder, John Howard. "The Kingdom as Social Ethic." In *The Priestly Kingdom: Social Ethics as Gospel*, 80–101. Notre Dame, IN: University of Notre Dame Press, 1984.

Yoder, John Howard. *The Politics of Jesus*. Grand Rapids, MI: Eerdmans, 1994.

Yoder, John Howard. *The War of the Lamb: The Ethics of Nonviolence and Peacemaking*, edited by Glen Stassen, Mark Thiessen Nation, and Matt Hamsher. Grand Rapids, MI: Brazos, 2009.

Yoho, Ted. Statement on Richard Spencer, October 16, 2016. https://www.facebook.com/plugins/post.php?href=https%3A%2F%2Fwww.facebook.com%2FCongressmanTedYoho%2Fposts%2F2185231301502836.

Index

For the benefit of digital users, indexed terms that span two pages (e.g., 52–53) may, on occasion, appear on only one of those pages.